"*Southern Criminology* takes the reader on a journey of critical imagination to offer a
future landscape for the discipline of criminology. This journey is challenging and
profound. The authors chart a route from the discipline's past to the promise of a
dawn for its future that anyone willing to travel with them will find intellectually
valuable and hugely rewarding. Take a risk. Take this journey. You will not be
disappointed."

Professor Sandra Walklate, *Eleanor Rathbone Chair of
Sociology, University of Liverpool and Editor in Chief of the*
British Journal of Criminology

"For most of its existence, criminology has been moulded by the intellectual perspectives
and ideological reflexes of the global North—a region that contains only a fraction of
the world's population and only a fraction of its experience of violence and social harm.
Southern Criminology promises to be a foundational document in a growing movement to
bring the rest of the world into the centre of criminological dialogue and action."

Professor Elliott Currie, *Department of Criminology, Law and Society,
University of California Irvine*

"This book is an inspiring project of retrieval of wisdom bubbling up from marginality
and domination in global structures of social relations. The ideas retrieved bridge global
divides rather than essentialize 'North' or 'South'. Dialogue across diverse divides helps
build new intercultural and interscalar understandings in a pathbreaking volume."

Professor John Braithwaite, *RegNet, ANU*

"This book presents a convincing argument about the need to develop a Southern
criminology to overcome the monopolization of criminology by the Northern part
of the world. It leaves us well informed on important issues, especially on the richness
and pertinence of incorporating Southern perspectives into the Global understanding of crime and violence. Far from trying to discredit the knowledge produced by
Northern criminology, this book proves a simple fact: that we can learn from each
other, and that knowledge can travel from Global South to North, South to South,
East to West and vice versa."

Professor Elena Azaola, *Mexican Criminologist,
del Centro de Investigaciones y Estudios Superiores en
Antropología Social, CIESAS*

SOUTHERN CRIMINOLOGY

Criminology has focused mainly on problems of crime and violence in the large population centres of the Global North to the exclusion of the global countryside, peripheries and antipodes. Southern criminology is an innovative new approach that seeks to correct this bias.

This book turns the origin stories of criminology, which simply assumed a global universality, on their head. It draws on a range of case studies to illustrate this point: tracing criminology's long fascination with dangerous masculinities back to Lombroso's theory of atavism, itself based on an orientalist interpretation of men of colour from the Global South; uncovering criminology's colonial legacy, perhaps best exemplified by the over-representation of Indigenous peoples in settler societies drawn into the criminal justice system; analysing the ways in which the sociology of punishment literature has also been based on Northern theories, which assume that forms of penality roll out from the Global North to the rest of the world; and making the case that the harmful effects of eco-crimes and global warming are impacting more significantly on the Global South. The book also explores how the coloniality of gender shapes patterns of violence in the Global South.

Southern criminology is not a new sub-discipline within criminology, but rather a journey toward cognitive justice. It promotes a perspective that aims to invent methods and concepts that bridge global divides and enhance the democratisation of knowledge, more befitting of global criminology in the twenty-first century.

Kerry Carrington is the Head of the School of Justice at Queensland University of Technology, Australia.

Russell Hogg is an Adjunct Professor in the School of Justice at Queensland University of Technology, Australia.

John Scott is a Professor in the School of Justice at Queensland University of Technology, Australia.

Máximo Sozzo is Professor of Sociology and Criminology at the Universidad Nacional del Litoral, Argentina. He is an Adjunct Professor in the School of Justice at Queensland University of Technology, Australia.

Reece Walters is a Professor in the School of Justice and Director of the Crime, Justice and Social Democracy Research Centre at Queensland University of Technology, Australia.

New Directions in Critical Criminology

This series presents new cutting-edge critical criminological empirical, theoretical, and policy work on a broad range of social problems, including drug policy, rural crime and social control, policing and the media, ecocide, intersectionality, and the gendered nature of crime. It aims to highlight the most up-to-date authoritative essays written by new and established scholars in the field. Rather than offering a survey of the literature, each book takes a strong position on topics of major concern to those interested in seeking new ways of thinking critically about crime.

Edited by Walter S. DeKeseredy, West Virginia University, USA

Revitalizing Criminological Theory
Towards a new Ultra-Realism
Steve Hall and Simon Winlow

Intersectionality and Criminology
Disrupting and revolutionizing studies of crime
Hillary Potter

Queer Criminology
Carrie L. Buist and Emily Lenning

Crime, Justice and Social Media
Michael Salter

Southern Criminology
Kerry Carrington, Russell Hogg, John Scott, Máximo Sozzo and Reece Walters

For more information about this series, please visit: www.routledge.com/New-Directions-in-Critical-Criminology/book-series/NDCC

SOUTHERN
CRIMINOLOGY

Kerry Carrington, Russell Hogg,
John Scott, Máximo Sozzo and
Reece Walters

Routledge
Taylor & Francis Group

LONDON AND NEW YORK

First published 2019
by Routledge
2 Park Square, Milton Park, Abingdon, Oxon OX14 4RN

and by Routledge
711 Third Avenue, New York, NY 10017

Routledge is an imprint of the Taylor & Francis Group, an informa business

© 2019 Kerry Carrington, Russell Hogg, John Scott, Máximo
Sozzo and Reece Walters

British Library Cataloguing-in-Publication Data
A catalogue record for this book is available from the British Library

Library of Congress Cataloging-in-Publication Data
Names: Carrington, Kerry, author.
Title: Southern criminology / Kerry Carrington [and three others].
Description: Abingdon, Oxon ; New York, NY : Routledge, 2019. |
    Series: New directions in critical criminology | Includes
    bibliographical references and index.
Identifiers: LCCN 2018024949| ISBN 9781138721296 (hardback) |
    ISBN 9781138721302 (pbk.) | ISBN 9781315194585 (ebook)
Subjects: LCSH: Criminology—Developing countries. |
    Crime—Developing countries.
Classification: LCC HV6030 .C373 2019 | DDC 364.09172/4—dc23
LC record available at https://lccn.loc.gov/2018024949

ISBN: 978-1-138-72129-6 (hbk)
ISBN: 978-1-138-72130-2 (pbk)
ISBN: 978-1-315-19458-5 (ebk)

Typeset in Bembo
by Swales & Willis Ltd, Exeter, Devon, UK

CONTENTS

ACKNOWLEDGEMENTS

First and foremost, we are delighted to reproduce *Mapa de Sudamérica Invertido* (1936) by Joaquín Torres García (1874–1949) for the paperback cover of the book, courtesy of the Estate of Joaquín Torres-García. The symbolism of the map inverts geo-political assumptions about Northern superiority, challenges visions of colonial landscape, and disrupts hegemonic perspectives of the global world order (De Armendi 2009: 5). We could hardly wish for a more fitting image for the cover. We are again also grateful for the outstanding professional editorial assistance provided by Jess Rodgers. We acknowledge the generous support of our colleagues from the Crime, Justice and Social Democracy Research Centre, Queensland University of Technology as well as that of our Executive Dean, Professor John Humphrey, and others from both the Global North and South for their contributions to the Southern criminology project. We also acknowledge the editorial support of the Routledge team, especially Tom Sutton and Hannah Catterall, and Walter DeKeseredy for his acceptance of this manuscript in the *New Directions in Critical Criminology* series. This project was inspired by Raewyn Connell's *Southern Theory*, De Souza Santos's quest for cognitive justice, and John Braithwaite's life long journey of Southernising criminology. We take this opportunity to express to them our deep gratitude for their pioneering, indeed, revolutionary bodies of work. Each of us thank our respective families and colleagues for the emotional and intellectual support they provide that sustains our collective vision for a better world—and one where the arc of history may indeed be bent towards justice in all its dimensions, cognitive as well as social and economic.

Lastly, parts of this book are naturally derivative of earlier pieces we have published on related topics and we expressly acknowledge the following publications.

Carrington K (2015) *Feminism and Global Justice*. London: Routledge.

Carrington K and Hogg R (2017) Deconstructing criminology's origin stories: A view from the Global South. *Asian Journal of Criminology* 12(3): 181–197. DOI: 10.1007/s11417-017-9248-7.

Carrington K, Hogg R and Sozzo M (2016) Southern criminology. *British Journal of Criminology* 56(1): 1–20. DOI: 10.1093/bjc/azv083.

Scott J, Fa'avale A and Thompson BY (2018) What can Southern criminology contribute to a post-race agenda? *Asian Journal of Criminology* 13(2): 155–173 DOI: 10.1007/s11417-017-9263-8.

Walters R (2018) Climate change denial—making ignorance great again. In Barton A and Howard T (eds) *Agnotology, Power and Harm: The Study of Ignorance and the Criminological Imagination*: forthcoming. London: Palgrave.

And the following chapters published in Carrington K, Hogg R, Scott J, and Sozzo M (eds) (2018) *Palgrave Handbook of Criminology and the Global South*. Switzerland: Palgrave Macmillan.

Barberet R and Carrington K. Globalizing feminist criminology: Gendered violence during peace and war. 821–845.

Brisman A, South N, and Walters R. Climate apartheid and environmental refugees. 301–321

Carrington K, Hogg R, Scott J, and Sozzo M. Criminology, Southern theory and cognitive justice. 3–17.

Hogg R and Brown D. Rethinking penal modernism from the Global South: The case of convict transportation to Australia. 751–754.

Scott J and Morton J. Understanding crime and justice in Torres Strait Islander communities. 587–609.

Sozzo M. Beyond the 'neo-liberal penality thesis'? Punitive turn and political change in South America. 659–685.

References

De Armendi N (2009) The map as political agent: Destabilising the North-South model and redefining identity in twentieth-century Latin American art. *St Andrews Journal of Art History and Museum Studies 13*: 5–17.

1

SOUTHERN CRIMINOLOGY AND COGNITIVE JUSTICE

There is no global justice without cognitive justice.

(de Sousa Santos 2014: viii)

In the Information Age, processes of empire building are as much about colonising knowledge, as they are about colonising territory (Hogg, Scott, and Sozzo 2017). There is a 'staggering amount of inequality in the geography of the production of academic knowledge' (Graham, Hale, and Stephens 2011: 14), with the United States (US) and the United Kingdom (UK) producing over half of it, yet comprising only 15 per cent of the global population (Population Reference Bureau 2013). This dominance has produced a hegemony of social scientific thought based on the experience of a small number of societies in the Global North where 'the bulk of the world's resources for research sit' (Connell 2017: 5). Until recently knowledge in the social sciences, including criminology, has generally been sourced from a select number of English speaking countries from the Global North, whose journals, conferences, publishers, and universities dominate the intellectual landscape (Connell 2007; Faraldo-Cabana 2018; Graham, Hale, and Stephens 2011; Hogg, Scott, and Sozzo 2017). Yet, theory, research agendas and innovations can be generated from the specific experiences of the Global South, and Northern thinking can be cross-fertilised by it in a way that enhances global epistemology (Connell 2014). This introductory chapter critically examines criminology's origin stories, which simply assumed a global universality even though they were specific to the conditions of crime affecting the Global North. This chapter interrogates whose voices, experiences, and theories are reflected in the discipline of criminology, and argues that challenging its Northern biases is more important now than ever before. Inspired by Southern theory, the chapter explains how Southern criminology can make a contribution to correcting the imbalance in the global organisation of criminological knowledge.

Around 85 per cent of the world's population live in the 'Global South', comprising the continents of Asia, Africa, Australia and Latin America and the island peoples of the Indian and Pacific Oceans (Worldometers 2018). One in ten of the global population exist on $US1.90 a day, and the vast majority of these live in the Global South, most in Sub-Saharan Africa (Collier 2007). Global inequalities in education, income, housing, gender, and health are concentrated in the Global South (World Bank 2016). Crime problems in the Global North, despite the disproportionate attention given them, generally pale in scale and significance alongside the violence (including armed conflicts, military coups, and grave human rights abuses) and other crimes that seriously threaten human security in many Global South countries. The countries with the highest rates of homicide, violence against women, corruption, and drug trafficking in the world are located in the South (United Nations Development Programme 2013; World Bank 2011). A large proportion of the world's police and around half the world's 10.2 million prisoners are also to be found in the Global South, across Asia, Africa, Oceania, and Latin America (Walmsley 2016). And yet, notwithstanding its apparent significance as a site of obvious (and critical) criminological interest, the Global South has remained marginal to the concerns and research agendas of criminology until quite recently. This is despite the constant reminders of how we now live in a globally connected world in which the fate of different peoples and countries are irrevocably entwined. Global challenges like climate change, refugee movements, the Global Financial Crisis, and terrorism emphatically underline the point.

In truth, however, global interdependence is not at all new even if it has taken novel forms and intensified in various ways in the recent past. Economies and polities in the Global South, together with their criminal justice institutions and their experiences of crime and violent conflict, have for long been interwoven with those of their erstwhile colonisers in the Global North. These histories and connections have also failed to attract much in the way of criminological interest until recently.

Criminology in the main, then, has been predominantly a Northern academic enterprise (Carrington, Hogg, and Sozzo 2016). Southern criminology aims to redress this bias; to enlarge the criminological imagination in order to encompass experiences and ideas from the Global South. To do so it is also essential to seek reasons for the neglect, to better understand the forces shaping the historical formation and present organisation of criminology as a field of academic knowledge. There were and are specific factors at work in the academic institutionalisation of criminology as a Northern enterprise, but this Northern dominance also reflects the broader history, pattern and dynamics of knowledge production in the social sciences. We, therefore, begin with Raewyn Connell's deep and critical engagement with this larger question, which has been so influential in framing the Southern criminology project.

Southern theory and epistemologies of the South

In *Southern Theory* (2007), Connell argues that a structural imbalance in the economy of knowledge has produced a hegemony of social scientific thought based on the experience of a small number of societies in the Global North, namely the countries of Western Europe (including Britain) and the US. The conventional (Northern) account depicts the rise of social science as a response to the profound problems—of social dislocation, urban change, migration, industrial conflict, and anomie—experienced by these societies as they underwent processes of rapid industrialisation, urbanisation, and modernisation in the nineteenth century (see, for example, Nisbet 1970). In this narrative the Global North, comprising countries depicted as *leading* the way to capitalist modernity and an advanced stage of civilisation, is treated as the normative benchmark for the economic, political, and social development of other countries entering the modern world. It was confidently assumed the social sciences produced from the experience of these Northern societies affords a sure guide to understanding and confronting processes and problems common to all societies undergoing modernisation. Thus, Connell argues, social science succeeded in representing itself, and being widely accepted, as universal, timeless, and placeless (Connell 2007). According to this logic, social phenomena in the 'periphery' would be investigated from the standpoint of universal theories and laws of development generated in 'modern' or 'Western' societies of the Global North. The South could be mined for data, as for other raw materials, and empirical studies might be conducted in Southern settings applying imported (Northern) theory, but little in the way of novel ideas or theoretical insights of anything more than local interest could be yielded by the social scientific enterprise in the South. Connell calls this 'metropolitan' thinking (Connell 2007: 215). We suggest that Connell's argument applies with equal force to the field of criminology.

Metropolitan thinking rests on a linear, panoramic, and unifying standpoint in which space, and geo-political and social difference, are erased in the imperial narrative of time. In this worldview, North Atlantic global dominance and leadership was a matter of historical precedence (Connell 2007: 38). Submerged is the fundamental historical reality that the processes of Western industrialisation and modernisation were not endogenous to a few particularly innovative or fortunate countries that led in some notional global race, but depended critically upon their imperial reach and power, the fact of empire. It was the conquest and colonisation of much of the rest of the world by North Atlantic powers in the period from the sixteenth to the twentieth centuries which provided them with the resources, labour, markets, and often know-how essential to their economic development. As dependency and world-systems theorists have argued for many years, capitalist modernity was global from the outset (Wallerstein 2004). Being 'under-developed' or economically 'backward' was not the 'normal' or 'natural' condition of particular countries so labelled, but commonly a consequence of their subordinate place in the global economic and political order. Likewise, social scientific knowledge and many of its key categories and concepts were not simply a product of efforts to confront the problems associated with modernisation in countries of the Global North, but were crucially shaped by the imperial context; and as such they 'embodied an intellectual response to the colonised world' (Connell 2007: 9).

Many other theorists have also taken issue with colonised constructions of knowledge, pointing out that metropolitan ideas are Eurocentric or Anglo-centric. Without doing justice to the full range of this literature and its insights, we point to some key thinkers whose ideas have influenced our development of Southern criminology. Boaventura de Sousa Santos, from Portugal, has dedicated his career to promoting global cognitive justice. Arguing there can be no global justice without cognitive justice (de Sousa Santos 2014: viii), de Sousa Santos urges a complete 'epistemological break' from the hegemony of Western thinking (2014: 163). Like Connell, he is critical of the way the history of the social sciences has projected itself as an emancipatory project while its modernist ideals remained based on the experience of metropolitan societies (2014: 71). However, unlike some post-colonial theorists who see little worth recovering anything from Northern theories, de Sousa Santos does imagine that a non-Occidentalist West is a possibility (2014: 114). Consequently, he rejects the reductionism and dualisms to be found in much post-colonial theory that reify concepts, such as indigenous knowledge, and stands them in outright opposition to Western scientific knowledge (2014: 212). Rather, he opts for the development of inter-cultural thinking and ways of knowing to escape the colonising effects of the global episteme. He defines these alternative knowledges and ways of understanding as necessarily limited and specific as opposed to the universalising claims and pretensions of metropolitan thought (2014: 212).

Brown (2018) points to the original ideas of Bengali social scientist Dipesh Chakrabarty (2000) as a valuable source for Southern criminology. Chakrabarty's method does not reject metropolitan thought outright, but seeks to de-centre these knowledges, to 'provincialize Europe' as Chakrabarty describes it and 'to open up unity and universals to plurality—without also denigrating the gains of Western thought and its categories' (Brown 2018: 95). This conceptual pragmatism acknowledges that how we think is so historically permeated by metropolitan thought it is not possible to reject it outright. It is however possible to de-centre, relativise, and democratise knowledge from the periphery.

A similar critique is advanced in the writings of Walter Mignolo. Born in Argentina, but based in the US for much of his academic career, he has published an extensive body of work excavating the geo-politics of knowledge, trans-modernity, and border thinking. Mignolo describes border thinking as 'the necessary epistemology to delink and decolonise knowledge and, in the process, build de-colonial local histories, restoring the dignity that the Western idea of universal history took away from millions of people' (Mignolo 2012: 10). Border thinking occurs in the spaces in between, the overlooked spaces of becoming and being. While epistemologies of the South exist, and have spawned innovative work in the social sciences, as Connell et al. (2017) remind us, they still very much exist in relation to the epistemologies of the North, which serve as their unstated referent (Connell et al. 2017: 29). In what follows we attempt to unravel some of these relations with respect to the development of criminology as a Northern-centric academic discipline and enterprise.

But, first it is necessary to further unpack these concepts of 'South', 'Southern', and 'Southernising'.

Conceptualising the South

The division of the contemporary world into North and South has come to be a more common way of talking about global divides and global social relations that used to be described using binaries like 'develop*ed*' and 'develop*ing*', 'industrial' and 'industrialis*ing*', the '*first*' and the '*third* world'. Economic discourse today often also divides the world into 'establish*ed*' and 'emerg*ing*' economies. These binaries explicitly privilege ideas of temporal succession, in which the first named (the Global North in contemporary parlance) designates the normative benchmark (the developmental destination) to which the rest of the world will naturally aspire. This is symptomatic of general metropolitan thinking. The discourse of North/South gained currency in the late 1970s in large part due to the work of the Brandt Commission (the Independent Commission on International Development Issues (ICIDI), chaired by the former chancellor of West

Germany, Willy Brandt). Established in 1977, the Commission sought to investigate and tackle existing and emerging challenges of international development, in particular the enormous inequalities between the countries of the Northern and Southern hemispheres. It published two reports with recommendations: *North–South: A Programme for Survival* (1980) and *Common Crisis: North–South Cooperation for World Recovery* (1983). What came to be known as the Brandt Line depicted the North/South economic divide on a map of the globe, based on GDP per capita. The line encircled the world at a latitude of 30° North, passing between North and Central America, above Africa, India, central Asia, and China, but thereafter descending South to place Japan, Australia, and New Zealand above the line, before sweeping North again to situate the islands of the Pacific in the South. The North/South discourse has the advantage that it registers space over time, but in most other respects underlying habits of thought that treat the North as normative and the South as in a process of 'catching up' remain largely unchallenged.

A useful starting point in questioning these habits is the work of art reproduced on the cover of this book. Uruguayan artist Joaquin Torres García's (1874–1949) *Mapa de Sudamérica Invertido* (1936) is, as both the title and image reveal, an upside-down map of South America. It could be seen as an early version of, or model for, a later genre of joke maps that variously reverse Southern and Northern hemispheres, insert countries or continents inside the borders of others and so on: cartography as playground rather than objective science. There is however a serious point to such amusing diversions. They challenge us to be more reflexive about 'cartographic structures of power' (Samson 2011: 244), to question the taken-for-granted objectivity and universality of the map. We are encouraged to see maps as cultural artefacts, powerful fictions that construct (rather than simply reflect) our worlds, shaping our understanding of them in ways that exclude and erase other possible ways of being and seeing. Torres García's map subverts a Eurocentric 'up and down' conception of the world. *Mapa de Sudamérica Invertido* is the artistic expression of the call in his 1935 'School of the South' manifesto for an autonomous art movement in Latin America that sought its inspiration locally and especially in the pre-Columbian past, rather than by reference to the North: '*nuestro norte es el sur'* ('our North is the South'). The image of the inverted map is ubiquitous in contemporary Latin American popular culture. It is a fitting symbol of the Southern criminology project and how we see the task of conceptualising, or reconceptualising, the South.

Conventional North/South discourse rests on a static view of the international order (Fonseca 2018), overlooking the seminal point that there is no North or South that are not also the products of centuries old interactions between regions and cultures spanning the globe. The modern world dominated by North Atlantic countries was global from the start. It depended, for example, on the prior globalisation of technologies (like printing and gunpowder, both invented in China) and knowledge accumulated from different cultures over many centuries (in mathematics and philosophy, for example, in which Islamic and Asian achievements were of central importance) (Sen 2006: 49–58); quite apart from the role of colonial wars and other foreign interventions in securing access to land, raw materials, manufacturing techniques, and labour to drive the economic development of Western capitalism (Beckert 2014; Gregory 2004). Given the simple facts of history, the principal significance of the 'South' and 'Southern' for us lies in the privilege conferred on the spatial over the temporal and over ideas of succession, hierarchy, universality, and closure central to Northern thought. For us 'the South' is a social construct that serves a number of purposes. It highlights and encourages autonomous knowledge-making in the Global South and advances claims for a more inclusive criminology. It provides a conceptual frame for resisting Northern hegemony in the production of knowledge and encouraging its on-going democratisation. Just as importantly, it seeks to explore and analyse global processes that shaped the worlds of both South and North and provides a vehicle for ensuring the events and relations of empire are inserted back into history and contemporary analysis and understanding. An essential task is to develop a more complex, layered, and dynamic conception of the South and of North/South relationships. We approach this not as the starting point, a pre-condition for getting underway as you might map a journey before embarking on it, but as part of the inquiry that is the journey. We begin therefore with some pointers only, some devices for orienting the inquiry, stressing once again that South and North are not homogeneous spaces or categories.

The modern world of nation states was sculpted from multi-racial empires—those of European imperial states—that by the nineteenth century spanned the globe. Imperial power was projected in a manner largely indifferent to the boundaries of North and South and to the ties to place and territory of the Southern peoples they encountered. Empire involved the movement (forced and free) and the intermixing of different peoples, institutions, cultures, and belief systems on a seismic scale (Anderson 2016). It was world-shattering for everyone involved and thus confounds any static conception or understanding of the North/South divide and relations. This is not to suggest that empire is or was ever one thing: monolithic, ideologically coherent, uniformly coercive (let alone benign) in its aims and methods (see, for example, Darwin 2013 on the British Empire). It is no accident, however, that conventional understandings of the division between North and South (with all the associated challenges of international development, such as those reflected in the Brandt Commission) roughly coincide with the divide between the old European imperial states and their former colonies. That there are some exceptions—the US, Canada, Australia, New Zealand—which, on account of being amongst the richest countries in the world, are regarded as being part of the Global North is evidence of the variety of visions, forms, and effects of empire.

The countries mentioned, constituting the contemporary 'Anglo-world', are products of what Belich (2011) describes as the 'settler revolution'; the expansion of Britain, its people, language, laws, institutions, and ways of life across the globe. He argues it sits in importance alongside the other momentous revolutions shaping the modern world (the American, French, and Industrial revolutions). Settler colonialism, according to Belich (2011: 23), managed to 'reach further and last longer than empire' (on settler colonialism, also see Veracini 2011; Wolfe 2006). Settler societies sought to replicate, and further cultivate, British ways of life in other, faraway places, as bastions of white civilisation in a rapidly changing and uncertain world. British colonial settler ambitions ultimately proved less successful in some other countries, including South Africa, Rhodesia/Zimbabwe, and Kenya, where majority indigenous populations ultimately prevailed over their colonisers. Other imperial European states established settler empires or aspired to do so (the Spanish and Portuguese in Latin America, the

French in Algeria), but they lacked the reach and depth of the British settlement empire. Belich describes the 'explosion' of the Anglo world from the late eighteenth century to the 1920s. He contrasts British imperial expansion with that of Spain, 'Europe's other great overseas settling society'. The British Empire grew 'from half the size of the Spanish world to over twice the size, overtaking the Russian world as well' (Belich 2011: 3, 4).

Like other nation states, these white Anglo settler states had to be carved from multi-racial societies. Vigorous assertions of white identity and the imperative of racial homogeneity as the essential foundations of national independence and democratic self-rule drove these settler nation-building efforts, what Lake and Reynolds (2008) describe as the making of 'white men's countries'. This was a symptom and critical dimension of what the African-American sociologist and political activist, WEB Du Bois (1920: 1), identified in the first decade of the twentieth century as yet another modern revolution— this time in thought and consciousness—namely, the appearance of a 'new religion of whiteness', 'dashing', as he put it, 'with ever increasing virulence . . . on the shores of our time'. A few years before, he had pointedly observed that 'the problem of the Twentieth Century is the problem of the color-line' (Du Bois 1903: 1). The claims of white precedence, privilege, and supremacy in multi-racial societies underpinned the dispossession, elimination, segregation, and sometimes expulsion of non-whites, and the adoption of racially discriminatory immigration programmes designed to further 'whiten' the population; what today would be understood as processes of ethnic cleansing. The settler states of Latin America engaged in the same practices (Gott 2007). A much longer history of inter-racial mixing of settler with indigenous and slave populations and the greater cultural distance from their metropoles saw Latin American countries denied membership, or at least full membership, of 'the white men's club' run by English-speaking peoples (see, for example, Lake and Reynolds 2008: 198). Even their own metropoles were regarded with ambivalence, as lacking the unique genius for self-government and love of freedom bestowed on the Anglo-Saxon and Nordic races by God and validated in the findings of nineteenth-century racial science. Others on the immediate periphery of Northern Europe, including the Irish and

Eastern Europeans, were treated with similar suspicion. That is to say, at various times and for certain purposes the *North* referred more narrowly to the Anglo-Saxon and Nordic races of Northern Europe. The unique virtues and long traditions of political freedom of the Northern European peoples were contrasted not only with the despotism of the East and the primitivism of tribal peoples, but also with the passionate, unruly, violent natures attributed to Southern and Eastern Europeans (and frequently the Irish) which left the latter ill-equipped to practice orderly forms of self-government. In early twentieth-century immigration policies in the Anglo world (the US, Australia) Southern and Eastern Europeans were often regarded as a 'semi-coloured race' whose numbers should be kept to a minimum (Lake and Reynolds 2008: 129–130, 163, 312; specifically on Australia, see Hancock 1961: 59, 126–127; on 'Nordic supremacy' in US immigration law and policy in the early decades of the twentieth century, see Daniels 2004: 45–58; and on the contingencies and struggles surrounding the achievement of whiteness for many immigrant groups in the Anglo-world, see Ignatiev 2009; Roediger 2005).

This confirms our earlier point concerning the fluid nature of the categories 'South' (and 'North') and the existence of layers of complexity that need to be acknowledged and explored in conceptualising these terms. Empire linked North and South, but in variegated forms and ways, such as to position certain (former) colonies of the geographical South (like Australia and New Zealand), and perhaps more ambiguously and for a limited time, others (like South Africa), in the Global North. Israel presents a further interesting variation on settler colonialism. These settler societies and others in the North need to be distinguished from the majority of colonised societies, while overlooking neither the experience of internal colonisation in the settler societies (of indigenous peoples, the descendants of slaves, non-white minorities, and other subaltern groups) nor the phenomenon of 'double colonisation' whereby settler states became in turn colonisers of their weaker neighbours (for example, the US in the Caribbean and the Pacific, Australia in Melanesia).

Race discourse is absolutely central to the complexities we have been describing and it is the protean qualities of racial categories (and, related to this, the fluidity of categories of North and South) in particular.

These questions are explored in more detail in Chapter 3 where we advance an analysis of race and an alternative to race-based conceptualisation from the South.

Depending upon circumstance and standpoint, therefore, it can be said that there is both a South within the North and a North within the South. Approaching this from a related but different perspective, world systems theory sought to capture the economic dynamics connecting North and South with an analysis of the interactions of capitalist centre, periphery and semi-periphery. Importantly, the North Atlantic world was characterised by economic, political, and cultural cleavages arising from the subordinate place assigned its own 'backward' periphery and semi-periphery. For example, the 'developed', industrial North versus the 'backward' Southern Mediterranean; England versus its Celtic fringe. These economic, political, and cultural relationships of dominance conditioned nation-building, practices of internal colonialism, racial discourse, and immigration/emigration *within* the North.

These relations within and between North and South are today being transformed once again by novel global economic changes and forces. As the engine rooms of global economic growth have shifted Eastward and Southward, deserting many of the old heartlands of industrial capitalism, the inter-dependencies, inequalities and tensions between regions *within* both North and South have intensified. A mega-rich elite grows and prospers in large parts of the South (China, Brazil, and India for example) amidst the continuing proliferation of urban slums and shanty towns that house the still vast ranks of the poor and displaced. A parallel process sees historically racialised subaltern groups further marginalised, their ranks expanded and augmented with others, so as to form an excluded class living in something like 'third world' conditions in large enclaves of the North (such as Detroit in the US). This is a prominent theme in the work of critical criminologists like Jock Young and Elliot Currie. Currie argued that 'we cannot begin to grasp either the nature or origins of America's outsized problem of violent crime (or of punishment) without placing the "Southern" legacy in the foreground' (Currie 2018: 44). He was referring to the huge disparities in death and injury due to violence that separate white from African Americans. These differences in the experience of violence in America are, he argued, white-washed, rendering the trauma, injustice, and suffering of African-Americans invisible (2018: 45). Chapter 2 returns to this vast disparity in homicide rates between white and African Americans in the context of an analysis of the unequal global distribution of violence.

To complicate matters further, globalising forces that serve to weaken states empower non-state actors (the rich, corporations, drug cartels, terror groups) to increasingly organise their economic and political affairs outside the effective reach of state laws and enforcement systems. The old liberal state order where crime and war occupied separate realms starts to disappear. These are conditions ripe for the appearance of authoritarian and demagogic politics—as we are witnessing in one country after another, from the Philippines to Russia to Turkey to the US and across many parts of Eastern and Western Europe—and (of direct relevance for criminologists) for the closely related pushing of punitive law and order and securitisation to the forefront of policy agendas. Thus North/South interdependencies, cleavages and structured inequalities while not new, are being newly, and dramatically, reconfigured by neo-liberal globalisation. In an interesting twist, the remnants of old empires re-appear in novel roles: Britain and its overseas territories and dependencies (the Channel Islands, Gibraltar, Bermuda, the British Virgin Islands, the Cayman Islands, and others) constitute 'the world's largest tax haven empire' (Tax Justice Focus 2016). These tectonic shifts in the global order ought, for many reasons, command the interest of criminology, but they demand a criminological gaze no longer confined by notions of national sovereignty and territoriality.

In rethinking the concept of the South, a yet further layer of complexity is more directly concerned with the structures of knowledge production in the contemporary social sciences and criminology. As Connell (2007) shows, the global production of knowledge in the social sciences has always been structurally skewed towards the Global North with the effects on the theoretical, research, and policy agendas of criminology already noted. Globalisation and the digital communications revolution offer the promise of a growing democratisation of knowledge production; however, their role in the increasing corporatisation and commercialisation of knowledge has served to consolidate rather than challenge or mitigate North Atlantic dominance, particularly that of Britain and the US (Hogg, Scott, and Sozzo 2017). Settler states like Australia and New Zealand (and Canada might also be included here) whose material prosperity positions them together with the rich North, nonetheless occupy a subordinate place in the global order of social scientific and criminological knowledge. For both settler-colonial societies and the formerly colonised societies of the South digital technologies (on-line, open access journals, internet-based methodologies) can be utilised to advantage, to create new forms of access and mobility, and to expand and strengthen the channels of autonomous knowledge production and dissemination in the South, rather than accepting the inevitability of their use to further extend and entrench Northern hegemony.

We have argued that the terra-centric bias of metropolitan criminology has paid insufficient attention to processes—the connectors—linking apparently separate worlds. The temporal—precedence, progress, hierarchy—has been privileged at the expense of the spatial (Lee 2018). In a modernity fundamentally shaped and defined by the preoccupation with change and progress, the market valorisation of rootlessness and the unprecedented mobility of peoples, it may seem strange that the settled life is treated as normative and itinerant, and nomadism and migration as harbingers of danger and disruption. As Brody pointed out in relation to the impact of 'expansionist agricultural cultures' on hunter-gatherer societies, the settler revolution which saw the spread of the former across large tracts of the globe was 'built on opposites':

> On the one hand, a passion to settle, on the other, fierce restlessness; a need to find and have and hold an Eden, alongside a preparedness to go out and roam the world . . . The urge to settle and a readiness to move on are not antagonists in the sociology of our era; they are, rather, the two characteristics that combine to give the era its geographical and cultural character.
>
> (Brody 2001: 87)

In the face of the blindness to this sociological reality, a more dynamic conception of the South and of North/South relationships, might usefully borrow insights from the spatial turn in social and cultural theory and from travelling theory. In the early 1990s, Carter argued (1992: 106), somewhat prophetically in light of the present flourishing of nativist politics in so many parts of the world, for the adoption of a 'migrational predisposition' as an attitude and ethos more appropriate to modern life:

> The formal end of the Cold War obliges us to face our double historical inheritance. The period of modernity has been characterized by the massive displacement of populations. We are almost all migrants; and even if we have tried to stay at home, the conditions of life have changed so utterly in this century that we find ourselves strangers in our own house. The true novelty is to live in an old country. But despite the normality of displacement, we find the migrant vilified. For alongside the fact of ethnic integration, we also witness a recrudescent nationalism, a yearning for the purification of racial roots and the extermination of alien elements.
>
> (Carter 1992: 106)

Carter advocates the development of 'a framework of thinking that makes the migrant central, not ancillary, to historical processes' (1992: 7–8). We accept, following Carter, that the adoption of something like his 'migrational predisposition' is essential to the development of a more complex and layered conceptualisation of the South and North/South relations. It is a disposition made the more urgent by changes—or the consciousness of those changes—since Carter made his argument.

One connector of the worlds of North and South is the most fundamental of all. It is the very planet we all inhabit: its oceans, weather systems, bio-diversity (note the allusion to universals—sun, moon—in Torres-García's *Mapa de Sudamérica Invertido*). The impacts of climate change—likely the gravest crisis facing humanity—travel everywhere, 'sweeping away all borders' (Latour 2017: 81). They disproportionately blight, harm and uproot the lives of those who contribute least to the causes, the poorest peoples in the Global South; they will surely initiate new wars and contribute to new generations of migrants and refugees; but as Latour points out, there is no refuge for anyone, no walls that can be erected, to protect against 'those shapeless, stateless migrants known as climate, erosion, pollution, dwindling resources and the destruction of habitat' (Latour 2017: 81). His point, to weave another seam into the 'migrational predisposition' commended by Carter, is that as the environment moves beneath our feet we are all becoming migrants in a further sense—'we are all migrating towards lands that need to be rediscovered and reoccupied' (Latour 2017: 79). Environmental degradation is closely interlinked with that fusion of contradictory desires identified by Brody (2001) as characteristic of settler cultures: the cycles of expansion, domination, settlement, and exclusion to which both people and nature are subjected. As Latour (1994) observed some years ago, the general analytical partitioning of human and natural worlds is an essential attribute of the 'modern critical stance', which is enabling in relation to the cycles of expansion and domination while bracketing out their effects. It may be the case then, as Hage recently argued, that when we remove that partition—when we cease to be modern in Latour's terms—the forms of domination of humans (racism) and those of nature (environmental destruction) appear not only as involving deeply unequal effects, but in a much more intimate relationship to each other: as sharing the same fundamental 'generative structures' (Hage 2017: 15). These questions are taken up in Chapter 5.

Criminology as Northern theory: deconstructing origin stories

Moral statistics, psychiatry, psychology, anthropology, craniology, phrenology, sociology, and law were among the many human sciences to first study crime and deviance (Garland 2011: 302). There is no single point of origin for the field or discipline but rather a number of origin stories in which various texts and authors are privileged, most involving men from the Global North (see, for example, the list of *Fifty Key Thinkers in Criminology*, Hayward, Maruna, and Mooney 2010). Origin stories of course present 'an individualistic picture of criminology as being shaped by a select group of geniuses rather than a messy, dynamic intellectual process characterised by collaboration and cross-fertilisation' (Hayward, Maruna, and Mooney 2010: xxv).

It is no historical accident that the institutionalisation of criminology as a 'science' of crime (criminal anthropology as it was initially known) coincided with the zenith of European imperialism and appeared in the close intellectual company of racial science and eugenics, essential branches in the legitimating armoury of that imperialism. Theories and concepts that grounded criminology's early claims to be a scientific endeavour, like 'atavism' and the 'born criminal', speak rather obviously to the prevailing social Darwinian intellectual climate and to the traffic in ideas and artefacts between imperial metropole and periphery (Carrington and Hogg 2017).

The North Atlantic world—academic departments, journals, congresses, conferences, publishers, networks—has dominated criminology ever since, as it has the global organisation of social scientific knowledge more generally (Connell et al. 2017: 21; Graham, Hale, and Stephens 2011; Hogg, Scott, and Sozzo 2017). More profoundly, the foundational concepts, theories, ideas, and methods in criminology produced by this intellectual milieu, were endowed with universal status, notwithstanding their provenance in experiences, concerns, and perspectives specific to a limited number of metropolitan countries in the Global North. Criminology has undergone much change and development since, but is still in vital respects haunted by the ghosts of Lombroso and the nineteenth-century positivists.

From the 1870s, Lombroso and his associates undertook an ambitious research program measuring, classifying, and recording their observations of thousands of prison inmates (Lombroso 1876 [2006]). There are abundant critiques of his methods and theories which need no rehearsing here. Our interest is in how Lombroso's theory of atavism was linked with a particular idea of 'the Southern' from the outset. As Bradley explains:

> The southern regions of Italy suffered from high levels of economic deprivation, and thus Southern Italians accounted for a high proportion of the Italian prison population. There were also powerful cultural connotations of the South with crime and atavism . . . The south was seen as backward and uncivilised.
>
> (Bradley 2010: 28)

Melossi also points out that the Italian Positivist School was built around the 'southern question' (Melossi 2008: 52–55). Lombroso was influenced, as were many intellectuals at the time, by Darwin's evolutionary theory (1859) and in particular the versions of social Darwinism developed by others, often with limited regard for Darwin's own positions (Bradley 2010: 25). Social Darwinism was a centrepiece of metropolitan thought which assumed that the developing/industrialising world provided the standard of modernisation and the model of civilisation validated by doctrines of natural selection. Nature decreed that others should follow if they were to survive and prosper. Social evolutionism 'naturalised global difference' (Connell 2007: 17), justifying the imperial domination of the Northern imperial states over the Global South. In evolutionary theory, the European spaces of modernity were represented as disciplined, measured, hierarchical, and inhabited by rational actors (Gregory 2004: 3). Modernity's other—the pre-modern—was represented as the 'primitive, wild, and corporeal, mysterious, capricious, and excessive; or as irregular, multiple, and labyrinthine' (Gregory 2004: 3–4).

Mimicking the methods of Charles Darwin (1859), Lombroso also collected a great many specimens of what he assumed to be 'atavistic stigma' from the 'oriental' and 'primitive cultures' of Asia, Africa, Australia, and New Zealand. The specimens, photos, and objects are today archived in the Museum of Criminal Anthropology in Turin, Italy. Lombroso compared the cranial and biological features of these prototypical atavistic specimens from the Global South with his observations of prisoners, most of whom just happened to be the 'darker', 'hairier', and muscular men from Southern Italy (Horn 2003: 43–51). Comparisons drawn were then deployed as evidence of evolution from the uncivilised (largely Southern) to the civilised (largely Northern) world. The idea that the criminal was a monster, an evolutionary degenerate from a primitive culture or species was, therefore, one of the central origin stories of criminology: 'Criminals were gothic monsters, strangers among the civilised' (Rafter 2011: 151). This Lombrosian idea translated into a twentieth-century criminal science that continued to link criminality with certain body types and characteristics. As Horn described it, 'Claims about the atavistic nature of criminality were dependent . . . not only on evolutionary and national narratives, but also on generative analogies that linked the bodies and behaviours of criminals, animals, children, savages, and women' (2003: 25–26).

In the closely related nineteenth-century theory of recapitulation, the development of the individual was posited as repeating the stages of evolutionary development of their ancestors. Thus, white children develop beyond an intellectual stage in which the adults of inferior races are supposedly trapped. As Herbert Spencer put it, 'the intellectual traits of the uncivilized . . . are traits recurring in the children of the civilized' (cited in Gould 1980: 217). Images and assumptions regarding the traits held to be innate to non-white races included: impulsiveness, lack of self-control, emotionalism, violent propensities, immorality, idleness, and so on. Criminal and delinquent archetypes incorporating precisely these traits—'traits' that are readily attributed to young men from the 'lower' classes and certain racial and ethnic minorities, as a phase in their development that explains their greater propensity for crime—continue to provide the foundation for what are offered as *general* theories of crime and delinquency (see, for example, Gottfredson and Hirschi 1990; Wilson and Herrnstein 1985). The theoretical elaboration of, and 'scientific' validation for, such claims may have become more sophisticated as nineteenth-century racial science became thoroughly discredited, but the core underlying assumptions remain intact to a surprising degree. They continue to underpin the focal concerns of criminal justice and control institutions and the principal theoretical and empirical agendas of a great deal of mainstream criminology (such as much life course criminology), to the substantial exclusion of what some might see as dangerous subjects more worthy of criminological attention (corporate offenders that inflict untold loss of life and other harm in unsafe workplaces, that destroy and degrade whole environments or engage in organised fraud and tax evasion on a colossal scale). The linking of universal constructions of 'race' to crime and violence is an issue of immense importance that we consider at length in Chapter 3.

The dominant tendency has been for theory generated in the Global North to be exported to the periphery (Connell 2017: 6), its essential task being relegated to that of applying the theory to local social problems in order to produce empirical findings whose relevance is generally confined to the local setting. The Global South has not, until recently, figured as an important focus or imaginary for criminology (Aas 2011: 407). Instead criminological theories developed in the Global North simply assume a transnational generalisability and transferability (Bowling 2011: 363). Where criminology has taken root in the Global South it has tended to simply borrow and adapt these metropolitan theories, like the social sciences more broadly (Connell 2014: 522). Consequently, criminologies of the periphery have, until recently, accepted their subordinate role in the global organisation of knowledge as one of merely applying concepts and theory imported from the Global North (Carrington, Hogg, and Sozzo 2016). There are manifold examples, including our own uncritical application of Foucauldian, feminist, and Marxist concepts in early works (Carrington and Hogg 2002).

By uncritically replicating concepts from the global metropole and adapting them to the Global South, the project of criminology has been oriented to vertical integration at the expense of horizontal collaboration and intellectual innovation. There are exceptions to this dynamic, to be found in critical, feminist, queer, green, post-colonial, and indigenous criminologies (see, for example, chapters in the recently published *Palgrave Handbook of Criminology and the Global South*, Carrington et al. 2018). Nevertheless, the tendency toward vertical integration has stunted the intellectual development and vitality of criminology, both in the South and globally by perpetuating the relative neglect of important criminological issues and perspectives of relevance to both North and South. If this is to change, the epistemological dominance of metropolitan thought cannot remain unquestioned.

So, what are the components, the core assumptions, of criminology as Northern theory in need of renovation? In common with the social sciences at large, criminology has tended overwhelmingly to be 'top-down, national, and "terra-centric"' (Christopher, Pybus, and Rediker 2007: 1). Its close association with European nationalism (as well as imperialism), made it highly state-centred, sharing the assumptions that salient events and fundamental patterns and processes of development were national and occurred essentially within the borders of states. It has shown little interest in those processes and forces that transcended national boundaries and linked apparently separate worlds. Its predominant focus has been on crime as a domestic social problem that disturbs the peace of the nation state and on those institutions— local and national criminal law enforcement agencies—which aim to prevent, police, and punish criminal offenders. While deeply problematic in a globalised era where crime and harms associated with it are increasingly borderless and transnational, the 'terra-centric' focus of criminology is even more problematic in the digital era. As Lee argues, the criminological gaze has been so focused on street crime, that it has been frightfully slow in understanding cyber-crime: 'These are peripheral spaces of a virtual world, not understood simply by applying existing theoretical constructs of a place-based, state-focused terrestrial criminology' (Lee 2018: 239).

The modern 'science' of criminology was erected on Hobbesian foundations and developed largely as an adjunct of the modern state and its characteristic forms and practices of rule. Taking a high level of internal peace for granted, as the very condition of its existence, criminology has rarely (at least until recently) transcended its narrow, introspective outlook, inquiring into the historically contingent and often violent foundations of social order, of how the conditions of peace it assumed were brought about in different geo-political settings; how states were made, how their rule (through justice institutions and otherwise) was exerted, and at what costs to other, existing ways of life, and how the reach of their power was extended into new worlds. Criminology has largely ignored the use of violence as a tool of states and nation-building and its role in war, conquest, and colonisation. What might be seen to be peculiarly apposite subjects for criminological inquiry have been almost entirely omitted from criminological research agendas.

As an essentially peace-time endeavour, most criminological research has, therefore, concentrated on justice as 'a domestic (national) project, confined to local or national interests' (Barberet 2014: 16), overlooking major historical and contemporary forms and trends in criminal justice practice outside the metropolitan centres of the Northern hemisphere and contemporary violent phenomena, like armed conflict, drug wars, and ethnic cleansing, that are more common in the Global South (Barberet 2014; Braithwaite 2015; Braithwaite and Wardak

2013; Hogg 2002). Rather, criminology largely confined its attention to studying the minor delinquencies that troubled (mostly without seriously threatening) the internal peace of stable liberal states, to their more efficient measurement (developing and improving crime statistics, victim surveys, and the like), and to refining the instruments for policing, controlling, punishing, and treating individual offenders (mostly drawn from the poor, young, and marginal sectors of society). A 'peace-time criminology' assumed a comfortable role in the institutional ensemble devoted to managing the normative boundaries of social life in liberal democratic societies.

Criminology has also been highly urban-centric, which accounts for its lack of interest, until recently, in rural crime (Donnermeyer and DeKeseredy 2013; Hogg and Carrington 2006). Modernisation theories in the social sciences conceived social ills like crime as disorders stemming from the processes of industrialisation and city life. Criminology has assumed that crime was primarily an urban phenomenon. Key concepts, such as anomie, social control, and social disorganisation, were central to the modernisation thesis (Young 2010: 91). Widely influential in the social sciences over the last century, this thesis links historical processes of industrialisation and urbanisation as central problems for the maintenance of social order (Nisbet 1970). Social problems of crime, delinquency, and violence are conceived as modern urban phenomena produced by the erosion of community and extended family structures and the demise of traditional forms of social solidarity that exerted informal social controls.

The most famous and enduring works of this kind of sociological theorising in the field of criminology emerged from the Chicago School of Sociology between 1920 and 1945. Chicago had undergone rapid population growth—from under 5000 in 1840 to 1.7 million by the turn of the twentieth century, surging to 3.4 million people during the 1920s (Bulmer 1984: 13). The city, like many other American cities, had experienced waves of migration, with over half its population born outside the United States, including a large immigrant community from Southern Italy. Hence the city provided an ideal social laboratory for the study of crime, disorder, race, and delinquency. Few would dispute the richness of the legacy yielded by the Chicago School which includes Shaw's *The Natural History of a Delinquent Career*

(1931), *The Jackroller* (1930), and (with McKay) *Juvenile Delinquency and Urban Areas* (1931), Anderson's *The Hobo* (1923), Thrasher's *The Gang* (1927), Wirth's *The Ghetto* (1928), to name a few of its major studies. It also exerted a major influence on later work in the field, including classics like Whyte's *Street Corner Society: The Social Structure of an Italian Slum* (1943), and Cohen's *Delinquent Boys* in which he describes the delinquent as the quintessential 'rough male' (Cohen 1955: 140). While in no way dismissing the value of this body of work, it does bear the heavy footprint of a form of sociological theorising centred on how unruly young men, mostly of immigrant and lower-class backgrounds, formed subcultures of delinquency which posed significant problems for maintaining social order in the rapidly growing cities of the Global North.

The assumption underpinning this large program of research was that rapid population growth, social disorganisation, and weakened social controls produced higher crime rates (Levin and Lindesmith 1937). Social disorganisation theory, with its focus on urbanisation, became something of an article of faith in much of twentieth-century criminology (Baldwin and Bottoms 1976: 1; Felson 1994; Nisbet 1970). The theory was generalised and its provenance to a particular place and time widely overlooked. While the modernisation thesis may capture the impact of nineteenth century-industrialisation on social order in the sprawling cities of the Global North, it ignores the dramatic impacts of industrial capitalism on the reconstruction of the global countryside. It also overlooks how patterns of crime and violence emerge outside the metropole, especially in rural contexts and contested border zones (Carrington, Hogg, and Sozzo 2016) (see also Chapter 2). The assumption also marginalises research into the distinctive character of crime in rural and regional locales (Barclay et al. 2007; Donnermeyer 2018; Donnermeyer and DeKeseredy 2013; Harkness, Harris, and Baker 2015; Hogg and Carrington 2006).

From a Southern standpoint, metropolitan criminology has overlooked the historical role of states and the actual direction of movement of people, ideas, and institutions that were central to shaping societies of the South as they were drawn into the orbit of the European imperial order. As Beckert (2014) shows in his magisterial history of global capitalism, European capitalism was engaged from the outset in the transformation of the *global* countryside in what was often a violent process of change. From the standpoint of the colonial periphery, it was not the domestic urban setting that was the primary site of world-shattering social change. The periphery, far from being the vestigial rural arcadia often assumed in Western social science, bears the heavy imprint of a 'globe-spanning system' that over several centuries variously involved the transportation of African slaves (some eight million between 1500 and 1800) to plantations in the Caribbean, Latin America, and the US; the extensive reliance on a range of other forced and racialised labour regimes (including domestic enslaving of indigenous peoples, indentured labour trafficked throughout the intra-imperial world and transported convict labour to found and/or build new colonial settlements); the expropriation of the lands of indigenous peoples; the violent suppression and criminalisation of resistance, often amounting to genocide; and the decimation of local economies (including deindustrialisation of domestic manufacturing industries) so that the demands of metropolitan capitalism for raw materials (like cotton) and a mass supply of cheap wage labour could be met. The advance of industrial capitalism in the metropole in the nineteenth century had as its counterpart the extension and intensification of state-sponsored 'war capitalism' in the periphery (Beckert 2014). The pattern finds parallels today in the ways in which the worlds of violence are interconnected by markets (in drugs, guns, and so on) and political intervention in new forms (military corporations, global security firms, sponsorship of local warlords).

Thus, however observant imperial states might have been of liberal principles 'at home' during 'normal' times, they typically had recourse to very different control practices in the colonial world. Ideas of policing by consent, minimal force, and respect for the rule of law readily gave way to other methods, including openly repressive models of policing, recourse to extreme military force including 'air control' or the bombing of civilians, regimes of executive detention and segregation, summary execution, flogging, collective punishment, exile, and other direct forms of coercive violence including outright massacre. Such measures might be taken or escalated in the face of uprisings, insurgencies, or widespread dissent, but many formed part of the normal repertoire of control measures and mechanisms of repression available to manage colonial populations. We explore these issues in more detail in Chapter 4 and identify some of the ways in which an engagement with the penalities of the Global South might contribute to an otherwise thriving punishment and society scholarship.

. . . What is Southern criminology?

The assumptions and concerns we have been discussing have ensured that criminology—as a theoretical, empirical, and policy project—has substantially overlooked the Global South (Carrington, Hogg, and Sozzo 2016). Southern criminology supports projects to fill this void, to transnationalise and democratise criminological practice and knowledge, to renovate its methodological approaches, and to inject innovative perspectives into the study of crime and global justice from the periphery. As an empirical project Southern criminology seeks to modify the criminological field to make it more inclusive of histories and patterns of crime, justice, and security outside the Global North. More fundamentally, Southern criminology is a theoretical project; it seeks to generate theory and not just apply theory imported from the Global North. This is in no way to dismiss the conceptual and empirical advances that criminology and social science have produced over the last century. Rather, as a democratising epistemology, Southern criminology seeks to modify the power imbalances which have privileged knowledges produced in the metropolitan centres of the Global North.

Southern criminology, therefore, eschews the standpoint of opposition. Our purpose is not to add another school to the growing catalogue of new criminologies, but rather we wish to promote a series of projects of retrieval, which might serve to bridge global divides, enlarge understanding, and foster intercultural dialogues and epistemologies. It is premised on the recognition that North and South are globally interconnected in ways and with effects, both historical and contemporary, which warrant careful inquiry and analysis in criminological research, theoretical, and policy agendas. Thus, rather than being simply and exclusively concerned with 'the South', it seeks to pursue the careful analysis of processes, interactions, and networks linking South and North which have been obscured by the metropolitan hegemony over criminological thought. Its purpose is not to denounce but to re-orient, not to oppose but to modify, not to displace but to augment. Metropolitan thinking captures a set of tendencies, rather than being a distinct, uniform body of theory. Our purpose in illustrating how metropolitan thinking has shaped the focus of criminology is to urge critical reflection on the colonising and hegemonic dynamics within criminological theory. We are not suggesting that the development of Southern criminology will suddenly overturn the knowledge/power relations that have shaped social science in general and criminology in particular, but it may usefully modify them in productive ways. It is the purpose of the following chapters to lay down some markers for how this might be undertaken in relation to certain selected topics and themes within criminology; to illustrate how the existing field might usefully be *Southernised*.

References

Aas KF (2011) Visions of global control: Cosmopolitan aspirations in a world of friction. In Bosworth M and Hoyle C (eds) *What Is Criminology?*: 406–442. Oxford: Oxford University Press.

Anderson C (2016) Global mobilities. In Burton A and Ballantyne T (eds) *World Histories from Below: Disruption and Dissent 1750 to the Present*: 169–196. London: Bloomsbury Academic.

Anderson N (1923) *The Hobo*. Chicago: University of Chicago Press.

Baldwin J and Bottoms A (1976) *The Urban Criminal*. London: Tavistock.

Barberet R (2014) *Women, Crime and Criminal Justice*. London and New York: Routledge.

Barclay E, Donnermeyer JF, Scott J, and Hogg R (eds) (2007) *Crime in Rural Australia*. Sydney: Federation Press.

Beckert S (2014) *Empire of Cotton: A New History of Global Capitalism*. London: Allen Lane.

Belich J (2011) *Replenishing the Earth: The Settler Revolution and the Rise of the Anglo-World, 1783–1939*. Oxford: Oxford University Press.

Bowling B (2011) Transnational criminology and the globalisation of harm production. In Bosworth M and Hoyle C (eds) *What Is Criminology?*: 361–379. Oxford: Oxford University Press.

Bradley K (2010) Cesare Lombroso (1835–1909). In Hayward K, Maruna S, and Mooney J (eds) *Fifty Key Thinkers in Criminology*: 25–29. London and New York: Routledge.

Braithwaite J (2015) Rethinking criminology through radical diversity in Asian reconciliation. *Asian Journal of Criminology* 10(3): 181–183. DOI: 10.1007/s11417-014-9200-z.

Braithwaite J and Wardak A (2013) Crime and war in Afghanistan. Part 1: The Hobbesian solution. *The British Journal of Criminology* 53: 179–196. DOI: 10.1093/bjc/azs065.

Brody H (2001) *The Other Side of Eden: Hunter Gatherers, Farmers and the Shaping of the World*. London: Faber.

Brown M (2018) Southern criminology in the post-coloniality: More than a 'derivative discourse'? In Carrington K, Hogg R, Scott J, and Sozzo M (eds) *Palgrave Handbook of Criminology and the Global South*: 83–104. Switzerland: Palgrave Macmillan.

Bulmer M (1984) *The Chicago School of Sociology*. Chicago: University of Chicago.

Carrington K and Hogg R (eds) (2002) *Critical Criminology: Issues, Debates and Challenges*. Cullompton: Willan.

Carrington K and Hogg R (2017) Deconstructing criminology's origin stories: A view from the Global South. *Asian Journal of Criminology* 12(3): 181–197.

Carrington K, Hogg R, and Sozzo M (2016) Southern criminology. *British Journal of Criminology* 56(1): 1–20. DOI: 10.1093/bjc/azv083.

Carrington K, Hogg R, Scott J, and Sozzo M (eds) (2018) *Palgrave Handbook of Criminology and the Global South*. Switzerland: Palgrave Macmillan.

Carter P (1992) *Living in a New Country: History, Travelling and Language*. London: Faber and Faber.

Chakrabarty D (2000) *Provincializing Europe: Post-Colonial Thought and Difference*, 2nd edn. Princeton: Princeton University Press.

Christopher E, Pybus C, and Rediker M (2007) Introduction. In Christopher E, Pybus C, and Rediker M (eds) *Many Middle Passages: Forced Migration and the Making of the Modern World*: 1–19. Berkeley: University of California Press.

Cohen A (1955) *Delinquent Boys*. New York: The Free Press.

Collier P (2007) *The Bottom Billion: Why the Poorest Countries are Failing and What Can Be Done About It*. Oxford: Oxford University Press.

Connell R (2007) *Southern Theory: The Global Dynamics of Knowledge Social Science*. Crows Nest: Allen & Unwin.

Connell R (2014) Rethinking gender from the South. *Feminist Studies* 40(3) 518–539. DOI: 10.15767/feministstudies.40.3.518.

Connell R (2017) Southern theory and world universities. *Higher Education Research and Development* 36(1): 4–15. DOI: 10.1080/07294360.2017.1252311.

Connell R, Collyer F, Maia J, and Morrell R (2017) Toward a global sociology of knowledge: Post-colonial realities and intellectual practices. *International Sociology* 32(1): 21–37. DOI: 10.1177/0268580916676913.

Currie E (2018) Confronting the North's South: On race and violence in the United States. In Carrington K, Hogg R, Scott J, and Sozzo M (eds) *Palgrave Handbook of Criminology and the Global South*: 43–60. Switzerland: Palgrave Macmillan.

Daniels R (2004) *Guarding the Golden Door: American Immigration Policy and Immigrants since 1882*. New York: Hill and Wang.

Darwin C (1839) *Journal of Researches into the Geology and Natural History of the Various Countries Visited by H.M.S. Beagle*. London: Colburn.

Darwin J (2013) *Unfinished Empire: The Global Expansion of Britain*. London: Penguin.

de Sousa Santos B (2014) *Epistemologies of the South: Justice Against Epistemicide*. Boulder: Paradigm Publishers.

Donnermeyer J (2018) The rural dimensions of a Southern criminology: Selected topics and general processes. In Carrington K, Hogg R, Scott J, and Sozzo M (eds) *Palgrave Handbook of Criminology and the Global South*: 105–120. Switzerland: Palgrave Macmillan.

Donnermeyer J and DeKeseredy W (2013) *Rural Criminology*. New York: Routledge.

Du Bois WEB (1903) *The Souls of Black Folk*. Chicago: AC McClurg and Co.

Du Bois WEB (1920) *Darkwater: Voices from within the Veil*. New York: Harcourt, Brace and Howe.

Faraldo-Cabana P (2018) Research excellence and Anglophone dominance: The case of law, criminology and social science. In Carrington K, Hogg R, Scott J, and Sozzo M (eds) *Palgrave Handbook of Criminology and the Global South*: 163–182. Switzerland: Palgrave Macmillan.

Felson M (1994) *Crime and Everyday Life: Insights and Implications for Society*. Thousand Oaks, California: Pine Forge Press.

Fonseca D (2018) Punishment at the margins: Groundwork for a revisited sociology of punishment. In Carrington K, Hogg R, Scott J, and Sozzo M (eds) *Palgrave Handbook of Criminology and the Global South*: 105–120. Switzerland: Palgrave Macmillan.

Garland D (2011) Criminology's place in the academic field. In Bosworth M and Hoyle C (eds) *What Is Criminology?*: 298–317. Oxford: Oxford University Press.

Gott R (2007) Latin America as a white settler society. *Bulletin of Latin American Research* 26(2): 269–289. DOI: 10.1111/j.1470-9856.2007.00224.x.

Gottfredson M and Hirschi T (1990) *A General Theory of Crime*. Stanford: Stanford University Press.

Gould S (1980) *Ever Since Darwin: Reflections in Natural History*. Harmondsworth: Penguin.

Graham M, Hale SA, and Stephens M (2011) Flick CM (ed.) *Geographies of the World's Knowledge*. London: Convoco! Edition.

Gregory D (2004) *The Colonial Present: Afghanistan. Palestine. Iraq*. Oxford: Blackwell Publishing.

Hage G (2017) *Is Racism an Environmental Threat?* Cambridge: Polity.

Hancock WK (1961) *Australia*. Brisbane: Jacaranda Press.

Harkness A, Harris B, and Baker D (eds) (2015) *Locating Crime in Context and Place: Regional and Rural Perspectives*. Annandale, NSW: Federation Press.

Hayward K, Maruna S, and Mooney J (2010) Introduction. In Hayward K, Maruna S, and Mooney J (eds) *Fifty Key Thinkers in Criminology*: xxv–xxxi. London and New York: Routledge.

Hogg R (2002) Criminology beyond the nation state. In Carrington K and Hogg R (eds) *Critical Criminology: Issues, Debates and Challenges*: 185–217. Collumpton: Willan.

Hogg R and Carrington K (2006) *Policing the Rural Crisis*. Sydney: Federation Press.

Hogg R, Scott J, and Sozzo M (2017) Special edition: Southern criminology—guest editors' introduction. *International Journal for Crime, Justice and Social Democracy* 6(1): 1–7. DOI: 10.5204/ijcjsd.v6i1.395.

Horn D (2003) *The Criminal Body: Lombroso and the Anatomy of Deviance*. New York: Routledge.

Ignatiev N (2009) *How the Irish Became White*. New York: Routledge.

Independent Commission on International Development Issues (Brandt Commission) (1980) *North–South: A Programme for Survival*. Cambridge MA: Brandt Commission.

Independent Commission on International Development Issues (Brandt Commission) (1983) *Common Crisis: North–South Cooperation for World Recovery*. Cambridge MA: Brandt Commission.

Lake M and Reynolds H (2008) *Drawing the Global Colour Line: White Men's Countries and the Question of Racial Equality*. Carlton: Melbourne University Press.

Latour B (1994) *We Have Never Been Modern*. Cambridge MA: Harvard University Press.

Latour B (2017) Europe as refuge. In Geiselberger H (ed.) *The Great Regression*: 78–87. Cambridge: Polity.

Lee M (2018) Crime and the cyber periphery: Criminological theory beyond time and space. In Carrington K, Hogg R, Scott J, and Sozzo M (eds) *Palgrave Handbook of Criminology and the Global South*: 223–244. Switzerland: Palgrave Macmillan.

Levin Y and Lindesmith A (1937) English ecology and criminology of the past century. *Journal of Criminal Law and Criminology* 27(6): 801–816.

Lombroso C (1876 [2006]) Gibson M and Hahn Rafter N (trans.) *Criminal Man*. Durham: Duke University Press.

Melossi D (2008) *Controlling Crime, Controlling Society: Thinking About Crime in Europe and America*. Cambridge: Polity Press.

Mignolo W (2012) *Local Histories/Global Designs: Coloniality, Subaltern Knowledges, and Border Thinking*. Princeton: Princeton University Press.

Nisbet R (1970) *The Sociological Tradition*. London: Heineman.

Population Reference Bureau (2013) *World Population Data Sheet*. Available at http://www.prb.org/Publications/Datasheets/2013/2013-world-population-data-sheet/data-sheet.aspx (accessed 10 October 2016, no longer available).

Rafter N (2011) Origins of criminology. In Bosworth M and Hoyle C (eds) *What Is Criminology?*: 143–154. Oxford: Oxford University Press.

Roediger D (2005) *Working Toward Whiteness: How America's Immigrants Became White*. New York: Basic Books.

Samson J (2011) Pacific history in context. *Journal of Pacific History* 46(2): 244–250. DOI: 10.1080/00223344.2011.607273.

Sen A (2006) *Identity and Violence: The Illusion of Identity*. London: Allen Lane.

Shaw C (1930) *The Jackroller: A Delinquent Boy's Own Story*. Chicago: University of Chicago Press.

Shaw C (1931) *The Natural History of the Delinquent Career*. Chicago: University of Chicago Press.

Shaw C and McKay M (1931) *Juvenile Delinquency and Urban Areas: A Study of Rates of Delinquents in Relation to Differential Characteristics of Local Communities in American Cities*. Chicago: University of Chicago Press.

Tax Justice Focus (2016) The corruption issue. *Newsletter of the Tax Justice Network*. (April).

Thrasher F (1927) *The Gang*. Chicago: University of Chicago Press.

Torres-García J (1936) *Mapa de Sudamérica Invertido*.

United Nations Development Programme (2013) *Human Development Report 2013: The Rise of the South*. New York: United Nations.

Veracini L (2011) Introducing Settler Colonial Studies. *Settler Colonial Studies* 1(1): 1–12. DOI: 10.1080/2201473X.2011.10648799.

Walklate S and McGarry R (eds) (2015) *Criminology and War: Transgressing the Borders*. London and New York: Routledge.

Wallerstein I (2004) *World-Systems Analysis: An Introduction*. Durham: Duke University Press.

Walmsley R (2016) *World Prison Population*, 11th edn. Institute for Criminal Policy Research.

Whyte WF (1943) *Street Corner Society: The Social Structure of an Italian Slum*. Chicago: University of Chicago Press.

Wilson JQ and Herrnstein R (1985) *Crime and Human Nature: The Definitive Study of the Causes of Crime*. New York: Touchstone Books.

Wirth L (1928) *The Ghetto*. Chicago: University of Chicago Press.

Wolfe P (2006) Settler colonialism and the elimination of the native. *Journal of Genocide Research* 8(4): 387–409. DOI: 10.1080/14623520601056240.

World Bank (2011) *World Development Report 2011: Conflict, Security, and Development*. Washington, District of Columbia: World Bank.

World Bank (2016) *Poverty and Shared Prosperity 2016: Taking on Inequality*. Washington, District of Columbia: World Bank.

Worldometers (2018) Population by region. Available at http://www.worldo meters.info/world-population/population-by-region/ (accessed 26 April 2017).

Young J (2010) Robert Merton (1910–2003). In Hayward K, Maruna S, and Mooney J (eds) *Fifty Key Thinkers in Criminology*: 88–98. London and New York: Routledge.

2

VIOLENCE, GENDER, AND THE GLOBAL SOUTH

Introduction

Criminology has tended to maintain a highly selective focus on violence in the large population centres of the Global North to the exclusion of the many more spaces and places that lie beyond them, such as the global countryside, peripheries, and antipodes (Hogg and Carrington 2006). The criminological gaze has, to an overwhelming extent, been a peace-time research endeavour focused on the problems of pacified nation states of the Global North (Barberet 2014: 16), albeit with a growing number of exceptions (Aas 2011; Barberet 2014; Braithwaite 2018; McGarry and Walklate 2016). It has had little to say about the violence of state and nation building, of empire and settler colonialism, of the expropriation of indigenous peoples (Cunneen 2001), and of enslavement and other forms of forced labour migration, or of the particular forms of gendered violence experienced by women in the Global South (Barberet and Carrington 2018). Yet countries in the Global South suffer most from cycles of extreme violence (World Bank 2015) and have the highest rates of homicide, ethnic and religious violence, and violence against women and minorities in the world (United Nations Development

Programme (UNDP) 2014). These countries include the places of the world most severely torn by violent conflict, the rapacious depletion of natural resources, environmental degradation, rising sea levels, population dislocation, political corruption, and poor, often autocratic, governance. This ensemble of mutually reinforcing threats to human security dwarfs the problems of violence that predominate the pages of published criminology. In a shrinking world with increasingly porous national borders, these issues are also highly consequential for South/North relations, and global security and justice. Yet the study of these problems has been largely overlooked (Carrington, Hogg, and Sozzo 2016). In this chapter we cannot provide a comprehensive account of violence in the Global South, but we do seek to outline the dimensions of the problem and consider some of the key driving forces behind it. The chapter argues that the distinctive shape and form that violence takes in the Global South has been structured by the coloniality of power and its mutual constitution with the coloniality of gender (Lugones 2008: 12). We begin with a broad overview of the unequal global distribution of criminal violence.

The unequal global distribution of criminal violence

The worst, most destructive and intractable forms of violence in the world today—civil war and ethnic cleansing—are the legacy of colonisation and decolonisation processes. These forms of violence have appeared across the Global South and in parts of the Global North (Eastern Europe, the former Yugoslavia) in the period since World War II. They have accompanied efforts to carve nation states from multiethnic colonial states whose borders were imposed by colonising powers without reference to the character and boundaries of pre-colonial societies. The founding of the United Nations (UN) in 1945 involved 51 member states; today there are 193 nation states. This has involved much shedding of blood by colonial powers seeking to hang onto their acquisitions, repress the resistance of subject peoples, and shape the post-colonial future of their former colonies; and also as a result of the violence unleashed in many places by the decolonisation process. Struggles between different peoples occupying the same territory to determine the composition and identity of the new nation are mostly what have driven civil wars, genocides, ethnic cleansings, grave human rights abuses, and refugee movements in the post-war period. In many post-colonial settings in Africa, Asia and the Middle East large-scale violent conflict or the threat or aftermath of it have been closer to the norm than the exception. The global Cold War frequently exacerbated these conflicts and triggered others elsewhere in the post-colonial world like Latin America, as these countries served as proxies for the rivalry between the superpowers. Large scale collective violence triggers other forms of serious violence due to the various legacies of poverty, inequality, environmental destruction, and weak and corrupt governance. A peace-time criminology largely conceived and developed within the framework of relatively stable and prosperous nation states has demonstrated little interest in these violent worlds, with some significant exceptions (Braithwaite 2018; see also McGarry and Walklate 2016).

Criminal violence (which includes homicide, racial and ethnic conflict, gendered violence, sexual violence, and collective violence) has more recently replaced armed conflict as one of the leading causes of death in the world (World Health Organization (WHO) 2014). Nine out of ten violent deaths now occur outside conflict zones. Each year, 1.6 million people die from criminal violence, accounting for 14 per cent of deaths for men and six per cent for women (WHO 2014: 2). The incidence of violence is highly uneven, with localities on the periphery in the Global South suffering most from high rates of criminal violence (UNDP 2014; World Bank 2015). By contrast homicide rates in high income countries have declined significantly since the turn of the twenty-first century—in fact by 39 per cent (from 6.2 to 3.8 per 100,000 population) (WHO 2014: vii).

Almost all (42 out of 43) of the countries ranked by World Health Rankings (n.d.) as having the highest rates of death by violence in the world are in the Global South. The overwhelming majority are in Africa, Latin America and parts of Asia (Afghanistan, Turkmenistan, Papua New Guinea (PNG), and the Philippines) (World Health Rankings n.d.). Honduras tops the list of countries for violence as a leading cause of death with a rate of 93 per 100,000, closely followed by El Salvador, Venezuela, Columbia, and Zimbabwe. South Africa ranks fourteenth with a rate of 26 per 100,000; Mexico ranks nineteenth with a rate of 19 per 100,000. Japan has the lowest rates in the world at 0.29 per 100,000. Other countries with a homicide rate less than one per 100,000 include China, Portugal, Spain, France, Australia, Ireland, and the Nordic countries in Europe. The United States is ranked in the middle with a rate of 5.6 per 100,000 (World Health Rankings n.d.).

Another way of illustrating the unequal distribution of violence is to examine rates of violence by cities. Of the 50 most violent cities in the world, 46 are in the Global South and only four are in the Global North (Central America is included in our conception of the Global South). Three are in Africa and 43 are in Central and South America (17 in Mexico; five in Venezuela, 17 in Brazil; three in Columbia; two in Honduras; and one each in El Salvador, Guatemala, Puerto Rico, and Jamaica) (Securidad, Justicia y Paz 2017). Rates of violence in post-apartheid South Africa have remained persistently high despite being 'freed from the economic, social and cultural fetters of racist autocracy' (Dixon 2013: 319). The distribution of violence, and especially lethal violence, is highly racialised in the world today. Violent cities and countries are mainly Latin American and African countries, some of them with large indigenous populations and some with descendants of slaves, so there is no surprise and nothing distinctive about the demographic profile described here. And it is not just the racialisation of violence that is significant, but also the legacies of colonisation, poverty, gross inequality, civil war, dictatorship, apartheid, and foreign control and intervention.

Four of the world's most violent cities are today located in the United States (US). They include St Louis and Detroit (places of migration of former slaves from the deep South) and Baltimore and New Orleans (American cities that operated the biggest slave trading markets in America before the Civil War in 1862 and the passing of the Fifth Amendment in 1870 that finally brought an end to slavery). At the height of the slave trade almost four million African slaves toiled the plantations of the deep South (Morgan 2007). After the end of slavery and the defeat of Reconstruction, Southern African Americans were left homeless, landless and dependent on exploitative white employers (Currie 2018: 54). Consequently, there are ongoing enclaves of the 'Southern' in the Global North, shaped by the historical processes of slavery and the coloniality of power (Currie 2018). The legacy of America's Southern pattern of development has devastated African-Americans through social forces that for generations curtailed their opportunities, shrunk their prospects, and subjected them to extreme racial discrimination (Currie 2018: 51–52). Today, homicide is the leading cause of death among African-American men. In the 15 years since the turn of the twenty-first century, there have been 124,000 homicides of African-Americans (Currie 2018: 46). The rate of homicide for African-Americans is 20 per 100,000 compared to 2.7 per 100,000 for white Americans (Currie 2018: 46). That is, numbers more akin to violent crime rates in parts of the Global South. This is at a time when violent crime rates have been in decline in the US—but only for its white population.

A similar pattern of violence occurs in other post-colonial settler societies. In Australia, for example, the homicide rate of both male and female Indigenous Australians is approximately five times higher than for non-Indigenous Australians (Cussen and Bryant 2015: 1). An analysis of 23 years of homicide data from 1989 to 2012 found that 70 per cent of homicides involving an Indigenous victim, also involved an Indigenous perpetrator (Cussen and Bryant 2015: 2). The analysis concluded 'Intimate partner homicides involving both an Indigenous victim and offender were almost double the proportion of non-Indigenous intimate partner homicides (38 per cent cf. 20 per cent)' (Cussen and Bryant 2015: 4). One of the case studies below explores the making of violent masculinities in the Global South and how these relate to the coloniality of gender and power.

Gendered violence and the Global South

A significant proportion of criminal violence in the world today is also gendered. This is because the majority of the victims of sexual harassment, sexual assault, and domestic assault are female and their perpetrators male (Cox 2016: 1). Violence against women and girls (VAWG) is a global issue with significant social, economic, and personal consequences. The World Health Organization undertook the first global estimate of prevalence rates of sexual and domestic violence against women. The study found that 35 per cent of all the women in the world had experienced violence by a partner or ex-partner and that 38 per cent of all female homicides were the result of domestic violence (WHO 2013). The burden of sexual and domestic violence, like criminal violence more generally, is distributed unequally with women from low to middle income countries of the Global South more susceptible to gendered violence (see also DeKeseredy and Hall-Sanchez 2018).

One of these regions is the South Asia-Pacific, where two out of three women have experienced gendered violence (Fulu et al. 2013). This figure is double the global average found by the WHO (2013) study referred to above. The South Asia-Pacific region accounts for 60 per cent of the world's population (United Nations Economic and Social Commission for the Asia and Pacific 2016). It includes 50 countries, from China in East Asia, to Vietnam in South-East Asia, from Afghanistan to Turkey in South Asia, and the Pacific which includes Australia, New Zealand, and the Pacific Islands. The influence of custom and religion in the making of local gender orders shapes both the prevalence and distinctive form of gendered violence across such a diverse array of countries in the South Asia-Pacific. Miedema and Fulu (2018) argue that global forces interact with local gender norms, practices, and ideologies to either reinforce or challenge violence against women in the Asia-Pacific. They use a Southern criminological perspective to include the histories and experiences of the Global South in feminist scholarship on interpersonal violence. They argue that the more patriarchal the local gender norms and practices are, the more likely women will be subject to interpersonal violence (Miedema and Fulu 2018: 870). This is why 'forms of violence, such as acid attacks, honour killings, and female genital mutilation disproportionately affect women of the global South' (Miedema and Fulu 2018: 867).

Women's social status, legal status, access to education, and participation in civil and political life drive the routine practices of gender in everyday life (Connell 2009). The local gender order affects the form and prevalence of gendered violence, especially where women's worth and value is tied closely to the institution of marriage (Miedema and Fulu 2018: 867–871). The exchange of a dowry for a bride is common in parts of South Asia. Women who exercise little or no choice over their marriage partner are likely to experience more gendered violence (Miedema and Fulu 2018: 871).

Additionally, girls and women exchanged for dowries during adolescence or as children are particularly vulnerable to sexual and domestic violence (Miedema and Fulu 2018: 871). Miedema and Fulu (2018) argue that the spread of patriarchal religious ideologies that justify child marriage (in places like Afghanistan, Indonesia, Maldives, Malaysia, and Pakistan) have consequently increased the risk of gendered violence in the Asia-Pacific. However, Miedema and Fulu also point out that the institution of marriage can act as a protective factor against violence (2018: 872). Fulu found that rates of domestic violence were lower in the countries of Asia where divorce and marriage are flexible, where gender roles are less unequal, and where local shame/honour customs are fairly moderate (Fulu 2014). Where regimes of shame are strict and enforced by religious police and/or extended families, honour-based violence is a significant issue for young women growing up in these local patriarchal gender orders.

Honour-based violence is a distinctive form of gendered violence associated with particular ethnic and religious cultures across the Global South (Mayeda, Vijaykumar, and Chesney-Lind 2018: 947). It occurs in Christian, Jewish, Hindi, Kurdish, and Muslim communities (Begikhani, Gill, and Hague 2015: 1–2). The main targets of honour-based violence are women and the main perpetrators are male relatives (Begikhani, Gill, and Hague 2015: 1–2). Honour-based violence occurs where family members inflict punishment for acts that they believe bring dishonour to family reputation (Mayeda, Vijaykumar, and Chesney-Lind 2018: 949). Dishonour includes a wide range of behaviours, such as sex outside marriage, immodesty, breach of dress codes, talking to strangers, refusing to marry in exchange for a dowry, appearing in public without a male relative, and falling pregnant outside marriage. Punishments vary in severity from isolation, withdrawal of family support and social ostracism to physical punishments, such as caning and stoning and, in the most serious instances, killing. International bodies, such as the UN, have been working globally to turn around the cultural and religious attitudes that underpin honour-based violence.

Rates of gendered violence in Australia are about half that of its neighbours in the Asia-Pacific. But it is still very costly—with a price tag of A$21.7 billion per year, covering health care and justice system costs (Price Waterhouse Coopers (PWC) 2015: 11). In Australia one in every six women have experienced violence by a partner or ex-partner, as have one in every 16 men (Australian Institute of Health and Welfare (AIHW) 2018: ix). On average, eight women are hospitalised per day in Australia due to domestic violence and one in five women have experienced sexual violence since turning 15 (AIHW 2018: 10). While nearly all rates of crime victimisation for non-violent offences have been declining in Australia, rates for sexual assault have been rising for decades (Australian Institute of Criminology 2005), rates of violence for Indigenous Australians are increasing, and the number of domestic violence homicides has remained fairly static for three decades (Bryant and Cussen 2015: 1). These generic figures for violence against women disguise those most vulnerable, who include: Indigenous women, women with disabilities, women who are pregnant, experiencing financial difficulty, or separating from partners (AIHW 2018: x). Women from rural Australia—both Indigenous and non-Indigenous—are also at higher risk of experiencing violence at the hands of their current or former partners (Owen and Carrington 2015). These disparities are important signposts of how the coloniality of gender has shaped the contours of contemporary patterns of violence in the Global South. Below we unpack what is meant by the coloniality of gender and how it arose from critiques of feminism by feminists of colour (Potter 2015).

Feminist theory and the coloniality of gender

The bulk of research on gendered violence, including feminist research, is undertaken in and on the countries and cities in the Global North. Yet as is obvious from the global distribution of gendered violence outlined above, it is a much bigger problem in the Global South. In this respect, feminist theory and research has reproduced structures of marginality and centrality between what Connell (2014a) calls the metropole and the periphery (2014a: 522)—the Global North and Global South (2014a: 526). This is not to suggest that feminist analyses from the Global North are faulty, simply that they are selective in privileging empirical referents and theoretical concepts derived from their geo-political specificities.

The core problem with feminist analyses identified mainly by feminists of colour is that universal categories of gender assumed a white woman and not a woman of colour (hooks 1982; Lugones 2008; Mohanty 1984; Sandoval 1991). Mohanty was perhaps one of the first to expose the Anglo-centric gaze of feminist theory in her now famous piece 'Under Western eyes' (originally published in 1984 and later re-published). The de-colonial philosopher Lugones (2008) argues that feminism constructed an idea of womanhood where all women were white:

> Erasing any history, including oral history, of the relation of white to non-white women, white feminism wrote white women large . . . They understood women as inhabiting white bodies but did not bring that racial qualification to articulation or clear awareness. That is, they did not understand themselves in intersectional terms, at the intersection of race, gender, and other forceful marks of subjection or domination.
>
> (Lugones 2008: 13)

Given the Northern-centric and white focus of much feminist criminology, it has become abundantly clear that this body of knowledge also needs to broaden its conceptual and spatial horizons by globalising research agendas to add voices from the Global South (Barberet 2014; Barberet and Carrington 2018; Carrington 2015; Renzetti 2013). Southern theories, subaltern studies, post-colonialism, indigenous knowledges, intersectionality, and feminisms of colour have done much to redress this structured inequality in the global economy of knowledge. Indeed, the concept of intersectionality was devised by feminists of colour as activists and scholars to overcome the whiteness of activism (Potter 2015: 41–42). Intersectionality is a useful corrective to the universalising tendencies of what Potter calls 'colour blind feminism' (2015: 43), as it does not privilege any particular axis of power. Crenshaw (1991) originally used the concept to re-appraise the politics of violence against women of colour as shaped by multiple, and not singular, axes power and domination. Importantly, it is an evolving concept that rejects universal constructions of women, opting instead for a plurality of diverse women of colour, race, class, ethnicity, culture, and religion (Carrington 2015). In the intersections and spaces of difference possibilities emerge that can accommodate a differential consciousness (Sandoval 1991: 349). This is a feminist consciousness that acknowledges women share alliances based on gender, but also acknowledges differences, especially those that arise from the power of coloniality in shaping the modern gender order.

A central challenge for feminist scholars now, then, is how to understand contemporary patterns of gendered violence, without confining victims/survivors to a unidimensional status of victimhood. Another challenge is how to criticise gendered violence linked to patriarchal practices based on ethnic and religious customs 'without perpetuating racist narratives that already plague South Asian and Middle Eastern countries' (Mayeda, Vijaykumar, and Chesney-Lind 2018: 958). One way of attempting to wrestle with this conundrum is to take into account the power relations of colonialism and neo-colonialism—what Lugones has termed the 'coloniality of gender' (2008). She argues that the coloniality of gender acts symbiotically with the projects and power of coloniality that, over centuries, racialised gender divisions from light to dark. Light-skin women, she argues, were inferiorised by a modern gender order that constructed them as passive subjects without agency, confining them largely to the private sphere for the purposes of nurturing and the reproduction of capitalism. Dark-skin women, on the other hand, were thrust into a gender system that was 'thoroughly violent' from the beginning (Lugones 2008: 16). Here, Lugones refers explicitly to the capitalist and sexual exploitation of African slaves and the vast indigenous genocide across the Americas.

Colonialism was a highly gendered, racialised, and violent historical process (Connell 2014b) that continues to shape the global structuring of vast social and geo-political inequalities. Below we explore examples of distinct patterns of violence in different parts of the Global South, shaped by the two axes of the coloniality of gender and race. This discussion confronts the fact that the Global South has the highest and most chronic rates of violence in the world. In these examples the constitution of violent masculinities will also emerge as a critical dimension of the coloniality of gender.

Drug wars, homicide, and femicide in Mexico

Globalisation has opened up new trade markets in the Global South increasing women's access to paid work and economic independence. In the 1990s, thousands of jobs became available in the *maquiladoras* (factories) that sprung up along the desert border of the Mexican state of Chihuahua following the establishment of the *1994 North American Free Trade Agreement* (US Customs and Border Protection 2018). The agreement, signed by Canada, the United States, and Mexico, removed trade barriers between the countries, turning this border zone into a hub of global manufacturing. This is the scene of one of the world's largest unsolved collective crimes of femicide. Between 1993 and 2016, 1642 girls and women were kidnapped, tortured, sexually mutilated, raped and killed in Juárez (Monárrez Fragoso 2018: 914). Ciudad Juárez, a city of around 2.5 million, is ranked the twentieth most violent city in the world (Securidad, Justicia y Paz 2017). For two decades, the Mexican criminal justice system failed to adequately investigate the murders of the female factory workers, many who had migrated from poor rural areas of Mexico in search of economic independence (Livingston 2004: 60). They were stigmatised as outsiders, as public women, who drank, worked, and socialised like men and were aligned with the stigma of sex work (Wright 2005: 289). Most victims were blamed for their own fate, diverting public attention from the role of corrupt government officials, police dereliction of duty, drug cartels, and complicit factory owners (Wright 2005). Livingston argues that the femicides reflect 'the gendering of production, the gendering of violence, and the relationship between the two' (Livingston 2004: 60).

Femicide—the killing of women by men—argues Monárrez Fragoso, is an on-going systemic risk faced by the *maquiladora* workers in Juárez, Mexico (Monárrez Fragoso 2018: 914). Monárrez Fragoso, who has lived and worked most of her life in this city, describes Ciudad Juárez as an example of 'global coloniality' (2018: 916). Globalisation opened the city to transnational corporations, most from the US, to cheap labour and industrial land with few restrictions and regulations. The illegal drug and arms trade between the US and Mexico use the same trade route through the *maquiladoras*. Illegal and legal capital coalesces in the dangerous deserts of the border zone. Corruption, ineptitude, and a lack of willingness by authorities to bring justice to the victims, has meant impunity for most of the offenders. The families of the victims have suffered and continue to suffer humiliating treatment by the justice system—most not believed, supported, or taken seriously. The disappearances continue and, at the time of writing, 104 young women remain missing (Monárrez Fragoso 2018). In an act of remembrance, an open air museum, murals, pink crosses, and photos of the missing girls adorn the streets of the city. These powerful symbols puncture the silencing of the victims and their families. Monárrez Fragoso insists on naming these mysterious disappearances as acts of systemic femicide. This framing 'allows us to think of [femicide] as a counter-hegemonic word with the power to denounce the gendered atrocity of systemic sexual [femicide]' (2018: 926).

Monárrez Fragoso draws critical attention to the overlapping and inextricably intertwined link between gendered violence (of which femicide is the most serious), and criminal violence in Mexico. As already mentioned, Mexico is home to 17 of the world's most violent cities (Securidad, Justicia y Paz 2017). The bulk of those killed on the border zones between Mexico and the United States include many thousands of men, mostly young men caught up in drug wars and arms smuggling. The border between Mexico and Texas is one of the world's most notorious zones for violent encounters between post-colonial masculinities associated with drug trafficking and law enforcement (Guerra 2015). Quintero and Estrada (1998) undertook a study of Mexican men living in the US-Mexican border zones. They found that 'machismo provides a special utility in the streets, where attitudes of dominance, pride and aggression are critical to the establishment and maintenance of street identities and defences' (Quintero and Estrada 1998: 158). For these men, machismo is attractive because it provides them with extremely effective survival skills—dominate and kill, or be dominated and be killed. However, they caution against interpreting machismo as an individualised 'risk factor' or psychological pathology, urging instead a sociological understanding of how the violence of poverty and exploitation of the border zone 'make some aspects of machismo a necessary means of engaging in certain life-worlds' (Quintero and Estrada 1998: 163). They point to the systematic exclusion of around half the population of local Latino men from the formal economy of the *maquiladoras* as macro factors that propel them into an informal economy of drug trafficking and arms smuggling (Quintero and Estrada 1998: 162).

While the idea of machismo has deep roots in a multitude of Latino and other cultural contexts, it has a particular historical connotation in Mexican culture, politics, and folklore (Paredes 1971: 330). The idea of machismo began to appear in Mexican songs and poems during the 1840s war with the United States (Paredes 1971: 334). The Mexican-American war ended in 1848 with the colonisation of vast swathes of Mexico by the American imperial powers under the *Guadalupe-Hidalgo Treaty* (Frazier 1998; see also *Treaty of Peace, Friendship, Limits and Settlement between the United States of America and the Mexican Republic*). What is now Texas was part of Mexico, and the city of Juárez, one of the most violent cities in the world, is perched between the two on that historically contested border. The coloniality of power has arguably had a role in the making of these very violent border masculinities. Beneath the cultural representation of machismo resides an inferiority, a vulnerability, an imperfection that is magically cast aside by the exaggeration of a gun-toting manliness (Paredes 1971: 339–340). Machismo is strategy of compensation 'shaped by a set of interrelated cultural and economic factors . . . in specific social contexts' (Quintero and Estrada 1998: 150).

The backlash hypothesis predicts that when women take on non-traditional roles, as the *maquiladora* workers did, men who are threatened by women's new found economic independence may resort to violence to re-subjugate them (Hautzinger 2003: 102). Hautzinger argues that these men are behaving 'more like foiled machos resorting to violence as a desperate, compensatory measure than dominating patriarchs maintaining control' (Hautzinger 2003: 98). Where masculinities are structurally threatened by historical gendered destabilisations, such as the feminisation of factory work and the invasion of American entrepreneurs on long-disputed borders, acting machismo may be an effective (albeit brutal) way of disguising or compensating for this vulnerability. At the conclusion to this chapter we return to the idea that violence can be a compensatory response to the coloniality of gender and power.

Terra Australis, frontier violence, and the coloniality of gender

The previous chapter conceptualised 'the South' as a social construct not so much for demarcating particular geographical regions as for exploring global processes of empire building and colonisation that shaped both the worlds of South and North. It is a vehicle for ensuring the events and relations of empire are inserted back into history and contemporary analysis and understanding. Australia, a relatively wealthy colonial settler society rich in natural resources, was one of the colonising projects of European imperial powers at a time of global empire building across the Global South on a grand scale.

Violence played a central role in the British colonisation of Australia in the eighteenth and nineteenth centuries—a continent fictitiously deemed to be *terra nullius* (empty continent). Its original human inhabitants were often depicted as simply part of the flora and fauna (Goodall 1996). 'Violence was the hallmark of the Australian frontier' (Broome 2003: 88), with an estimated 2000 white settlers and 20,000 mainland Aboriginal inhabitants killed in the frontier wars (Broome 2003: 96). Recently, a team of historians has gathered evidence of 150 massacres of Aboriginal people across eastern Australia (the states of Tasmania, Queensland, New South Wales, and Victoria) over an 80-year period of pastoral and agricultural settlement from 1872 (University of Newcastle 2017). These researchers estimate that when evidence from the other states is included there will more than 200 documented massacres Australia-wide. Describing such racially inspired forms of violence on the Australian frontier, Reynolds has argued that 'the admired bush values of egalitarianism, mateship solidarity and anti-authoritarianism' are linked not only to the conditions of isolation and adversity prevailing amongst the itinerant rural working class on the frontier, but also to the role of this class as 'part of a caste of racial overlords forcing submission from a recently conquered and dispossessed underclass' (1999: 132). He continues:

The ubiquitous presence of the 'subject race' enhanced in a way not possible otherwise the equality of all whites, who were not black . . . Complicity in atrocity, abuse and abduction added greatly to the sense of solidarity. When race was the issue all white men stuck together, boss and worker, bond and free, Protestant and Roman. Nothing more strengthened anti-authoritarianism than the profound division between the city and the bush over how the blacks should be treated. Nothing government did called forth more contempt and greater resistance than the endeavour to bring white men to justice for murdering blacks. And on no other issue was anti-authoritarianism so successful as with this one.

(Reynolds 1999: 132–133)

White male identity was constituted in these conditions of racial domination.

Colonisation involved dispossession, mass killings, forced segregation, vigilantism, and a variety of forms of discriminatory and oppressive administrative action (Attwood and Foster 2003; Cowlishaw 2004; Reynolds 1989). The justice system and laws of the colonial settlers replaced the customary laws of the Indigenous peoples (Reynolds 1989). For almost 200 years, Indigenous Australians were denied meaningful citizenship. They were segregated on missions and reserves where virtually all aspects of their lives were administered under 'protection' or 'welfare' laws (McCorquodale 1997). Their children were not permitted to attend public schools, almost 6000 children were removed from families, and Aboriginal farm hands and stock men worked the land for white settlers in return for rations in many remote parts of the country (Cowlishaw 2004). These extensive human rights abuses were all part of the project of building a 'white man's country' on the Australian continent (Lake and Reynolds 2008).

The legacies of colonisation and frontier violence reach into the present, through inter-generational trauma and loss, adversely impacting on Indigenous health and rates of violence today (AIHW 2014). These impacts include extreme levels of familial and interpersonal violence and day-to-day contact with the criminal justice system as both victims and offenders (Cunneen 2001; Hogg and Carrington 2006; Australian

Law Reform Commission 2018). Compared with non-Indigenous Australians, the rate of partner homicides is twice as high, the rate of hospitalisation for domestic violence up to 32 times higher (AIHW 2018: xi), homicide rates are five times higher, and 'rates of assault are much higher among Indigenous people than non-Indigenous people' (AIHW 2015: 134). While rates of violence are increasing, there are still very few violence prevention programs that aim to strengthen Indigenous family life and community well-being (AIHW 2015).

Cunneen argues that Eurocentric knowledges, such as those rooted in Anglo-centric criminology, fail to grasp how or why victimisation of violence is linked to historical colonial practices (2018: 26). He argues that domestic violence law and policy fails to grasp the 'the way different culturally determined priorities can impact on the decisions that a person makes, for example, to leave their kinship group and "country"' (2018: 27). For instance, these policies simply assume that Indigenous women will report family or partner violence to the police in circumstances where they risk having their children removed from their care if they did. Another problematic assumption is that Indigenous women will leave a violent partner and uproot themselves from their country. These assumptions do not take into account, as Cunneen argues, their ontological differences. Walklate and Fitz-Gibbon conclude: 'Already othered as women, they become further marginalised by the very policies intended to intervene on their behalf because such policies fail to capture the nature of their lives as they are actually lived. The colonized becomes doubly colonized' (Walklate and Fitz-Gibbon 2018: 858). A recent piece of qualitative research with three mainland Indigenous communities, led by Blagg, argues it is important to break with the orthodox approach of criminalising men for acts of domestic and family violence (Blagg et al. 2018: 7). Instead they call for a 'country-centred' approach that works collaboratively and flexibly with Indigenous organisations and practices to prevent and respond to domestic and family violence (Blagg et al. 2018: 6). These would include initiatives such as alcohol reduction, enhancing social and emotional well-being, dealing with inter-generational trauma, using alternatives to custody and criminalisation, and placing Elders in courts.

Alongside the violent dispossession of Indigenous peoples, the making of colonial Australia depended on the expropriation and exploitation of the countryside through the industries of agriculture, pastoralism, and mining. The great challenge for the British colonisers was how to populate the harsh interior to extract its rich resources. Acting as if the land was vacant, white settlers (initially many of whom were squatters) occupied the vast Australian interior according to the imported (English) yeoman model of the family farm (Hogg and Carrington 2006). This model of settlement was inherently patriarchal as women were not permitted to own property, inheritance passed properties to sons, and women's work was generally confined to the home (Alston 1995; Poiner 1990).

There is substantial evidence that violence is a significant problem for non-indigenous rural communities in Australia (Alston 1997; Barclay et al. 2007; Hogg and Carrington 2006), and that the form this violence takes has historically been shaped by the coloniality of gender. Both men and women in rural Australia experience on average about a third more violence in their lives than men and women who live in urban environments. Male death rates in rural Australia are 31 per cent higher for assault, 33 per cent higher for suicide, and 38 per cent higher for other external injuries or causes (AIHW 2010: 27). Men and women in remote and very remote Australia have higher standardised prevalence ratios (SPRs) for a range of violence related harms and deaths (see also AIHW 2005: 106, Table 1.4.5.2). The rate ranges from 1.20 times greater in Inner Regional areas to 2.61 times in Very Remote areas. In New South Wales—one of Australia's largest states—39 of the top ranking 50 localities for assault, domestic assault, sexual assault and breach of apprehended violence orders are located in rural communities (Carrington and Hogg 2016). Four out of five rural based Indigenous communities and half the mining communities were also in the top 50 for New South Wales (Carrington and Hogg 2016).

Yet most scholarly research about violence has privileged the urban environment as the ideal laboratory of criminological research, neglecting the study of violence in rural contexts, with some exceptions (Hogg and Carrington 2006; Donnermeyer 2018; Donnermeyer and DeKeseredy 2013). Criminology emerged during the social and economic upheaval of the late nineteenth and early twentieth centuries amidst anxieties about urbanisation, industrialisation, revolution, and social disorder. Hence, as explained in the previous chapter, much of criminology has focused on studying the petty delinquencies and disorders of the sprawling metropolises in the Global North. Some of the authors of this book have undertaken many years of empirical research in rural Australia, research that debunked the myth that rural societies are relatively crime-free (see Carrington and Scott 2008; Hogg and Carrington 2006). Not only was rural Australia historically a place where racial violence was perpetrated on a large scale, it also fostered a rural gender order that normalised and hid much violence against women. The colonising project in Australia restricted white women's labour to the private sphere of the family or family farm. Historically, the substantial labours of rural women were rendered largely invisible as was the violence they experienced within this environment (Alston 1995; Poiner 1990).

There are thus two distinctive patterns that form the contours of rural violence in this 'white man's country'—one light, the other dark—a schematic that Lugones (2008) refers to as an aspect of the coloniality of gender. In the case of Indigenous Australians, violence is made highly visible in rural Australia. Whereas, in the case of gendered violence involving white victims and perpetrators, it is rendered largely invisible by the same architecture of rural life. The social ordering of the private and public spaces of small townships insulates families from visibility, drawing a veil of privacy over any violence that might occur within them (Hogg and Carrington 2006). The lack of anonymity and high density of local social networks, local gossip networks, fear of retaliation, and the risk of social ostracism also inhibit the reporting of violence. Even if victims wanted to seek help, the provision of domestic and sexual violence services in rural localities is often non-existent, difficult to access, or fragmented (Owen and Carrington 2015).

The demography of many parts of rural and remote Australia, which is often polarised between dwindling white Anglo populations and relatively large, youthful and growing Indigenous populations, has exacerbated racial tensions and fuelled anxieties around Indigenous crime and violence (see Hogg and Carrington 2006). Consequently, the most common response to high rates of violence (and disorder) in rural Australia is to stress its roots in Indigenous communities, which are represented as the antithesis of rural norms (see Hogg and Carrington 2006). Violence is treated as an Indigenous, not a rural, issue. It is subject to concerted efforts to measure, research, and explain it, recurrent law and order campaigns draw attention to it as a political issue, and intense efforts are made to criminalise it (Cunneen 2001). Yet little attention is focused on the violence of colonisation in its various forms and phases, the inter-generational wounds it inflicted, and how these continue to shape patterns of violence in and among Indigenous peoples in Australia. Little attention is also drawn to the historical and contemporary frontier violence of men whose labours were central to the making of rural Australia, and the cultural narratives that went with it.

In frontier white settler societies, such as Australia, Canada, and the United States, colonisation went hand in hand with the idea of specific 'frontier' masculinities, which achieved distinctive symbolic ascendancy in colonial societies. Men who settled the harsh Australian frontier were underwritten by narratives of conquest and power over nature. Frontier masculinities are associated in popular culture with visible markers of strength, physicality, courage, and power (Hogg and Carrington 2006: 164). Rural men today continue to have an embodied relationship with the land and nature (Saugeres 2002). They work in conditions in which the comfort of the body is denied. Masculinity is defined through the tasks performed, the physical features of men, or the type of work on the land as farmers, miners, or pastoralists (Carrington and Scott 2008). An important element in defining rural masculinity is an ongoing struggle with nature. Importantly, they control nature rather than it controlling them. On the other hand, rural women have been defined by their indirect relationship with the land, and doubts about the durability of their bodies and physical capacity to engage in rural labours like mining, pastoralism, or agricultural work (Little 2006: 370). Pioneering studies of gender and rural social life conducted over the last two decades have consistently shown rural masculinity to be narrowly constructed around traditional conceptions of gender (Alston 1995; Poiner 1990). This patriarchal rural gender order is however undergoing significant de-stabilisation. The globalisation of agriculture and resultant rural crisis has led to significant farm losses (Cocklin and Dibden 2005; Gray and Lawrence 2001; Lockie and Bourke 2001). Modern industrial farming has shifted from the local to the global stage, with a growing emphasis on science and technology and the need for technical expertise (Little 2006: 371). At the same time the growth of dependence on women's off-farm labour has empowered women as economic actors in the public life of rural communities (Little 2006: 372). The consequent threats to the identity of white rural men are contributing factors in the heightened rates of domestic violence in rural Australia (Carrington and Scott 2008; Owen and Carrington 2015). These threats are also contributing factors to the much higher rates of male self-harm, injury, and suicide in rural Australia (AIHW 2010).

The imaginary story of frontier Australia promotes a narrative proclaiming the progressive advance of white settler civilisation, the conquering of wilderness, and the taming of men. In national mythology the miner—alongside the farmer and the pastoralist, the other fabled figure of the Australian frontier—has either been idealised as an exploited proletariat hero or demonised as an exploiter of pristine nature (Lahiri-Dutt 2012). The exaggerated masculinity of the mining industry has also seen women relegated to the private space of the home (Lahiri-Dutt 2012) if they are present at all. Mining is still regarded as an industry too tough, dark and dirty for women (Murray and Peetz 2010: 6). What is not well-understood is how gendered social relations are maintained in mining towns and the role of violence in constructing local gender orders. Gender here cannot be considered simply as a dichotomous relation between the sexes, but should also be seen in terms of differentiation within genders and relations between masculinities and femininities that are conditioned by other social factors, such as class and status. Miners are associated with extreme forms of patriarchal authority—or what might otherwise be called hyper-masculinity (Connell 1995)—prone to acting out violence as a strategy of subjugation, or a way of re-asserting authority and control when threatened (Carrington, McIntosh, and Scott 2010).

Mining communities remain places of transformation in the national psyche. They are often not viewed as 'communities', but as temporary places that come and go, rise and fall, according to cycles of bust and boom. Mining towns have rarely figured as places for the study of violence, as it is popularly understood. What is absent, even in the histories of mining towns, is an understanding of violence as an everyday event. And while mining and agricultural communities may differ in terms of economics and politics, they notably share a social order which is grounded in fairly rigid gender norms (Alston 1995; Hogg and Carrington 2006). The social ordering of these frontier towns not only divides men and women, but creates hierarchies among men which fuel male on male violence, as well as violence against women (Carrington and Scott 2008). Indeed, a recent study of alcohol consumption and violent crime in Western Australia discovered that the presence of significant mining activity was a major risk factor for alcohol-related assaults and violence against women (Gilmore, Liang, and Chikritzhs 2015).

Australia has undergone a succession of mining booms, with the most recent boom only just coming to an abrupt end with falling commodity prices. One of the significant changes in the mining sector over that period was a shift in the very nature of mining regimes, from production centred on industrial mining towns to post-industrial mining regimes that maximise resource extraction through continuous production processes organised around block roster shifts reliant on non-resident, contract, fly-in/fly-out (FIFO) labour accommodated temporarily in work camps (see Carrington, Hogg, and McIntosh 2011; Scott, Carrington, and Hogg 2012).

It is common for men in these camps to gather at local pubs and clubs in the local towns at the end of shift. They become incorporated into a localised culture of masculinity and violence through their participation in drinking rituals (Campbell 2000: 563). Pubs in the mine-fields have often become venues for confrontation between rival masculinities where brawling and alcohol related violence are an everyday occurrence (Carrington et al. 2010). It is clear that the mining boom and workplace patterns and cultures have produced significant tensions between outsiders and local men, which are frequently 'resolved' through violence. In such instances, alcohol-related violence can be regarded as an attempt by groups to 'make sense of their place' amidst economic upheaval and restructuring, and what might be considered the anomic impacts of super-capitalism on their daily work routines (Carrington, Hogg, and McIntosh 2011).

The power of global mining corporations to dominate their workers, land-holders, towns, governments and Indigenous peoples is alarming. As Paul Cleary puts it:

> [T]he industry has been able to dictate terms to compliant state and federal governments. It has erased small communities and towns, occupied vast tracks of prime farmland; constructed ports and liquefied natural gas plants in the Great Barrier Reef; diverted entire rivers and built on top of 30,000 year old sacred sites.
>
> (Cleary 2012: xxi)

Globalisation of agricultural and mining production processes pose challenges to the rural gender order in a variety of ways. As seen above, tensions may emerge in mining regions between established and outsider male groups which are expressed as conflicts over control of resources, notions of belonging and various status indicators. Hyper-masculinity and the expression of anger may symbolically compensate for this sense of loss, disruption and disorder. Performing acts and rituals that exaggerate male physicality and brute strength is one strategy available to men who are threatened by large-scale global powers that turn them into dispensable FIFO workers and contain them in camps that often resemble desert detention centres. We now turn to the final example of how the coloniality of gender and power contributes to the shape of violence in the Global South.

Violence and climate change in the Pacific Ocean

While climate change is a global issue, its impacts are felt disproportionately in the Asia-Pacific—home to many of the poorest and most conflict-affected nations in the world (World Population Review 2017) (see Chapter 5). A study of 57 countries, including samples from 'western and non-western countries', found that 'climate change may acutely increase violence in areas that already are affected by higher levels of homicides and other social dislocations' (Mares and Moffett 2016: 297). Populations displaced by environmental or man-made disaster 'are particularly vulnerable to threats to security and physical integrity, loss of contact with children and family members, inadequate and insecure shelter, discrimination in aid distribution, psycho-social stress and sexual and gender-based violence' (Office of the High Commissioner of Human Rights, The Pacific 2011: 1). Displaced people also face significant vulnerability in refugee camps; notorious places for the infliction of violence, sexual assault, human trafficking, and exploitation of women and children (Barberet and Carrington 2018; Roeder 2014).

Bougainville, an autonomous island of Papua New Guinea, is home to climate change refugees from the Carteret Islands, forced to relocate in 2015 due to rising sea levels (Beldi 2016). It also has the highest rates of violence against women in the Asia-Pacific (Fulu et al. 2013). A staggering 80 per cent of men surveyed in Bougainville admitted to committing violence against women. Of these men, 41 per cent said they had used both physical and sexual violence against women. Raping women was also pervasive, with 64 per cent of men from Bougainville admitting to having committed rape (Fulu et al. 2013: 5–6). The violence death rate for PNG (inclusive of Bougainville) is in the high to mid range (World Health Rankings n.d.). This country underwent a horrific civil war from 1988 to 1998. Bitter conflict emerged over the Bougainville copper mine (one of the biggest in the world), between Indigenous land owners and PNG shareholders over the distribution of profits and royalties. Civil war erupted between factions loyal to the Bougainville Revolutionary Army and factions loyal to Papua New Guinea (Braithwaite 2010). Approximately 20,000 islanders (from both PNG, generally and Bougainville, specifically) were killed during the civil war. At the peak of the violence, the PNG leadership enlisted private mercenaries from a company called Sandline to protect the mine's operations. The tactic catastrophically back-fired and the plan collapsed amid international condemnation (Braithwaite 2010).

While Bougainville is gradually transitioning to independence from PNG, after a long and complex multi-staged negotiation backed by the UN, it is clear that criminal violence has replaced armed conflict as a significant hindrance to peace building in a post-conflict era. At the beginning of this chapter we highlighted the fact that criminal violence has replaced armed conflict as the main cause of death in the Global South. Bougainville is symptomatic of this trend and much of this violence is gendered. It is alarming that women and children from distant tribal cultures in the Pacific Ocean are forced to relocate to this island. They face a particularly insecure future. The broad and increasingly influential concept of 'human security' recognises that criminal violence is a signal of fragility and a significant hindrance to economic and social development. The Sustainable Development Goals adopted by world leaders at the UN in 2015 also reflect this idea (United Nations 2016a). Goal 16 focuses on: building peaceful and inclusive societies, access to justice, and accountable institutions (United Nations 2016b). Target 16.1 commits all signatory states to 'significantly reduce all forms of violence and related death rates everywhere' (United Nations 2016b). In the following section we provide a necessarily selective overview of responses to the prevention and reduction of criminal violence in the Global South.

Responses to gendered violence in the Global South

Violence is distributed unequally in the world, with 90 per cent occurring in middle to low income countries, most of which populate the Global South (Butchart, Mikton, and Kieselbach 2012). It is also the case that violence has been declining in the high-income economies of the world (mainly the Global North) over the last three decades (Eiser 2015). Yet most of the research about violence is conducted in and on high income economies (Eiser 2015). Of the studies on interpersonal violence for example, 70 per cent are based on the experiences of urban communities in high-income English-speaking countries mainly from the Global North (Arango et al. 2014: 1). Only 11 per cent were conducted in Africa and seven per cent in South Asia (Arango et al. 2014: 19). This imbalance is not simply a question of quantitative output, but also a question of cultural and intellectual hegemony (Connell 2007: 215). This body of research also tends to draw on concepts and theories of relevance to violence and its prevention in the Global North (Carrington 2015). These theories are not necessarily translatable to understanding the complexities of violence in culturally diverse, low income and post-conflict, post-colonial, or neo-colonial contexts (Carrington 2015). So there is an urgent need to expand our knowledge about how to reduce and prevent violence for the low and middle income countries that populate the bulk of the Global South.

The United Nations has been one of the leading international authorities at the forefront of encouraging member countries to commit to the elimination of criminal violence. One of the Sustainable Development Goals is that countries introduce laws that effectively penalise violence (United Nations 2016b). While 80 per cent of countries in the world have such laws, only 57 per cent enforce them (WHO 2014: ix). There remains a significant gap between passing laws that criminalise violence and introducing the supports and programs necessary to respond to, prevent, and reduce criminal violence.

The UN has also set a sustainable development target that all countries should have laws to protect women and girls from violence by 2030 (United Nations 2016b). Over the last 25 years there have been significant increases in the number of countries introducing laws against sexual and domestic violence. A study of trends in legal protection against sexual and domestic violence of 141 countries, between 2013 and 2017, found the number of countries with laws punishing domestic violence rose from 70 to 75 per cent (Tavares and Wodon 2018: 5). Most countries in Latin America, and all countries in the Asia-Pacific, now have legislation criminalising domestic violence, but only one in three in the Middle East, North Africa, and sub-Saharan Africa have such laws (Tavares and Wodon 2018: 5). Legal protections against sexual violence are weaker. There are no laws against sexual violence in one in three countries in the world (Tavares and Wodon 2018: 5). The biggest gaps are in respect to rape in marriage with more than one billion women worldwide lacking this legal protection (Tavares and Wodon 2018: 8). Again, Middle East and North African countries had the fewest legal protections for girls or women against sexual violence. Even where there are laws to protect women and children against gendered violence, their implementation is either non-existent or problematic. The consensus in the feminist literature is that victims of gendered violence 'who seek redress through the criminal justice process find the process at best ambivalent and at worst, destructive' (Douglas 2012: 121). There is also concern that a simple punitive approach to gendered violence may not necessarily aid its prevention.

In Kenya, for example, the criminalisation of female genital mutilation (FGM) simply led to deep resistance and the practice went underground (Bunei and Rono 2018: 901–902). Bunei and Rono outline a history of failed attempts to outlaw FGM in Kenya from 1982. FGM was finally criminalised in 2011, but since then the practice, especially in rural areas 'remains obstinately high' (Bunei and Rono 2018: 906). Cutters are protected by a communal network of support for the practice. Non-circumcised women are discriminated against, regarded as unfit for marriage and community status. Bunei and Rono argue that instead of adopting a universal regulatory approach, as encouraged by the UN, countries from the Global South need to implement multi-pronged strategies to eliminate FGM including capacity building, alternative income streams for cutters, alternative cultural practices that no longer stigmatise non-circumcised women, alternatives to child marriage, and the elevation of women's status (2018: 902).

Importantly, they point to the role of men and boys in changing cultural attitudes and practices as a key component in bringing about an end to FGM (2018: 909). Increasingly, men are recognising they too have an important role in violence prevention. While most men do not commit violence, those who do are influenced by wider cultural and environmental factors (Flood 2006: 26). Hence, 'we have no choice but to address men and masculinities if we want to stop violence against women' (Flood 2006: 26). Violence prevention must address the constructions of masculinity that normalise and reward men for committing violence.

Primary prevention, which seeks 'to intervene to prevent' criminal violence before it occurs, is regarded as the key to strengthening human security (UN Women 2015). Yet it is seriously under researched, because most research has focused on the impact of post-victimisation interventions with individual victims and offenders (PWC 2015: 17). Additionally, most of this research has focused on models of intervention in the Global North (Ellsberg et al. 2015), while women in the Global South are subject to higher prevalence rates of gendered violence (WHO 2013: 46–47).

The WHO has identified VAWG as a 'global health problem of epidemic proportions' (WHO 2013) which adversely impacts on the health of millions of women disproportionately from low to middle income countries of the Global South. The WHO provides resources and models of violence prevention for different kinds of violence. It also runs public campaigns to end violence on specific issues, such as FGM, and on violence against women generally. The United Nations has established a trust fund to support $14 million worth of initiatives each year to eliminate violence against women. The fund supports grassroots campaigns to prevent violence. For example, Puntos de Encuentro, an all-women's media agency from Nicaragua, was funded to create a soap opera about the risk of sexual exploitation and trafficking of young women (UN Trust Fund to End Violence against Women 2014: 6). The trust funded an initiative based in Uganda called Raising Voices. The initiative provided mentoring to 13 local anti-violence organisations in Uganda, Botswana, Burundi, Ethiopia, Kenya, and the United Republic of Tanzania. The fund has also supported a multi-country Gender Inclusive City program aimed at enhancing women's safety. The cities included: Petrozavodsk, Russia; Dar es Salaam, Tanzania; Delhi, India; and Rosario, Argentina. Women's centres across the four cities surveyed women about their experiences and what they thought would enhance their safety. Program leaders were able to use the results to seek changes to urban planning policy, practice, and budget allocations in ways that enhanced women's security (UN Trust Fund to End Violence against Women 2014: 13). These are some examples of novel initiatives created at a local level, but supported by the donors to the UN Trust, to help reduce violence against women. Of course, one of the limitations of these initiatives is that they are piecemeal, not systemic, and are likely to have a limited impact, especially when the funding ends.

One of the most innovative and systemic responses to addressing violence against women by the nation state emerged in Latin America. In 1985, Brazil was the first country in Latin America to establish women's police stations (WPS). Since then, WPS have been established in Argentina, Bolivia, Brazil, Ecuador, Nicaragua, Peru, and Uruguay, and more recently in Sierra Leone, India, Ghana, India,

Kosovo, Liberia, the Philippines, South Africa, and Uganda. A 2011 United Nations Women (Jubb et al. 2011) evaluation found that WPS in Latin America enhanced women's access to justice and their willingness to report, increased the likelihood of conviction, and enlarged access to a range of other services such as counselling, health, legal, financial, and social support. Of those surveyed for the evaluation, 77 per cent in Brazil, 77 per cent in Nicaragua, 64 per cent in Ecuador, and 57 per cent in Peru felt that WPS had reduced violence against women in their countries (Jubb et al. 2011).

WPS emerged historically at a time of re-democratisation in Latin America. They were designed to enhance women's confidence in the criminal justice system, encourage reporting, prevent re-victimisation, and send a message to the community that gendered violence was no longer tolerated and men who abuse women will be made accountable (Hautzinger 2007: 137). However, Hautzinger who studied these police stations in Brazil in the 1990s concluded that they fell short of expectations as they were seriously under-resourced (Hautzinger 2003: 248).

Since then, in 2006, Brazil passed the *Mariah de Penha Law* (Law No. 11.340) which shifted interpersonal violence from a civil to a criminal offence and provided much needed additional funding for WPS, strengthening collaboration across the government and non-government sectors to provide additional support to victims of domestic violence (Perova and Reynolds 2017: 190). A more recent study of WPS in Brazil used female homicides as a proxy measure for assessing their effectiveness. They compared 2074 municipalities from 2004 to 2009 and found that 'women's police stations appear to be highly effective among young women living in metropolitan areas' (Perova and Reynolds 2017: 188). They found the homicide rate dropped by 17 per cent for all women, but for women aged 15–24 in metropolitan areas the reduction was 50 per cent (or 5.57 deaths reduction per 100,000) (Perova and Reynolds 2017: 193–194). They also undertook qualitative research with victims, service providers, and key informants, and discovered three main barriers that discourage women (especially from smaller/rural communities) from accessing the services of WPS. These barriers are: economic dependency, fear of retaliation, and high levels of tolerance for gendered violence in the normative structure of local communities (Perova and Reynolds 2017: 195).

The wider institutional and political environment will have an enormous impact on whether police stations for addressing gendered violence operate as designed. As in Brazil, WPS were introduced in Argentina during a period of re-democratisation (Carrington 2015). Buenos Aires established its first women's police station at La Plata in 1988. Buenos Aires currently has 125 WPS in operation and aims to have 135 by the end of 2018. In 2009, Argentina introduced Law 26.485, Comprehensive protection law to prevent, punish and eradicate violence against women (*Ley de Protección Integral para prevenir, sancionar y erradicar la Violencia contra las Mujeres en los Ámbitos en que desarrollen sus Relaciones Interpersonales*). The act introduced a new offence called femicide, established a department for gender policy in the Ministry of Security, and implemented a national action plan to prevent, assist, and eradicate violence against women.

In 2015, the *Ni una Menos* (Not one Less) campaign against femicide saw the largest ever public protest with around 70,000 people flooding the streets of Buenos Aires. Marches across the country were attended by governors, judges, thousands of police, politicians, and leaders of the Catholic Church (*Buenos Aires Herald* 2015). Central to the success of the public campaign was the widespread grassroots involvement of hundreds of WPS across the country. They produced leaflets, posters and widely circulated the message at the *barrio* level. By raising public awareness about the impact of gendered violence, WPS in Argentina have played an important preventative role in changing the cultural attitudes that normalise violence against women.

Women's only transport services are becoming increasingly popular as a means to prevent gender-based violence across countries in the Global South. Women's only train carriages have been established in parts of India (Anuja and Sharma 2015) and Japan (Mitsutoshi and Burgess 2012), and women's only buses have been established in Mexico (Dunckel-Graglia 2013) and Papua New Guinea (UN Women 2014). Dunckel-Graglia conducted a survey of female commuters in Mexico City. Based on her study she concludes 'that Mexico City is an example where women-only transportation has played a role in changing the traditional gender norms which have reinforced violence against women commuters' (Dunckel-Graglia 2016: 624). While not a solution to gender-based violence, studies of women's only transport have found that they reduce the incidence of harassment of female transit users, while enhancing women's freedom to be mobile, independent, empowered, and able to earn a living and commute without fear (Tudela Rivadeneyra et al. 2015). Importantly, women's only transportation is not a solution to women's unequal access to mobility or public space.

There is a good deal of debate among feminists about the politics of women's police stations and women's only transport. Some feminists regard segregation as a deepening of gender divides and would rather men just respect women, so they can travel safely (Dunckel-Graglia 2016: 97). Others argue that such services have a primary preventative impact by bringing public attention to violence against women, thus creating the impetus for long-term cultural change. Others still have problems with the criminalisation of men for violence against women, as they argue that it impacts disproportionately on men from low socio-economic, indigenous, and ethnic minorities. Hence these interventions may not solve the problem but rather entrench the cycle of criminalisation. This is one of the objections to the impact of domestic violence interventions in Indigenous communities in Australia for example (see, Blagg et al. 2018; Cunneen 2018, 2002).

The coloniality of gender and violence

It has not been possible to do justice to the diversity of violence in this single chapter. Instead, we have attempted to describe in general terms the unequal distribution of global violence, and to illustrate how most of it is racialised, gendered, and disproportionately a much larger problem in the countries of the Global South. We selected just a few examples to illustrate how patterns of violence are shaped by the coloniality of gender and power. In these examples the constitution of violent masculinities, shaped by a diverse array of historical, economic, and social factors, emerged as a critical dimension of the coloniality of gender. Men experiencing powerlessness in the labour market in Juárez, partly as a consequence of the influx of young female factory workers, legitimise their violence as a means of momentarily reversing the structural subordination of their own Latino masculinity. Men living on the edge of drug wars live by a mantra to kill or be killed. For them, machismo is a resource for survival. Men in the minefields in the global countryside use violence against other men (and sometimes women) as a way of re-asserting their lost privileges in the hierarchy of masculinities, in the face of globalising de-humanising FIFO work regimes. White men in rural Australia sometimes resort to violence (turned inward and toward others) in response to the loss of their historic patriarchal privileges and racial dominance. Indigenous men in Australia inflict lethal violence and experience lethal violence at rates five times of those of white men. Reflecting on the condition of dark-skin men in white European society, Fanon observed that the internalisation of the abject can produce a self-loathing manifest as violence turned inward (Fanon 1967). Tragically, violence turned inward accounts, in part, for the very high homicide rates and catastrophic rates of domestic violence between Indigenous peoples.

Connell argues it is vital to comprehend the coloniality of gender— how the social and historical making of masculinities in the South were shaped by legacies of colonialism (Connell 2014a). For those countries in the Global South colonised by the European and Northern powers, 'the process and settlement was itself a site for the creation of masculinities' (Connell 2014c: 8). Frontier masculinities remain deeply troubled by the legacies of colonialism that not only transformed the global countryside and created new trade routes that extended the reach of market economies, but radically transformed gender relations in the process, disrupted hierarchies of power between groups of men, and dislodged unquestioned patriarchal control and authority from the labouring classes. In the contemporary world, globalising forces have increasingly destabilised traditional constructs of gender at the same time as creating enormous inequalities, exacerbating men's loss of patriarchal control over women as wives and co-workers especially (Connell 2014a). Male violence in this context can be a form of compensation for losing power and an attempt to re-subjugate others (Hautzinger 2003: 93). It is a reaction to loss of patriarchal control, rather than an assertion of it. For where male power is firmly entrenched, as it is in the metropole, in the board rooms of the global agricultural and mining corporations, and the multinational factories that operate on the Mexican border, there is little need for physical force to uphold their almost unfettered dominance (Hautzinger 2003: 102). This is how the coloniality of power works to entrench global inequalities on a world scale that shape patterns of everyday violence on the periphery.

References

Aas KF (2011) Visions of global control: Cosmopolitan aspirations in a world of friction? In Bosworth M and Hoyle C (eds) *What Is Criminology?*: 406–442. Oxford: Oxford University Press.

Alston M (1995) *Women on the Land: The Hidden Heart of Rural Australia.* Sydney: University of New South Wales Press.

Alston M (1997) Violence against women in a rural context. *Australian Social Work* 1(1): 15–22. DOI: 10.1080/03124079708415203.

Anuja A and Sharma A (2015) Gender contests in the Delhi Metro: Implications of reservation of a coach for women. *Indian Journal of Gender Studies* 22(3): 421–436. DOI: 10.1177/0971521515594279.

Arango D, Morton M, Gennari F, Kiplesund S, and Ellsberg M (2014) Interventions to prevent or reduce violence against women and girls: A review of reviews. *Women's Voice, Agency, and Participation Research Series* 10. Washington, District of Columbia: World Bank Group.

Attwood B and Foster G (eds) (2003) *Frontier Conflict: The Australian Experience.* Canberra: National Museum of Australia.

Australian Institute of Criminology (AIC) (2005) Trends in recorded sexual assault. *Crime Facts* 105. Canberra: AIC.

Australian Institute of Health and Welfare (AIHW) (2005) *Rural, Regional and Remote Health.* Canberra: AIHW.

Australian Institute of Health and Welfare (AIHW) (2010) *A Snapshot of Men's Health in Regional and Remote Australia.* Canberra: AIHW.

Australian Institute of Health and Welfare (AIHW) (2014) *National Key Performance Indicators for Aboriginal and Torres Strait Islander Primary Health Care: Results from December 2013. Cat. no. 146.* Canberra: AIHW.

Australian Institute of Health and Welfare (AIHW) (2015) *Trends in Hospitalised Injury, Australia: 1999–2013.* Canberra: AIHW.

Australian Institute of Health and Welfare (AIHW) (2018) *Family, Domestic and Sexual Violence in Australia.* Canberra: AIHW.

Australian Law Reform Commission (ALRC) (2018) *Pathways to Justice: An Inquiry into the Incarceration Rate of Aboriginal and Torres Strait Islander Peoples*. Sydney: ALRC.

Barberet R (2014) *Women, Crime and Criminal Justice*. London and New York: Routledge.

Barberet R and Carrington K (2018) Globalizing feminist criminology: Gendered violence during peace and war. In Carrington K, Hogg R, Scott J, and Sozzo M (eds) *Palgrave Handbook of Criminology and the Global South*: 821–846. Switzerland: Palgrave Macmillan.

Barclay E, Donnermeyer JF, Scott J, and Hogg R (eds) (2007) *Crime in Rural Australia*. Sydney: Federation Press,

Begikhani N, Gill A, and Hague G (2015) *Honour-Based Violence*. Surrey: Ashgate.

Beldi L (2016) Carteret climate refugees seek home. *ABC News*, 7 August. Available at http://www.abc.net.au/news/2016-08-07/carteret-climate-refugees-new-home/7693950.

Blagg H, Williams E, Cummings D, Hovane V, Torres M, and Woodely K (2018) *Innovative Models in Addressing Violence against Indigenous Women: Final Report*. Sydney: ANROWS.

Braithwaite J (2010) *Reconciliation and Architectures of Commitment: Sequencing Peace in Bougainville*. Canberra: ANU Press.

Braithwaite J (2018) Criminology peacebuilding and transitional justice: Lessons from the Global South. In Carrington K, Hogg R, Scott J, and Sozzo M (eds) *Palgrave Handbook of Criminology and the Global South*: 971–990. London: Palgrave Macmillan.

Broome R (2003) The statistics of frontier conflict. In Attwood B and Foster SG (eds) *Frontier Conflict and the Australian Experience*: 79–87. Canberra: National Museum of Australia.

Buenos Aires Herald (2015) Protest puts femicides on the agenda. 3 June. Available at: http://www.buenosairesherald.com/article/190742/protest-puts-femicides-on-the-agenda.

Bunei EK and Rono JK (2018) A critical understanding of resistance to criminalization of female genital mutilation in Kenya. In Carrington K, Hogg R, Scott J, and Sozzo M (eds) *Palgrave Handbook of Criminology and the Global South*: 901–912. Switzerland: Palgrave Macmillan.

Butchart A, Mikton C, and Kieselbach B (2012) *Violence Prevention Alliance, Global Campaign for Violence Prevention, Plan of Action Plan 2012–2020*. Geneva: World Health Organization.

Campbell H (2000) The glass phallus: Pub(lic) masculinity and drinking in Rural New Zealand. *Rural Sociology* 65(4): 562–581. DOI: 10.1111/j.1549-0831.2000.tb00044.x.

Carrington K (2015) *Feminism and Global Justice*. London and New York: Routledge.

Carrington K and Hogg R (2016) Violence in rural Australia. In Stubbs J and Tomsen S (eds) *Australian Violence: Crime, Criminal Justice and Beyond*: 49–66. Annandale, New South Wales: Federation Press.

Carrington K and Scott J (2008) Masculinity, rurality and violence. *British Journal of Criminology* 48(5): 641–666. DOI: 10.1093/bjc/azn031.

Carrington K, Hogg R, and McIntosh A (2011) The resource boom's underbelly: The criminological impact of mining development. *Australian and New Zealand Journal of Criminology* 44(3): 335–354. DOI: 10.1177/0004865811419068.

Carrington K, Hogg R, and Sozzo M (2016) Southern criminology. *British Journal of Criminology* 56(1): 1–20. DOI: 10.1093/bjc/azv083.

Carrington K, McIntosh A, and Scott J (2010) Globalization, frontier masculinities and violence: Booze, blokes and brawls. *British Journal of Criminology* 50(3): 393–413. DOI: 10.1093/bjc/azq003.

Cleary P (2012) *Mine-Field: The Dark Side of Australia's Resources Rush.* Collingwood: Black Inc.

Cocklin C and Dibden J (eds) (2005) *Sustainability and Change in Rural Australia.* Sydney: University of New South Wales Press.

Connell R (1995) *Masculinities.* Berkeley: University of California Press.

Connell R (2007) *Southern Theory: The Global Dynamics of Knowledge Social Science.* Crows Nest: Allen & Unwin.

Connell R (2009) *Gender*, 2nd edn. Cambridge: Polity Press.

Connell R (2014a) Rethinking gender from the South. *Feminist Studies* 40(3): 518–539.

Connell R (2014b) The sociology of gender in Southern perspective. *Current Sociology* 62(4): 550–567. DOI: 10.1177/0011392114524510.

Connell R (2014c) Margin becoming centre: For a world-centred rethinking of masculinities. *International Journal for Masculinity Studies* 9(4): 217–231. DOI: 10.1080/18902138.2014.934078.

Cowlishaw G (2004) *Blackfellas, Whitefellas, and the Hidden Injuries of Race.* London: Wiley-Blackwell Publishing.

Cox P (2016) *Violence against Women: Additional Analysis of the Australian Bureau of Statistics' Personal Safety Survey, 2012.* Sydney: ANROWS.

Crenshaw K (1991) Mapping the margins: Intersectionality, identity politics, and violence against women of colour. *Stanford Law Review* 43(6): 1241–1299.

Cunneen C (2001) *Conflict, Politics and Crime: Aboriginal Communities and the Police.* Sydney: Allen and Unwin.

Cunneen C (2002) Preventing violence against women through programs which target men. *UNSW Law Journal* 25(1): 242–250.

Cunneen C (2018) Indigenous challenges for Southern criminology. In Carrington K, Hogg R, Scott J, and Sozzo M (eds) *Palgrave Handbook of Criminology and the Global South*: 19–42. Switzerland: Palgrave Macmillan.

Currie E (2018) Confronting the North's South: On race and violence in the United States. In Carrington K, Hogg R, Scott J, and Sozzo M (eds) *Palgrave Handbook of Criminology and the Global South*: 43–60. Switzerland: Palgrave Macmillan.

Cussen T and Bryant W (2015) Indigenous and non-Indigenous homicide in Australia. *Research Practice* 37. Canberra: Australian Institute of Criminology.

DeKeseredy W and Hall-Sanchez A (2018) Male violence against women in the global South: What we know and what we don't know. In Carrington K, Hogg R, Scott J, and Sozzo M (eds) *Palgrave Handbook of Criminology and the Global South*: 883–900. Switzerland: Palgrave Macmillan.

Dixon B (2013) The aetiological crisis in South African criminology. *Australian & New Zealand Journal of Criminology* 46(3): 319–334. DOI: 10.1177/0004865813489697.

Donnermeyer J (2018) The rural dimensions of a Southern criminology: Selected topics and general processes. In Carrington K, Hogg R, Scott J, and Sozzo M (eds) *Palgrave Handbook of Criminology and the Global South*: 105–120 Switzerland: Palgrave Macmillan.

Donnermeyer J and DeKeseredy W (2013) *Rural Criminology*. New York: Routledge.

Douglas H (2012) Battered women's experiences of the criminal justice system: Decentring the law. *Feminist Legal Studies* 20(2): 121–134.

Dunckel-Graglia A (2013) Pink transportation in Mexico City: Reclaiming urban space through collective action against gender-based violence. *Gender and Development* 21(2): 265–276. DOI: 10.1080/13552074.2013.802131.

Dunckel-Graglia A (2016) Finding mobility: Women negotiating fear and violence in Mexico City's public transit system. *Gender, Place and Culture* 23(5): 624–640. DOI: 10.1080/0966369X.2015.1034240.

Eiser M (2015) Holding violence down. *New Scientist* 2 July: 1–3.

Ellsberg M, Arango D, Morton M, Gennari F, Kiplesund S, Contreras M, and Watts C (2015) Prevention of violence against women and girls: What does the evidence say? *The Lancet* 385(9977): 1555–1566. DOI: 10.1016/S0140-6736(14)61703-7.

Fanon F (1967) *Black Skin, White Masks*. New York: Grove Press.

Flood M (2006) Changing men: Best practice in sexual violence prevention. *Women against Violence* 18: 26–36.

Frazier DS (ed.) (1998) *The United States and Mexico at War: Nineteenth-Century Expansionism and Conflict*. New York: Macmillan Reference USA.

Fulu E (2014) *Domestic Violence in Asia: Globalization, Gender and Islam in the Maldives*. London: Routledge.

Fulu E, Warner X, Miedema S, Jewkes R, Roselli T, and Lang J (2013) *Why Do Some Men Use Violence against Women and How Can We Prevent It? Quantitative Findings from the UN Multi-Country Study on Men and Violence in Asia and the Pacific.* Bangkok: United Nations.

Gilmore W, Liang W, and Chikritzhs T (2015) The wild West: Associations between mining and violence in Western Australia. *Australian Journal of Rural Health.* DOI: 10.1111/ajr.12228.

Goodall H (1996) *Invasion to Embassy: Land in Aboriginal Politics in New South Wales 1770–1972.* Sydney: Allen & Unwin.

Gray I and Lawrence G (2001) *A Future for Regional Australia: Escaping Global Misfortune.* Melbourne: Cambridge University Press.

Guerra SI (2015) La chota y los mafiosos: Mexican American casualties of the border drug war. *Latino Studies* 13(2): 227–244. DOI: 10.1057/lst.2015.12.

Hautzinger S (2003) Researching men's violence: Personal reflections on ethnographic data. *Men and Masculinities* 6(1): 93–106. DOI: 10.1177/1097184X03253139.

Hautzinger S (2007) *Violence and the City of Women.* Berkeley: University of California Press.

Hogg R and Carrington K (2006) *Policing the Rural Crisis.* Sydney: Federation Press.

hooks b (1982) *Feminist Theory: From Margins to Center.* Boston: South End.

Jubb N, Comacho G, D'Angelo A, Hernández K, Macassi I, Meléndez L, Molina Y, Pasinato W, Redrobán V, Rosas C, and Yáñez G (2011) *Women's Police Stations in Latin America: An Entry Point for Stopping Violence and Gaining Access to Justice.* Quito: CEPLAES, IDRC.

Lahiri-Dutt K (2012) Digging women: Towards a new agenda for feminist critiques of mining. *Gender, Place & Culture: A Journal of Feminist Geography* 19(2): 193–212 DOI: 10.1080/0966369X.2011.572433.

Lake M and Reynolds H (2008) *Drawing the Global Colour Line: White Men's Countries and the Question of Racial Equality.* Carlton: Melbourne University Press.

Little J (2006) Gender and sexuality in rural communities. In Cloke P, Marsden T, and Mooney P (eds) *Handbook of Rural Studies*: 366–378. London: Sage.

Livingston J (2004) Murder in Juárez: Gender, sexual violence and the global assembly line. *Frontiers* 25(1): 59–76. DOI: 10.1353/fro.2004.0034.

Lockie S and Bourke L (eds) (2001) *Rurality Bites.* Annandale: Pluto Press.

Lugones M (2008) The coloniality of gender. *Worlds and Knowledges Otherwise* 2(Spring): 1–17.

Mares DM and Moffett K (2016) Climate change and interpersonal violence: A 'global' estimate and regional inequities. *Climate Change* 135(2): 297–310. DOI: 10.1007/s10584-015-1566-0.

Mayeda DT, Vijaykumar R, and Chesney-Lind M (2018) Constructions of honor-based violence: Gender, context and Orientalism. In Carrington K, Hogg R, Scott J, and Sozzo M (eds) *Palgrave Handbook of Criminology and the Global South*: 947–968. Switzerland: Palgrave Macmillan.

McCorquodale JC (1997) Aboriginal identity: Legislative judicial and administrative definitions. *Australian Aboriginal Studies* 2: 24–35.

McGarry R and Walklate SL (eds) (2016) *The Palgrave Handbook of Criminology and War*. London: Palgrave Macmillan.

Miedema SS and Fulu E (2018) Globalization and theorising intimate partner violence from the global South. In Carrington K, Hogg R, Scott J, and Sozzo M (eds) *Palgrave Handbook of Criminology and the Global South*: 867–882. Switzerland: Palgrave Macmillan.

Mitsutoshi H and Burgess A (2012) Constructing sexual risk: 'Chikan', collapsing male authority and the emergence of women-only train carriages in Japan. *Health Risk and Society* 14(1): 41–55. DOI: 10.1080/13698575.2011.641523.

Mohanty C (1984) Under Western eyes: Feminist scholarship and colonial discourses. *Boundary 2* 12(3): 333–358. DOI: 10.2307/302821.

Monárrez Fragoso J (2018) Feminicide: Impunity for the perpetrators and injustice for the victims. In Carrington K, Hogg R, Scott J, and Sozzo M (eds) *Palgrave Handbook of Criminology and the Global South*: 913–930. Switzerland: Palgrave Macmillan.

Morgan K (2007) *Slavery and the British Empire: From Africa to America*. Oxford: Oxford University Press.

Murray G and Peetz D (2010) *Women of the Coal Rushes*. Kensington: University of New South Wales Press.

Office of the High Commissioner of Human Rights, The Pacific (2011) *Protecting the Human Rights of Internally Displaced Persons During Natural Disasters: Challenges in the Pacific*. Suva: United Nations.

Owen S and Carrington K (2015) Domestic violence (DV) service provision and the architecture of rural life: An Australian case study. *Journal of Rural Studies* 39(June): 229–238. DOI: 10.1016/j.jrurstud.2014.11.004.

Paredes A (1971) The United States, Mexico, and machismo (Steen M, Trans.). In Bauman R (ed.) *Folklore and Culture on the Texas-Mexican Border*: 215–234. Austin: CMAS Books.

Perova E and Reynolds SA (2017) Women's police stations and intimate partner violence: Evidence from Brazil. *Social Science and Medicine* 174: 188–196. DOI: 10.1016/j.socscimed.2016.12.008.

Poiner G (1990) *The Good Old Rule: Gender and Other Power Relationships in a Rural Community*. Sydney: Sydney University Press.

Potter H (2015) *Intersectionality and Criminology*. London and New York: Routledge.

Price Waterhouse Coopers (PWC) (2015) *A High Price to Pay: The Economic Case for Preventing Violence against Women.* Melbourne: VicHealth.

Quintero GA and Estrada AL (1998) Cultural models of masculinity and drug use: 'Maschismo,' heroin, and street survival on the U.S.-Mexico Border. *Contemporary Drug Problems* 25(1): 147–167. DOI: 10.1177/009145099802500107.

Renzetti C (2013) *Feminist Criminology.* London: Routledge.

Reynolds H (1989) *Dispossession: Black Australians and White Invaders.* Sydney: Allen & Unwin.

Reynolds H (1999) *Why Weren't We Told?* Ringwood: Viking.

Rice M (1990) Challenging orthodoxies in feminist theory: A black feminist critique. In Roeder Larry W (ed.) (2014) *Issues of Gender and Sexual Orientation in Humanitarian Emergencies.* Switzerland: Springer International Publishing.

Sandoval C (1991) U.S. third world feminism: The theory and method of oppositional consciousness in the postmodern world. *Genders* 10: 1–24. DOI: 10.5555/gen.1991.10.1.

Saugeres L (2002) The cultural representation of farming landscape: Masculinity, power and nature. *Journal of Rural Studies* 18(4): 373–384. DOI: 10.1016/S0743-0167(02)00010-4.

Scott J, Carrington K, and McIntosh A (2012) Established-outsider relations and fear of crime in a mining town. *Sociologia Ruralis* 52(2): 147–169. DOI: 10.1111/j.1467-9523.2011.00557.x.

Securidad, Justicia y Paz (2017) *Listado de las 50 ciudades más violentas del mundo en 2017.* Available at http://www.seguridadjusticiaypaz.org.mx/ranking-de-ciudades-2017 (accessed 12 April 2018).

Tavares P and Wodon Q (2018) *Ending Violence against Women and Girls: Global and Regional Trends in Women's Legal Protections against Domestic Violence and Sexual Harassment.* Washington, District of Columbia: The World Bank.

Tudela Rivadeneyra A, Lopez Dodero A, Mehndiratta SR, Bianchi Alves B, and Deakin E (2015) Reducing gender-based violence in public transportation strategy design for Mexico City, Mexico. *Transportation Research Record* 2531: 187–194. DOI: 10.3141/2531-22.

United Nations (2016a) *Sustainable Development Goals.* Available at http://www.un.org/sustainabledevelopment/sustainable-development-goals/ (accessed 25 May 2017).

United Nations (2016b) Goal 16: Promote just, peaceful and inclusive societies. *Sustainable Development Goals.* Available at www.un.org/sustainabledevelopment/peace-justice/ (accessed 1 February 2018).

United Nations Development Programme (UNDP) (2014) *Human Development Report 2014 – Sustaining Human Progress: Reducing Vulnerabilities and Building Resilience.* New York: United Nations.

United Nations Economic and Social Commission for the Asia and Pacific (2016) *Population Data Set.* Available at http://www.unescap.org/resources/2016-escap-population-data-sheet (Accessed 18 February 2018).

United Nations (UN) Trust Fund to End Violence against Women (2014) *Within our Reach: Solutions to End Violence against Women and Girls.* New York: United Nations Entity for Gender Equality and the Empowerment of Women (UN Women).

United Nations (UN) Women (2014) Women and the environment. Available at http://www.unwomen.org/en/news/in-focus/end-violence-against-women/2014/environment (accessed 1 February 2018).

United Nations (UN) Women (2015) *A Framework for Prevention to Underpin Action to Prevent Violence against Women.* Geneva: United Nations.

University of Newcastle (2017) Mapping the massacres of Australia's colonial frontier. *Newsroom,* 5 July. Available at https://www.newcastle.edu.au/newsroom/featured-news/mapping-the-massacres-of-australias-colonial-frontier.

US Customs and Border Protection (2018) *North American Free Trade Agreement 1994.* Available at https://www.cbp.gov/trade/nafta (accessed 1 February 2018).

Walklate S and Fitz-Gibbon K (2018) Criminology and the violence(s) of Northern theorizing: A critical examination of policy transfer in relation to violence against women from the global North to the global South. In Carrington K, Hogg R, Scott J, and Sozzo M (eds) *Palgrave Handbook of Criminology and the Global South*: 847–866. Switzerland: Palgrave Macmillan.

World Bank (2015) Violence against women and girls. *Brief,* 4 April. Available at http://www.worldbank.org/en/topic/socialdevelopment/brief/violence-against-women-and-girls (accessed 7 June 2015).

World Health Organization (WHO) (2013) *Global and Regional Estimates of Violence against Women: Prevalence and Health Effects of Intimate Partner Violence and Non-Partner Sexual Violence.* Geneva: WHO.

World Health Organization (WHO) (2014) *Global Status Report on Violence Prevention 2014.* Geneva: WHO.

World Health Rankings (n.d.) Causes of death by country: Violence. Available at http://www.worldlifeexpectancy.com/cause-of-death/violence/by-country/ (accessed 1 February 2018).

World Population Review (2017) Asia population 2018. Available at http://worldpopulationreview.com/continents/asia-population/ (accessed 1 February 2018).

Wright M (2005) Paradoxes, protests, and the Mujeres de Negro of Northern Mexico. *Gender, Place, and Culture* 12(3): 177–192. DOI: 10.1080/09663690500202376.

Legislation cited

Law No. 11.340 of 7 August 2006 [Brazil].

Law No. 26.485 (2009) *Ley de Protección Integral para prevenir, sancionar y erradicar la Violencia contra las Mujeres en los Ámbitos en que desarrollen sus Relaciones Interpersonales* [Argentina].

Treaty of Peace, Friendship, Limits and Settlement between the United States of America and the Mexican Republic (1848).

3

RETHINKING RACE AND CRIME FROM THE GLOBAL SOUTH

The central point of Southern theory and Southern criminology is to challenge the hierarchy of the global episteme and to insert colonialism into the analysis of contemporary criminal justice systems and problems, from multiple perspectives and subaltern voices including indigenous ones, that reckon with both the historical violence of colonisation and 'coloniality of gender'. There is no intrinsic indigenous experience, just as there is no intrinsic black or white or other racial experience, be it one of universal oppression or dominance.

Post-colonial criminology has begun to carve a territory in furthering the understanding of the historical impact of colonial and imperial practices on the over-representation of Indigenous and formerly enslaved peoples in current criminal justice systems in settler societies, such as Australia, the Americas, and parts of Africa and Asia. While post-colonial perspectives in criminology widen the analysis of identity and criminalisation, the concept of race, itself often the product of colonial relations, remains a central, privileged concept in criminology. This is problematic because concepts of race are a functional fiction of colonialist epistemologies (Chalmers 2014).

So, how might Southern criminologies understand difference and belonging in post-colonial societies? In this chapter we examine the concept of race as an artefact of Northern thinking, albeit one of global significance. We argue that dominant understandings of race, and even concepts such as ethnicity, have dominated thinking about difference globally, influencing practices not only in criminology and other social sciences, but also the everyday functioning of law and criminal justice systems in many post-colonial societies of the Global South. Outdated and inadequate terminology relating to racial and ethnic categories can generate simplistic or deterministic accounts of the behaviours and experiences of cultural groups and inadvertently reconfigure existing power relationships between such groups (Garland, Spalek, and Chakraborti 2006). So, the challenge to this politics of difference comes in not imitating the colonial rhetoric of difference, but in locating discursive gaps whereby new ways of understanding and practising belonging may be articulated.

Problematising race and ethnicity

In pre-modern times, the people who inhabited diverse global regions were typically accorded identity according to place and locality, religion and language. Up until the modern period, race was a folk idea interchangeable with terms such as 'species', 'type', 'kind', and 'breed'. The history of the concept 'race' is recent and the term only emerged when population groups from different continents made contact with each other (Smedley and Smedley 2005). During the seventeenth century, biological race was used to refer to populations interacting in North America. Modernity resulted in a stronger focus on race. In contrast to religious identity, race was presented as a scientific reality (Battiste 1998; Smedley and Smedley 2005). As an ideology, race provided an important rationale for slavery, which baulked at the ideals of the American and French revolutions in terms of democracy, civil rights, equality, and justice (Jackson 1998; Smedley and Smedley 2005). European empires similarly adopted race to rationalise the contradictions and injustices of capitalism and imperialism. The idea that the world's population could be divided into distinct racial groups was highly pervasive during the nineteenth century when European powers were dividing the world into colonial spheres of influence. In this way, modern racial schema, while showing geographic variation, has been adopted globally to understand difference, in both popular and official discourse.

There is no question of the significance of race in criminology, itself an enterprise embedded in nineteenth-century scientific dogma. Criminology has always posited race as a major correlate of crime (Parmar 2016). Without race, positivist criminology is impossible (Peterson 2012; Bowling and Phillips 2012) (see Chapter 1). On one level, resources in society, including police, are organised around notions of race. On another level etiological explanations of crime, especially street crime, draw significantly on notions of race. Race, and to a lesser extent ethnicity, are key sociodemographic variables used by criminologists to describe victims of crime and offenders and, less often, criminal justice practitioners (Phillips and Bowling 2003: 269).

While the idea of race, whether understood as a biological or cultural essentialism, has been durable in the social sciences, it is clear that the meanings given to race are highly variable, both culturally and historically (Walsh and Yun 2011); however, certain meanings have become reified. Such processes do not occur in a social and political vacuum, but are the product of global power relations which have spatial dimensions and may be considered ideological and, in turn, hegemonic. The dominated and oppressed often share a language of race which, when most politically effective, is articulated in a manner which reduces complex social phenomena into antagonistic dichotomies, such as black/white.

Of course, defining race is fraught with difficulty and while social scientists are often quick to acknowledge the difficulties in defining imprecise variables and concepts, there seems to be a general reluctance among criminologists to wrestle with the challenges of race. In the absence of any challenge, criminologists have been ready to accept the validity of data structured around dominant racial categories. Both the United States (US) Census and National Crime Survey allow respondents to provide data on racial origin, yet neither applies universal criteria (LaFree and Russell 1993: 281–282). The US Census Bureau currently has six definitions of race. A question on race has been in all iterations of the US Census since the first in 1790.

Although categories have fluctuated over time, two have remained stable, these being black and white (Ladson-Billings 1998). North Americans define as black anyone who has known African ancestors. Yet, 'black' is ambiguous, especially owing to the historical significance of the 'one drop' rule, which developed during and after slavery and defined a black person as any person with any known African ancestry (Botham 2009). Although these laws are no longer recognised, many Americans of 'mixed' ancestry still assume a black identity. According to the US Census Bureau, you are defined as white if your ancestors were from Europe, Middle East, North Africa, or North East Asia. More recently, there are so-called 'mixed' or 'multiracial' individuals, who challenge traditional notions and assumptions about race because they cannot be easily placed into pre-existing racial categories. Rather than reject the idea of race, new categories have been created for such people (Shih et al. 2007).

Problems of classification also exist for 'non-black' minorities. 'Hispanic' for example, can include a variety of ethnicities and nationalities and people who are classified as 'white, non-white and 'other' (LaFree and Russell 1993: 282). Indeed, it would seem that census categories have been designed to tell who is white or, more significantly, who is not white. However, despite claims to such, whiteness is not a biological determination, but a political one. To take one example, Mexican ancestry was originally deemed white in the census, but over time, political, social, cultural, and economic shifts placed Mexicans out of that category (Ladson-Billings 1998).

The US census is not unique. The British census uses an 18-point racial classification scheme. In Britain, as in the US, the crude category of 'Asian' compounds data on diverse religious populations, including Muslims originating from the Asian continent. Indeed, Muslim populations, who represent a diverse range of nationalities and ethnicities in Western countries, are often overlooked in criminological research and yet the term 'race' is used with impunity or, out of convenience, they are racialised (Garland, Spalek, and Chakraborti 2006).

The politics of racial identification was highlighted in the United States in 2015 with the case of Rachel Dolezal, a leader within the National Association for the Advancement of Colored People, who took a 'black' identity in her adult life, but was revealed by her parents to be biologically 'white'. She received criticism for 'pretending' to be black, her inauthenticity being the product of her biological heritage. And yet, this very situation highlights how 'race' is defined in a very localised manner. In Australia, in 2012 media reported that Dallas Scott, an Aboriginal man, had experienced difficulty in proving his Aboriginality, lacking documentary evidence of his heritage and cultural affiliations. The situation is not unusual in the Australian context, but what attracted media interest was that Scott has dark skin and 'looked like' an Aboriginal man. Scott eventually managed to formally certify his heritage, but his case highlighted the complexity of defining biological and cultural heritage. Similarly, in 2010 it was reported that a young Aboriginal woman was 'shocked and humiliated' to hear that she might not look 'Indigenous' enough for a job promoting an Aboriginal employment initiative. The employer was quoted as stating that the applicant was 'lovely' and 'perfect', but added but 'if you're promoting Italian pasta, and you put Asians there, how's that going to look? Wouldn't you pick an Italian to promote the Italian pasta?'. She went on: 'I wouldn't have picked her for Aboriginal at all . . . to me she looked like an Aussie girl' (Snow 2010). These cases throw open the conundrum, is it possible to be 'black' and not be biologically black? Of course, for many people racialisation is not a choice, but is something that is inescapable. Further, given historical policies of assimilation in Australia, it is not uncommon for people to discover Indigenous heritage, having previously viewed themselves and/or been viewed by others as non-Indigenous. These examples indicate that belonging remains largely determined by skin colour, but that interpretations are inconsistent. These problems are not new in the Australian context.

> In 1935 a fair-skinned Australian of part-Indigenous descent was ejected from a hotel for being an Aboriginal. He returned to his home on the mission station to find himself refused entry because he was not an Aboriginal. He tried to remove his children but was told he could not because they were Aboriginal. He walked to the next town where he was arrested for being

an Aboriginal vagrant and placed on the local reserve. During the Second World War he tried to enlist but was told he could not because he was Aboriginal. He went interstate and joined up as a non-Aboriginal. After the war he could not acquire a passport without permission because he was Aboriginal. He received exemption from the *Aborigines Protection Act* and was told that he could no longer visit his relations on the reserve because he was not an Aboriginal. He was denied permission to enter the Returned Servicemen's Club because he was.

(Read 1996 in Gardiner-Garden 2003)

These examples also highlight some similarities in how race is popularly understood in both Australian and American contexts, especially when it comes to legislative definitions of Aboriginal. However, administratively the Australian Federal Government defines an Aboriginal as someone who: is of Aboriginal descent; identifies as an Aboriginal person; and, is accepted as an Aboriginal person in the community in which they live (AIATSIS 2018; McCorquodale 1997). This would indicate Aboriginality is not solely defined by skin colour and this definition has been accepted in some court judgments. But while this may prevent biology being a primary measure of belonging, it also raises new questions around cultural belonging.

Gardiner-Garden (2003) observes there are problems with both definitions of 'race' in that they are tautological and there is no indication of 'blood-quantum' required to prove descent or how this might be collected and assessed. The three-part definition can be problematic as it is 'unclear as to what constitutes a "member of the Aboriginal race", when self-identity as an Aboriginal might not be all pervasive and when the Aboriginality of the community doing the accepting is brought into question'. Moreover, in contrast to New Zealand, the Australian Census does not allow for an individual to be identified as being both Aboriginal and belonging to another group, the expectation being that a person of mixed origin will identify as Aboriginal (McCorquodale 1997). In the United States, to be eligible for Bureau of Indian Affairs services, an Indian (Native American) must be: a member of a Tribe recognised by the Federal Government; have one-half or more Indian blood of tribes Indigenous to the United

States, or; must, for some purposes, be of one-fourth or more Indian ancestry (McCorquodale 1997).

In an attempt to address problems associated with racial terminology, ethnicity has been employed as a substitute for race, mostly in sociology and to a lesser extent in other social sciences, such as criminology where the term has failed to gain any traction (Phillips and Bowling 2012; Walsh and Yun 2011). The term is a little more complex than race, because it usually involves grouping people who share a common cultural, linguistic, or ancestral heritage (Smedley and Smedley 2005). In contrast to race, ethnicity is not static, but it is constantly in flux, being shaped by a range of social, economic, and political forces. Moreover, ethnicity is only one source which people or groups may draw upon in terms of establishing an identity. All people are ethnically located, but some ethnicities are marked more than others at particular times and places (Jackson 1998).

While ethnicity is regarded as more helpful than race by many social scientists trying to understand the differences between social groupings, it also presents some conceptual problems. For example, is there a shared ethnicity common to all people who are born and grow-up in a particular nation or place? Can a person have multiple ethnic identities? Here, ethnicities come to resemble Anderson's (1983) imagined communities, in which people who exist within the symbolic and material boundaries of an ethnic group will mostly never have any interaction with their fellow-members, yet there might exist among such people a sense of shared values and community. The problem with ethnicity is that it comes to represent everything that is cultural and is too elastic to provide definite or consistent meanings.

The borders of ethnicities are constantly being negotiated and, as such, are subject to constant shifts of meaning and practice (Ratcliffe 2004: 30). In dominant discourses, race tends to be conceived in terms of black and white groups, while ethnicity is often used to refer to immigrant groups. Ethnicity, as it has been applied in the social sciences, is also viewed in terms of bounded groups, with immutable boundaries, and there is a failure to consider the fluidity of ethnic identity and the cultural hybridity of the post-colonial period. Often ethnic categories are applied in a way that replicates racial terminology and are too broad to be meaningful (that is, Asian, Mixed, Chinese), with static categories failing to capture the diverse ways in which peoples' identities are aligned. Nationality is sometimes presented as a proxy for ethnicity and visible markers of ethnic difference are taken for granted (Parmar 2016). At another level, ethnic attributes such as 'Asianess' have been used to explain lower levels of crime in both the United States and United Kingdom (UK). As Webster (1997) argues, such attributes homogenise dynamic and differentiated cultures and are not valid predictors of behaviours, instead concealing the internal diversity of the groups to which such attributes are applied (Webster 1997: 78).

On a broader level, we have very limited knowledge or appreciation of how class, gender, ethnicity, and generation intersect, largely because race, as discussed, is essentialised and bounded. Citizenship, religion, nationality and culture are frequently elided in dominant criminological discourses (Parmar 2016). And while 'race' may be a fuzzy and imprecise term, racialising practices have some substance and regardless of imputed motives and intents, such practices are not merely the product of prejudicial law enforcement, but are also perpetuated in criminological discourses. It is the very fuzziness of racial terminology that makes it politically useful. That the category race does not withstand scrutiny from any scientific or rational standpoint, does not undermine its immense utility and power in everyday social and political life (racists not being overly inconvenienced by their own lack of theoretical rigor).

Racialising Indigenous Australians

Racist practices of marginalisation and exclusion should be a focus of critical research, as this might avoid dubious truth claims regarding racial groups. Yet, Parmar (2016) argues that the concept of racism is taken for granted in criminology and that criminology has contributed to the 'hollowing out of the concept of racism and a culture of racial equivalence, whereby a multitude of disparate scenarios and interactions are referred to as "racist" and thus deemed equivalent' (Parmar 2016: 36). One example of this is that racial or ethnic identities or processes of racialisation are often assumed in criminological literature to be produced in a top-down manner, being something done to others by individuals or institutions, such as the media. That is, powerful (typically 'white') individuals, groups or institutions construct such identities and those who are racialised have limited means to resist such categorisation, owing to structural constraints or because they lack consciousness of their condition. If they do respond, it is less action than reaction and such reactions are considered to be the primitive and naive responses of dupes who play into the hands of their oppressors (Knepper 2008). As criminology itself has shown, the reality is far different and criminologists do very well not to construct, perpetuate and apply racial categories of dubious heritage.

'Racialisation' was coined by Balibar and Wallerstein (1991) to refer to discrimination of individuals and groups based on perceived racial attributes. Racialisation refers to a process where individuals or groups are identified as belonging to races and possessing racial characteristics. Social structures and institutions can also be stratified along racial lines as part of such a process. The process can happen from without and within a group, however, racialisation is typically described as something done detrimentally to others as part of a power relationship. This noted, it can be instilled with positive attributes by subordinate groups resisting marginalisation. Racialisation is also a practice employed by dominant groups as a form of self-racialisation. This provides an account of the ontology of racialised groups, as distinct from races (Hochman 2017). The classic work on racialisation of crime was Hall et al. (1978), who showed how a new ('new' to the UK, but borrowed with all its fearful and racialised connotations from the US) form of crime, 'mugging', came to be seen geographically and ethnically as a 'black crime' requiring extreme political and policing interventions. Racialisation allows for an examination of the social processes that lead some crimes to be defined in terms of race.

Racialised societies see racial groups as biologically or culturally discrete and exclusive, hierarchical and consider culture to be inherited. Both physical features and behaviour are seen as innate and differences among races are considered profound and unalterable. In such societies, racial classifications are stipulated in legal and social systems (Smedley and Smedley 2005). As will be shown here, Australia is a racialised society, although this is a characteristic it shares with other former settler colonial societies, such as the United States. What is notable here, however, is that race has not always existed in Australasian cultures and there is much to indicate that Indigenous Australian peoples had no equivalent concept to understand and organise difference and belonging.

Australian criminologists and political activists cannot escape adopting racial terminology which divides the Australian population into racialised groupings and largely ignores the complex ways in which difference is experienced and practised in diverse Australian contexts. Questions of race and crime in Australia largely revolve around Indigenous peoples. This is in contrast to the Global North where Indigenous peoples are relatively invisible in discussions of race and crime and are mostly absent in criminology textbooks. Indeed, in the US, Indigenous social problems have more often been framed as welfare, as opposed to criminal problems. However, criminal matters are significant as Indigenous communities suffer overrepresentation in imprisonment and killing by police, despite much attention being focused on African-American communities (Belko 2004; Marcus 2016; Wagner and Rabuy 2017). Similarly, and as highlighted in Chapter 4, Indigenous peoples in Australia are vastly over-represented within the criminal justice system, usually in relation to violence and public disorder offences (Hogg and Carrington 2006). This is partially explained by the highly visible presence of many Indigenous groups in rural and urban centres, which places them at risk of increased levels of policing (Hogg and Carrington 2006). Higher rates of offending in Indigenous communities can also be understood as a consequence of colonial processes, which have led to the dislocation of Indigenous people from their land and the deracination of their cultures, a point which we will take up in greater detail in Chapter 4 (Hogg and Carrington 2006; Reynolds 1989).

Given the high proportion of Indigenous people residing in rural and remote communities, such places are often viewed as sites of racial conflict and/or crime in the Australian context. With respect to this, crime outside the city in Australia is not so much spatialised as it is racialised. The crime problem in rural Australia is largely interpreted as a product of Indigenous pathology or 'race' relations (see Scott and Hogg 2015). Ironically, the racialisation of crime in Australian contexts provides a contrast with the United States, where inner-city crime has been characterised as a racial phenomenon, associated with African-American populations. This immediately suggests that dominant ways of thinking about crime in the Global North, especially the notion of rural areas being relatively crime free and bucolic sites, may be inappropriate in the Australian context (see Scott, Barclay, and Hogg 2007). Further, many of the theories used to explain crime in the Global North, which have attempted to explain crime in highly urbanised settings, may also be inadequate to explain the racialisation of crime in the Australian context. In the Global North, the issue of racism in rural and isolated areas is often overlooked (Chakraborti and Garland 2004). Rural minority ethnic households are largely invisible in Northern research, either as a result of urban-centrism or because they are numerically insignificant (Garland, Spalek, and Chakraborti 2006: 427).

There are inherent problems to be accounted for when considering Indigenous Australian justice, which reflect the way Indigenous belonging is experienced and interpreted. 'Aboriginal' is a racialised term employed to control and homogenise heterogeneous peoples and to align with indicators of well-being and belonging that people given this label have not created and which may be in conflict or exclude their own localised indicators of well-being (Chalmers 2014). There are numerous Indigenous cultures on the Australian mainland, which the colonial misnomers of 'Aboriginal' or 'Indigenous' tend to obscure. Chalmers (2014) is highly critical of conceptual frameworks which conflate culturally distinct and diverse Indigenous Australian cultures using antiquated colonial terms such as 'Aboriginal'. The term 'Indigenous' is amorphous and often used to construct a counter discourse of dominant accounts of racial belonging.

According to Chalmers (2014) elements of racial thinking are formalised for Indigenous peoples because *their* race is subject to legal definition, administration, and control in the Australian context. Legislation has been fundamental in the creation of racial discourse in the Australian context, which operates to create a pan-Aboriginality, obfuscating diverse ways of belonging and knowing. At the heart of the colonialist legal constructions of Indigenous peoples is a biologically essentialised legal personality that has been variously constructed in terms of colour, 'blood quantum', 'race' and genealogical 'descent' (Chalmers 2014; Gardiner-Garden 2003; McCorquodale 1997). Colonialist epistemologies have constructed these administrative and legal definitions of Aboriginality in ways that falsely unify hundreds of Indigenous nations, thereby producing the present-day fiction that there is a singular 'Aboriginal' (legal) identity (Chalmers 2014: 50). At a legal and social level, this biologically essentialised construct becomes counterposed with an equally false binary oppositional construct of the 'non-Aboriginal' Australian, or the 'normal' Australian (Chalmers 2014). The present-day legal construction of Aboriginality thus becomes a way of identifying what is deemed a certain type of unacceptable 'difference', in order that such difference can be subjected to disciplining forces (laws and policies) aimed at its assimilation into what is deemed an acceptable sameness ('normal', 'Australian') (Chalmers 2014). In accordance with this logic, 'Aboriginality' presently exists as a category of disadvantage for the purpose of targeting specialised laws and policies for its eventual erasure in the colonial matrix (Grosfoguel 2011: 7–16) of 'Australian' sameness.

'Indigenous' crime problems

As noted above, the term 'Aboriginal' in Australia is highly racialised, the legacy of colonial thinking, which failed to distinguish between the myriad of cultures that existed on the Australian mainland, conflating these into one ethnicity and/or Aboriginal 'race'. Furthermore, two Indigenous groups are officially recognised in Australia, these being Aboriginals and Torres Strait Islanders. Criminologists and policy makers speak in general terms of Aboriginal and Torres Strait Islander (TSI) peoples, 'ATSI' being a category used in the Australian Census and in all official criminal justice data, both federally and at a state level. The term conflates the Melanesian culture of the Torres Strait Islands with the various cultures of mainland Australia (Beckett 1990; Singe 1979). In presenting cultural homogeneity, this terminology has rendered Torres Strait Islander peoples relatively invisible. As the Department of Aboriginal and Torres Strait Islander Partnerships (DATSIPD

2015) makes clear, a significant issue for TSI peoples is recognition and respect as a distinctive people. Described as a 'minority within a minority' (Shnukal 2001), it is staggering that in 2018 we know virtually nothing about justice practices in the Torres Strait Islands. Existing policy and statements concerning 'ATSI' peoples are incomplete and inaccurate until this is rectified. The limited available data suggests that TSI communities experience crime and justice distinctly and differently from mainland Indigenous cultures.

The Torres Strait Region has a unique geography, history, politics, and culture, which distinguishes TSI people from people living in other regions of Australia. The features of the region have provided TSI people with a degree of autonomy and cultural continuity not afforded to other Indigenous peoples of the Australian mainland. There are over 100 islands in the region, which are spread over 48 000 square kilometres. Islanders live in 18 permanent communities spread over 17 islands, but continue to visit traditionally owned islands for fishing, gardening, food collection, and recreation (Shnukal 2001). The TSI region is classified by the ABS as 'very remote Australia' (Queensland Government Statistician's Office (QGSA) 2016c: 35). The geographic isolation of the region has fostered a relatively high level of cultural homogeneity, supported by isolation. Until relatively late in their development, there was limited access to telecommunications technologies in the Islands (Robertson 2010: 474).

Pre-European contact, the TSI peoples did not regard themselves as a single homogenous or unified group, despite sharing some cultural links through warfare, trade, and ceremonial exchange, some of which were also shared with the peoples of New Guinea and the Cape York region. Indeed, each island could be distinguished from its neighbours through linguistic and cultural differences (Robertson 2010; Shnukal 2001). It was not until the Queensland *Torres Strait Islanders Act 1939* that TSI peoples were considered a separate people. As a result of this legislation, the people of the TSI Region were classified as Polynesian in the first post-war census in 1947. Community Police were also appointed at this time. Community Policing was to remain under the *Torres Strait Act 1971* (Qld) and *Community Services Torres Strait Act 1984* (Qld). In 2007, the Queensland Police Service set up stations on Thursday Island and Horn Island, but responsibility for policing on all other inhabited islands remained the responsibility of local councils. In the 1954 and 1961 Census the peoples were classified as 'Pacific Islanders', but were then classified as 'Aboriginal' and excluded from official figures in the 1966 Census. It was not until 1971 that a separate 'Torres Strait Islander' category was used for the first time (Shnukal 2001).

The islands were annexed comparatively late by the British in 1872 and 1879, with the Islanders becoming British subjects and their islands Crown lands. The first European settlement in the region was in 1863. At Federation, and in contrast to mainland Indigenous peoples, Islanders became Australian citizens though were denied many rights and benefits enjoyed by non-Indigenous Australians (Lawrence 2007; Shnukal 2001). The islands have always enjoyed a relative degree of autonomy very distinct from Indigenous mainland experience. The longest serving (1885–1904) resident magistrate on the Islands instituted a system of Island councils to replace the previous system of island leaders which allowed islanders to conduct their own community affairs through their own police and court system. Robertson (2010: 466) states:

> The nature of European incursion into the Torres Strait is distinctly different to the incursion on the mainland. While mainland Aboriginal communities were steadily dispossessed of their lands, confronted with cultural assimilation and forced to the fringes of an intrusive settler society, islanders, in contrast, experienced limited dispossession. There has been no significant permanent settlement of Europeans beyond the administrative centre of Thursday Island. Segregation, assisted by the region's remoteness and assimilation have characterized colonial rule. Islanders, in contrast to the mainland indigenous communities, did not contend with the conflicting interests of settlers, only the imposition of a colonial order . . . Islanders have been subjected to *colonial rule*, while mainland indigenous communities have been the casualties of the European settlement of the Australian continent.
>
> (Robertson 2010: 465–466, emphasis in original)

Today the Torres Strait Island Region, which includes the tip of Cape York, is home to approximately 5000 people who identify as Torres Strait Islander. Politically, the TSI Region remains relatively autonomous. The Torres Strait Regional Authority was established in 1954 to allow local people to govern their own affairs according to 'Ailan Kastom' (pigeon English term for 'Island Customs'). Ailan Kastom combines a mix of Christianity and older practices associated with the authority of Elders and sea and market garden-based economies (Cooperative Research Centre for Aboriginal Health (CRCAH) et al. 2006: 4). Each Island elects its own council and the 20 representatives meet monthly from 17 local Islands to administer a wide range of local government functions. Among other things, each council is responsible for employing Island police, administering local courts and controlling entry onto land granted in trust to TSI peoples. Local cultural life remains strong in the TSI region and over 75 per cent of TSI people living in the TSI Region speak a language other than English at home (CRCAH et al. 2006: 4). Rates of religious participation are very high in the TSI, with the 2011 Census recording 81.1 per cent of people affiliated with a Christian religion, which compared with the Queensland average of 64.3 per cent of people affiliated with a Christian religion (QGSA 2016b: 15).

Australian born people account for over 90 per cent of the population born in the TSI region, compared with 73.7 per cent for the rest of the state of Queensland (QGSA 2016c: 9). Residential mobility in the Torres Strait Region is relatively low (QGSA 2016a: 7–9). Education and vocational training attainment and household wealth in the TSI Region is relatively high in the context of Indigenous peoples, though this was lower than non-Indigenous Queenslanders (QGSA 2016: 15–17, 39). Approximately three quarters of the population experience high levels of social disadvantage (QGSA 2016c: 34). There is much income inequality in the TSI Region, with Indigenous households earning considerably less than non-Indigenous households and the region having a higher proportion of lower income households when compared to both Indigenous and non-Indigenous populations throughout the rest of Queensland (QGSA 2016a: 22–30). Internet connectivity amongst Indigenous households in the TSI Region is almost half that of the non-Indigenous population in the TSI and living in the rest of Queensland (QGSA 2016a: 36).

An Australian Law Reform Commission Report (1986) described TSI peoples as 'strictly monogamous, mostly church married'. The most significant area of customary practice on the Islands was that of adoption, especially of extra-marital children, by grandparents or other members of extended family. A high percentage of Indigenous people (37.1 per cent) in the Torres and Torres Strait region are children, aged between 0–14 years of age, which is significantly higher than the state average (19.6 per cent) for the same group. In contrast, relatively fewer Indigenous people living in the region (4.6 per cent) were aged 60 years of age and over, when compared with the non-Indigenous population of Queensland (QLD) (13.4 per cent) (QGSA 2016a: 5). In 2015, the median age in the TSI Region was 26.5 years of age, compared with the rest of Queensland with a median age of 36.9 years of age (QGSA 2016b: 6). In the TSI Region in 2011, 49.2 per cent of total families were couple families with children, compared to 42.8 per cent of total families throughout Queensland. 66.6 per cent of total households within the TSI were one family households, compared to the 70.7 per cent of such households throughout Queensland (QGSA 2016c: 16–17).

A Queensland government report observed that raising children on the Islands is a shared responsibility and while parents are primarily responsible, extended family also play a significant role. Family can also include close friends and respected community members (CRCAH et al. 2006: 7). This results in extensive supervision of youth, which can provide support for young people, but can also be seen by them as invasive (CRCAH et al. 2006: 7). Research has indicated a strong sense of traditional culture exists in the Islands, expressed in a desire to include the teaching of traditional languages and cultures in schools. This includes the teaching of traditional practices, such as food gathering and gardening. Elders were actively involved in teaching traditional cultural practices and those who engaged in these were considered less likely to be impacted by what were seen as negative influences, including Western cultural practices. Cultural retention appears stronger in the more remote Northern islands. A high value was also placed on formal education (CRCAH et al. 2006: 8).

Offences against the person are higher in region when compared with the state rate, while offences against property are lower in the TSI region compared with the rest of Queensland (QGSA 2016c: 38). The *Annual Bulletin for Queensland's Discrete Indigenous Communities*

(DATSIP 2014–2015) offers comparative data for eight Indigenous Communities in QLD, including the TSI Region. This data indicates a declining trend and/or relatively low rates in offences against the person, substantiated notifications of child abuse and finalised rates of child protection orders in the TSI Region. In terms of assault rates, the TSI ranks lowest among four larger Indigenous communities (DATSIP 2015). The figures remain unexamined and unexplained, but demonstrate that crimes rates in the TSI region are distinct from other Indigenous regions in QLD. The socioeconomic variables cited above offer some possible explanations for the relatively low rates of Indigenous crime in the Torres Strait Region.

The above data suggests that TSI people are a relatively homogenous group. Ecological conditions also suggest that TSI peoples cannot be conflated with the diverse cultures of the Australian mainland. Torres Strait Island people form a majority ethnic group in the Islands, whereas, in many mainland communities with high Aboriginal populations, the Aboriginal population constitutes a minority grouping. Indeed, racial conflict does not appear to be a precipitating factor in crime in TSI communities, in contrast to many mainland settings (DATSIP 2015). In this way, the TSI region is unique in the Australian experience. Further, Australia cannot simply be framed as a 'post-colonial' society, in the same way as other former parts of the British Empire, such as India, where the dominant, but often minority, white population of colonists went home following independence or relocated to other British settler societies (Moreton-Robinson 2003: 29).

Giving context to the Torres Strait Island experience

Previous Australian research has suggested that crime can be prevented and controlled in rural and regional areas through strong economic conditions, high levels of civic participation, and strong parental supervision (Carcach 2000; Carcach and Huntley 2002). Certainly the TSI region presents as an economically disadvantaged region, so it is the latter factors relating to what has often been referred to as 'social capital' that will be our focus in examining the relatively low rates of crime in the TSI region. While little research in Australia has looked at crime and the ecology of island places, research also suggests that such environments, when demonstrating strong social bonds and interdependencies, require relatively little legal intervention. Pratt and Melei (2018), for example, provide the Pacific Island nation of Tuvalu as an example of a place which shows that Northern dispositions towards law and order politics have not been global. However, they do note that a move towards secular forms authority in Tuvalu has been accompanied by a rise in individualism which threatens to challenge customary obligations and traditional forms of social cohesion.

There are several indicators of social capital in the TSI data, despite a perception of Indigenous Australian communities as being violent places with high rates of victimisation. Social capital describes features of social organisation, such as relations of honesty, cooperation, reciprocity, engagement, and mutual obligation that exist between people within social networks, social structures, and social institutional arrangements. It develops within groups and across groups (Putnam 1993). It is notable in the data presented above that social indicators relating to the TSI region show relatively high levels of institutional engagement, for example, in terms of organised religion, schooling, and employment, and attachment to families. Braithwaite (1989) observes that in control theory the most significant social bonds are to family, school and, occasionally, church.

Research in Australia on rural communities and crime suggests that factors such as the level of community participation, economic change, family disruption, concentration of Indigenous residents, Indigenous contacts with the justice system, and forms of social capital may assist in explaining crime rate variations in remote locations (McIntosh et al. 2008). Until recently, remote community justice research has been especially rare in Australia, despite the immense rural expanses of the continent (Scott, Barclay, and Hogg 2007). This has resulted in urban-centric crime prevention strategies and policy development. This neglect is all the more puzzling given the long-term interest criminology has shown in the ecological distribution of crime. The limited research has indicated that crime in rural Australia is extremely diverse and that incidence of crime ranges from relatively low in bucolic communities (see O'Connor and Gray 1989) to comparatively high in some places (Hogg and Carrington 2006). The discussion of high rates of violence in frontier communities will be taken up further in Chapter 4.

The literature on Indigenous justice notes that crime rates vary considerably between different Indigenous communities and between different locations (Hogg and Carrington 2006; Lawrence 2007). This raises the question as to what are the differences between these communities and what might be the defining elements of a strong Indigenous community? Such knowledge may tell us if crime rates (about which much is known) are linked to the strength of bonds between community members. There is, however no consensus in the literature on the meaning of the phrase 'strong Indigenous communities'. Complex forms of social capital have been associated with Indigenous communities with :dense networks based on kinship, social classes, language groups, land-owning clans, and ceremonial groups (Lawrence 2007: 5).

This noted, Indigenous 'communities' in Australia do not necessarily display kinship, integration, and common purpose. While the idea of community has symbolic impute, it is also a political construct built on a broad terrain of history and politics. In Australia, this terrain is marked by historical and contemporary dislocation. In spite of political efforts to present a coherent political voice at a national level (see, for example, *Uluru Statement* 2017), at local levels Indigenous peoples are often politically divided, this fracturing being in part a product of the colonial and spatial politics whereby peoples were displaced from traditional groupings and culture and separated on reserves and missions, as noted in Chapters 2 and 4. Indigenous groups in rural Australia are usually located on former reserves and missions that were constructed through the colonial process which often resulted in different and sometimes traditionally antagonistic groups being forced to live together. This construction of 'community' took people away from their traditional lands (a process discussed in Chapter 4) and prevented the use of customary ways of dealing with conflict (such as temporary exile) (Goodall 1996). Therefore, the term 'community' may not apply to the complex ways of belonging, inter-relationships and diverse groups of Indigenous people that exist in some rural places (Barclay and Scott 2013).

While conservative law and order discourse presents 'Aboriginal' people as symptomatic of crime problems in rural Australia and in some inner-city enclaves, the counter discourse of the left, which often describes Indigenous belonging in terms of 'community' defined by geographic boundaries, fails to appreciate the complex social inter-actions and networks which inform belonging (Yuval-Davis 2006). There is no such thing as a universal community—communities always have boundaries that define not only what is included in the realm of community, but what is excluded. Without such boundaries belong-ing would be meaningless. Further, communities are not havens of reciprocity and mutuality, but are hierarchical formations, structured through power differentials. In this way, terms such as 'community' replicate some of the problems inherent in racial discourses which reify complex sociocultural articulations.

A 'Southern' account of belonging

While documentation and analysis of racist practices will continue to inform criminological accounts of race-based societies and the racialisation of criminal justice, an account of belonging may pro-vide a useful alternative to race when trying to understand cultural organisation and how it informs crime. Yuval-Davis (2006: 197) argues that we need to distinguish between belonging and the poli-tics of belonging. Belonging is about emotional attachment, feeling 'at home' and feeling 'safe and secure' (Yuval-Davis 2006). When it is threatened it is prone to naturalisation and can be politicised. The politics of belonging refers to specific political projects which articulate particular ways of belonging for specific groups, which are themselves constructed through such projects. Belonging is not just about individual social location and identity, but also how persons are valued and judged.

In post-colonial spaces, subjectivities, including notions of belonging, home, and place are marked by the often conflicting spheres of migration and dispossession. Non-Indigenous belonging is associated with legends of pioneers, ownership, and achieve-ment, and is linked to a racialised social status that confers privileges (Moreton-Robinson 2003: 23–24). In racialised societies, descent becomes the dominant mode through which belonging is defined and organised. Indigeneity is defined by the racially aligned criterion of descent, linking Aboriginality to biological features of genetic lineage. To be Aboriginal is to be biologically descended from pre-invasion peoples (Chalmers 2014: 47). While this may limit the possibilities for cultural exchanges and progressive alliances with non-Aboriginal peoples, post-modern theorists have argued that in conditions of diaspora, multiple and hybrid cultural identities emerge which provide possibilities for counter hegemonic discourses (Moreton-Robinson 2003: 28). Racial categorisation also involves excluding non-Aboriginal people from participation in pre-invasion ontologies, which Chalmers argues included categories that were more inclusive of outsiders (Chalmers 2014: 47). Terms such as 'black' and 'white' can exclude individuals and groups from political struggles (Modood 1997).

De Sousa Santos (2007, 2014) has termed the marginalisation and repression of alternative ways of knowing 'epistemicide' and called for 'cognitive justice' in the face of epistemic violence. He observes how the colonial process was intimately bound to the subjugation of Indigenous knowledge. Chalmers (2014) problematises the idea of 'Aboriginality' in the Australian context, especially definitions, which draw on colonial racial criteria and contrasts these with local Yanyuwa (Northern Australian people) ways of understanding belonging. In the Yanyuwa language no word equates with race, despite it now being a concept for Aboriginal people and of Aboriginal people, who have been racialised. Local criteria for belonging, in the case of the Yanyuwa, involves a two stage process based around situating a person firstly in a social context and then in an environmental context. This process means that when one changes from an outsider to having a position in the Yanyuwa society they can relate appropriately to other people and the environment around them. This process of customary adoption applies to all people. Yanyuwa belonging has some shared characteristics with other Indigenous Australian cultures, especially with regard to the emphasis on the relationship of the body with the land (Moreton-Robinson 2003: 23–24). This Southern account of belonging offers a fluid alternative to the biological essentialism of race.

Conclusion

As a political project applying what has sometimes been termed 'strategic essentialism', the hegemony of race seems assured, as it is used by the powerful to express status and racialise, but also presents as a means to organise and resist power for those who have been racialised. In contrast to race, which offers a static and universalist representation of cultural processes and identities, belonging offers a more fluid and open means of accounting for human diversity, processes of integration, and social conflict. The focus of this criminology should be less about who we are, but how we are. There are Southern alternatives for belonging, some of which draw on Indigenous Australian epistemologies. Yet as a distinct Indigenous Australian culture we know virtually nothing about TSI epistemologies and how these influence bonding and how the ecology of the region, this being isolated island communities, impacts on justice. While criminology has long speculated on the ecology of rural and isolated communities, virtually nothing is known of how island environments influence crime prevention and control. The neglect is surprising given Australia's location in the Southern Pacific. Research into other Melanesian cultures has significantly informed contemporary practices of restorative justice, which have been documented, adapted, and widely adopted in jurisdictions throughout the world, including Australia (Braithwaite 1989). Perhaps here lies an opportunity for Southern criminology to develop an account of Island justice, which will inform the already rich field of spatial criminologies.

References

Anderson B (1983) *Imagined Communities*. New York: Verso.

Australian Institute of Aboriginal and Torres Strait Islander Studies (AIATSIS) (2018) Indigenous Australians: Aboriginal and Torres Strait Islander people. Available at http://aiatsis.gov.au/explore/articles/indigenous-australians-aboriginal-and-torres-strait-islander-people (accessed 2 May 2018).

Australian Law Reform Commission (1986) Recognition of Aboriginal customary laws. *Report* 31. Canberra: Australian Government.

Balibar E and Wallerstein I (1991) *Race, Nation, Class: Ambiguous Identities*. London: Verso.

Barclay E and Scott J (2013) Community policing in Australia's Indigenous communities. In Nalla M and Newman G (eds) *Community Policing in Indigenous Communities*: 153–162. Boca Raton, Florida: CRC Press—Taylor & Francis Group.

Battiste M (1998) Enabling the Autumn seed: Toward a decolonised approach to Aboriginal knowledge, language, and education. *Canadian Journal of Native Education* 22(1): 16–27.

Beckett J (1990) *The Torres Strait Islanders: Custom and Colonialism*. Melbourne: University of Cambridge Press.

Belko W (2004) John C. Calhoun and the creation of the Bureau of Indian Affairs: An essay on political rivalry, ideology, and policymaking in the early republic. *The South Carolina Historical Magazine* 105(3): 170–197.

Blaustein J (2015) *Speaking Truths to Power: Policy Ethnography and Police Reform in Bosnia and Herzegovina*. Oxford: Oxford University Press.

Botham F (2009) *Almighty God Created the Races: Christianity, Interracial Marriages, and American Law*. Chapel Hill: The University of North Carolina Press.

Bowling, B and Phillips C (2012). Ethnicities, racism, crime and criminal justice. In Maguire M, Morgan R, and Reiner R (eds) *The Oxford Handbook of Criminology*. 5th edn. New York: Oxford University Press.

Braithwaite J (1989) *Crime, Shame and Reintegration*. Cambridge: Cambridge University Press.

Carcach C (2000) Regional development and crime. *Trends and Issues in Crime and Criminal Justice* 160. Canberra: Australian Institute of Criminology.

Carcach C and Huntley C (2002) Community participation and regional crime. *Trends and Issues in Crime and Criminal Justice* 222. Canberra: Australian Institute of Criminology.

Carrington K, Hogg R, and Sozzo M (2016) Southern criminology. *British Journal of Criminology* 56(1): 1–20. DOI: 10.1093/bjc/azv083.

Chakraborti N and Garland J (2004) England's green and pleasant land? Examining racist prejudice in a rural context. *Patterns of Prejudice* 38(4): 383–398. DOI: 10.1080/0031322042000298446.

Chalmers G (2014) Indigenous as 'not-Indigenous' as us?: A dissident insider's view on pushing the bounds for what constitutes 'our mob'. *Australian Indigenous Law Review* 1(2): 47–55.

Cooperative Research Centre for Aboriginal Health (CRCAH), Telethon Institute for Child Health Research and Department of Families, Community Services and Indigenous Affairs (2006) Growing up in the Torres Strait region: A report from the Footprints in Time trials. *Occasional Paper* 17. Canberra: Australian Government, Department of Families, Community Services and Indigenous Affairs.

Department of Aboriginal and Torres Strait Islander Partnerships (DATSIP) (2015). *Annual Bulletin for Queensland's Discrete Indigenous Communities 2014–15*. Queensland Government.

de Sousa Santos B (2007) Beyond abyssal thinking. *Eurozine*, 29 June. Available at http://www.eurozine.com/journals/revista-critica-de-ciencias-sociais/page/5/ (accessed 17 March 2017).

de Sousa Santos B (2014) *Epistemologies of the South: Justice Against Epistemicide.* Boulder: Paradigm Publishers.

Gardiner-Garden J (2003) Defining Aboriginality in Australia. *Current Issues Brief* 10. Parliamentary Library, Department of Parliamentary Services, Parliament of Australia. https://www.aph.gov.au/About_Parliament/Parliamentary_Departments/Parliamentary_Library/Publications_Archive/CIB/cib0203/03Cib10#intro.

Garland J, Spalek B, and Chakraborti N (2006) Hearing lost voices: Issues in researching 'hidden' minority ethnic communities. *British Journal of Criminology* 46(3): 423–437. DOI: 10.1093/bjc/azi078.

Goodall H (1996). *Invasion to Embassy: Land in Aboriginal Politics in New South Wales 1770–1972.* St Leonards, New South Wales: Allen & Unwin.

Grosfoguel W (2011) Decolonizing post-colonial studies and paradigms of political-economy: Transmodernity, decolonial thinking and global coloniality. *Transmodernity: Journal of Peripheral Cultural Production of the Luso-Hispanic World* 1(1): 1–37.

Hall S, Critcher C, Jefferson T, Clarke J, and Roberts B (eds) (1978) *Policing the Crisis: Mugging, the State and Law and Order.* London: Macmillan.

Hart MA (2010) Indigenous worldviews, knowledge, and research: The development of an indigenous research paradigm. *Journal of Indigenous Voices in Social Work* 1(1): 1–16.

Hochman A (2017) Replacing race: Interactive constructionism about racialised groups. *Ergo: An Open Access Journal of Philosophy* 4(3): 61–92. DOI: 10.3998/ergo.12405314.0004.003.

Hogg R and Carrington K (2006) *Policing the Rural Crisis.* Annandale, New South Wales: Federation Press.

Jackson P (1998) Constructions of whiteness in the geographical imagination. *Area* 32(2): 99–106. DOI: 10.1111/j.1475-4762.1998.tb00053.x.

Knepper P (2008) Rethinking the racialization of crime: The significance of black firsts. *Ethnic and Racial Studies* 31(3): 503–523. DOI: 10.1080/01419870701492018.

Ladson-Billings G (1998) Just what is critical race theory and what's it doing in a nice field like education? *International Journal of Qualitative Studies in Education* 11(1): 7–24. DOI: 10.1080/095183998236863.

LaFree G and Russell K (1993) The argument for studying race and crime. *Journal of Criminal Justice Education* 4(2): 273–289. DOI: 10.1080/10511259300086141.

Lawrence R (2007) Research on strong Indigenous communities. *Indigenous Justice Clearing House, Brief* 1(April). Australian Institute of Criminology and Attorney General's Department of New South Wales.

Males M (2014) Who are police killing? *Center on Juvenile and Criminal Justice*, 26 August. Available at http://www.cjcj.org/news/8113.

Marcus J (2016) Bringing Native American stories to a national audience. *Neiman Reports*, 11 February. Available at http://niemanreports.org/articles/bringing-native-american-stories-to-a-national-audience/.

McCorquodale JC (1997) Aboriginal identity: Legislative, judicial and administrative definitions. *Australian Aboriginal Studies* 2: 24–35.

McIntosh A, Stayner R, Carrington K, Rolley F, Scott J, and Sorensen T (2008) *Resilience in Rural Communities: Literature Review*. Armidale, New South Wales: Centre for Applied Research in Social Science, University of New England.

McKay D (2017) Uluru Statement: A quick guide. *Research Paper Series* 2016–17. Parliamentary Library, Department of Parliamentary Services, Parliament of Australia.

Modood T (1997) Difference, cultural racism and anti-racism. In Werbner P and Modood T (eds) *Debating Cultural Hybridity: Multicultural Identities and the Politics of Anti-Racism*: 154–172. Atlantic Highlands, New Jersey: Zed Books.

Moreton-Robinson A (2003) I still call Australia home: Indigenous belonging and place in a white postcolonizing society. In Ahmed S, Castada C, Fortier A, and Sheller M (eds) *Uprootings/Regroundings: Questions of Home and Migration*: 23–40. New York: Bloomsbury Publishing.

O'Connor M and Gray D (1989) *Crime in a Rural Community*. Sydney: The Federation Press.

Parmar A (2016) Intersectionality, British criminology and race: 'Are we there yet?' *Theoretical Criminology* 20(4): 419–429. DOI: 10.1177/1362480616677496.

Peterson R (2012) The central place of race in crime and justice: The American Society of Criminology's 2011 Sutherland Address. *Criminology* 50(2): 303–327. DOI: 10.1111/j.1745-9125.2012.00271.x.

Phillips C and Bowling B (2003) Racism, ethnicity and criminology: Developing minority perspectives. *British Journal of Criminology* 43(2): 269–290. DOI: 10.1093/bjc/43.2.269.

Pratt J and Melei T (2018). One of the smallest prison populations in the world under threat: The case of Tuvalu. In Carrington K, Hogg R, Scott J, and Sozzo M (eds) *Palgrave Handbook of Criminology and the Global South*: 729–750. Switzerland: Palgrave Macmillan.

Putnam R (1993) *Making Democracy Work: Civic Traditions in Modern Italy*. Princeton: Princeton University Press.

Queensland Government Statistician's Office [QGSA] (2016a) Indigenous profile. *Queensland Regional Profile, Custom Region Compared with Queensland*. Brisbane, Queensland: Queensland Treasury.

Queensland Government Statistician's Office [QGSA] (2016b) Resident profile: People who live in the region. *Queensland Regional Profile, Custom Region Compared with Queensland.* Brisbane, Queensland: Queensland Treasury.

Queensland Government Statistician's Office [QGSA] (2016c) Time series profile: The region over time. *Queensland Regional Profile, Custom Region Compared with Queensland.* Brisbane, Queensland: Queensland Treasury.

Ratcliffe P (2004) *'Race', Ethnicity and Difference: Imagining the Inclusive Society.* Maidenhead, Berkshire: Open University Press.

Reynolds H (1989) *Dispossession: Black Australians and White Invader.* St Leonards, New South Wales: Allen and Unwin.

Robertson J (2010) Evolutionary identity formation in an Indigenous colonial context: The Torres Strait experience. *Nationalism and Ethnic Politics* 16(3–4): 465–482. DOI: 10.1080/13537113.2010.527236.

Scott J and Hogg R (2015) Strange and stranger ruralities: Social constructions of rural crime in Australia. *Journal of Rural Studies* 39: 171–179. DOI: 10.1016/j.jrurstud.2014.11.010.

Scott J, Barclay E, and Hogg R (2007) There's crime out there, but not as we know it: Rural criminology—the last frontier. In Barclay E, Donnermeyer J, Scott J, and Hogg R (eds) *Crime in Rural Australia*: 1–12. Annandale, New South Wales: Federation Press.

Shih M, Bonham C, Sanchez D, and Peck C (2007) The social construction of Race: Biracial identity and vulnerability to stereotypes. *Cultural Diversity and Ethnic Minority Psychology* 13(2): 125–133. DOI: 10.1037/1099-9809.13.2.125.

Shnukal A (2001) Torres Strait Islanders. In Brundle M (ed.) *Multicultural Queensland 2001: 100 Years, 10 Communities, A Century of Contributions*: 28–32. Brisbane: Multicultural Affairs Queensland, Department of the Premier and Cabinet.

Singe J (1979) *The Torres Strait: People and History.* Brisbane: University of Queensland Press.

Smedley A and Smedley B (2005) Race as biology is fiction, racism as a social problem is real: Anthropological and historical perspectives on the social construction of race. *American Psychologist* 60(1): 16–26. DOI: 10.1037/0003-066X.60.1.16.

Snow D (2010) Indigenous applicant not black enough for the job. *Sydney Morning Herald*, 4 November: 1.

Wagner P and Rabuy B (2017) Mass incarceration: The whole pie 2017. *Press Release*, 17 March. Prison Policy Initiative. Available at https://www.prisonpolicy.org/reports/pie2017.html.

Walsh A and Yun I (2011) Race and criminology in the age of genomic science. *Social Science Quarterly* 92(5): 1279–1296. DOI: 10.1111/j.1540-6237.2011.00818.x.

Webster C (1997) The construction of British 'Asian' criminality. *International Journal of the Sociology of Law* 25(1): 65–86. DOI: 10.1006/ijsl.1996.0034.

Yuval-Davis N (2006) Belonging and the politics of belonging. *Patterns of Prejudice* 40(3): 197–214. DOI: 10.1080/00313220600769331.

Legislation cited

Community Services Torres Strait Act 1984 (Qld).

Torres Strait Act 1971 (Qld).

Torres Strait Islanders Act 1939 (Qld).

4

SOUTHERN PENALITIES

Introduction

In their introduction to *The Sage Handbook of Punishment and Society*, Simon and Sparks (2013a) describe the contours of contemporary 'punishment and society' scholarship. Stressing its intellectual strengths and vitality and underlining its multi-disciplinary character and 'openness to new and less familiar bodies of knowledge', they argue that future research must reflect 'the need to extend the study of punishment-in-societies beyond the traditional heartlands of the north-Atlantic cultural space and into the global south and east' (Simon and Sparks 2013b: 4).

This is most welcome as a prospectus for future research. Yet there does remain a certain ambiguity in the switch from a field described as 'punishment and society' to the reference to 'punishment-in-societies'. Could this reflect an underlying assumption that in pushing back the geographical boundaries of 'punishment and society' scholarship theories and perspectives developed in the Global North nevertheless remain the unspoken conceptual referent for narrating the history and grounding the analysis of penality in other societies? Are we to infer that theory generalised from North Atlantic experiences provides a universal framework of analysis, with penality in the Global South relegated to serving as merely a testing ground for Northern theory: a case of placeless theory being applied to local empirical particulars?

On the other hand, what Simon and Sparks describe as the 'primacy of topic over perspective' in the field opens up the possibility of a deeper engagement with, and on-going reconstruction of, punishment and society scholarship. It is in this latter spirit that we seek in this chapter to examine certain Global South experiences and developments in penality of historical and contemporary significance. One aim is to demonstrate that unacknowledged and under-theorised histories and geographies are folded into the experience of North Atlantic societies upon which most punishment and society scholarship has been based. In so doing we revisit and reconsider the dominant narrative of penal modernism from the standpoint of Southern penality and show that this may add a further layer of understanding to penal developments in Northern societies as well as contributing to our knowledge of penal trajectories, practices, and cultures of particular societies of the Global South. For example, Marie Gottschalk in her contribution to the *Sage Handbook* sought to explain the deeper cultural, political, and institutional roots of United States (US) penal exceptionalism, suggesting that 'the history of punishment in the USA is more a Southern story' (2013: 206). She was, of course, referring to the US South. Yet, that story also obviously points much further South. It calls for a recognition that modern penal cultures and practices in both the Global North and South were in their development linked to the statecraft of imperial states, forced migrations, servitude in various forms, and the use of punishment as a mode of labour control and racial subordination. In the black belt of the American South trafficked African slaves replaced transported convicts and indentured laborers as the foundation of the Southern plantation economy and culture which, in turn, shaped post-slavery forms of state, politics, and penality in these regions and beyond. Some of that is familiar historical ground, but other ways in which global processes (imperial expansion, convict transportation, forced migrations of other kinds) shaped modern penality are much less familiar, and even less likely to be incorporated into dominant penal modernist narratives.

The same hegemonic habits of thought and intellectual practices also commonly pervade attempts to explain contemporary penal developments, most notably perhaps in the 'neo-liberal penality thesis' and its variants, where it is assumed a general punitive turn in penal policy and practice is to be explained by the global spread of a uniform neo-liberalism (see, for example, Wacquant 2009). In the final section of the chapter we question such forms of generalisation by examining developments in Global South settings, in particular Latin America, to underline the importance of seriously engaging with national, regional, and local difference and nuance in penal policy and practice.

This chapter is organised around three general and closely related themes that we argue are highlighted by adopting a Southern perspective. We first discuss the importance of an historical sociology of punishment that looks beyond national borders and the nation state. Second, we consider the value of adopting an expansive view of penality that explicates close links with processes that have been formative in colonial rule and settler nation building. Finally, we demonstrate the need to eschew frameworks of analysis that examine penality in Global South countries as (imperfect) exemplars of penal narratives derived from developments in the Global North, and argue for the need for frameworks that instead attend to the specificities of Southern penalities.

Penality beyond national borders: looking out from 'incarcerative' to 'excarcerative' modes of punishment (De Vito and Lichtenstein 2015: xiv)

> I was perplexed. How were Empire and penal colonies so absent from the penological canon? How would the historical sociology of punishment look if we gazed outwards towards—or even first opened our eyes beyond—Europe and North America?
>
> (Anderson 2016: n.p.)

The penal modernist narrative elaborated within the revisionist sociology of punishment that has flourished since the 1970s is dominated by the image of punishment as confinement: a linear historical movement in which the pre-modern age of political absolutism, bodily punishment, torture, and forced labour gave way to liberal political institutions, scientific reason, national progress, and the disciplinary prison. The narrative rests on further core assumptions. The most fundamental of these is the idea that the nation state is the natural and obvious unit within which to frame analyses of penality. Penal policy is to be understood as an instrument of states directed at their internal governance. Modern penal development has been analysed almost exclusively by reference to the trajectory of the nation state (or sometimes, in federal systems of government, sub-state jurisdictions); that is, as a phenomenon occurring within national borders driven by the domestic politics, economics, and culture of the liberal state. Cross border influences are, of course, acknowledged. In the global era, such influences are increasingly subject to examination, prompting researchers to consider issues like: 'policy transfer' (how penal policy 'travels'); the 'diffusion' of penal ideas; and the impact of particular national political contexts on the reception of ideas (see for example, Newburn 2010 and the series of studies in the edited collection Newburn and Sparks 2004). Nevertheless, the core processes in question are often regarded as being internal to the state.

In addition, such inquiries tend to be set against a further, rather insistent and fundamental underlying assumption: that just as the North Atlantic societies led the way in shaping the modern world, the penal forms pioneered in these societies (especially the prison) naturally make their way across the globe as other societies are led to emulate the penal precedent set by them. This has created the basis for a rapidly developing contemporary comparative penology in which imprisonment rates are used as a tool for cross-national comparison of penal systems, for judging their relative punitiveness and so on (two of the best-known examples are Cavadino and Dignan 2006 and Lacey 2008).

One consequence of this North Atlantic, state-centric bias is that close to no attention has been given to the ways in which modern penality has been shaped by 'historical processes and relationships that transcend nation states and that connect apparently separate worlds' (Curthoys and Lake 2005: 5). Viewing penality from the South necessitates recognition that certain formative processes shaping modern penality transcended national borders, rendering the tendency to focus exclusively on national and endogenous drivers of penal development partial and misleading.

As Clare Anderson's quote at the beginning of this section makes clear, penality was deeply implicated in the European colonisation of 'new worlds' in the early modern and modern periods. The transportation of convicts to overseas destinations was a feature of the colonisation projects of all European imperial states without exception, although some used it on a much larger scale than others. Penal power was an important component of imperial statecraft with implications for both how punishment was enacted in metropoles and its role in the governance and development of colonial societies. Scant attention has been accorded to it within Global North punishment and society scholarship, which has been centrally concerned with generalisation based on the trajectory of penal modernisation *within* metropolitan societies and, in particular, related to the rise and global spread of the penitentiary prison. Indeed, more attention was paid to these global dimensions of penal development by earlier punishment and society scholars (see, for example, Rusche and Kirchheimer 2003 [1939]).

Amongst contemporary scholars it has been left almost entirely to historians to study the character, scope, and impact of convict transportation. A growing community of energetic global historians have researched the dimensions of penal transportation, mapped sites and routes, and explored the variety of convict regimes and their impacts on economy and society in a wide range of colonial settings (Anderson 2009, 2016; Anderson et al. 2015; Anderson and Maxwell-Stewart 2013; De Vito and Lichtenstein 2013, 2015; Maxwell-Stewart 2012, 2015; Nicholas 1988a).[1] In the early modern period of European colonisation of the New World, the Portuguese were the pioneers, transporting convicts to meet labour and military needs in its Latin American colonies. In particular, convicts were sent to Brazil from early in the fifteenth century until Brazilian independence in 1822. From the mid-nineteenth century until 1932, the military administered a convict system in Portugal's African colonies of Angola and Mozambique that operated alongside the national penitentiary system established in Portugal in the same period. After serving a period of penance in prison at home, offenders were sent to the overseas colonies to both redeem themselves through labour and, more importantly, to contribute that labour to the building of colonial infrastructure. Convicts were also sent to Africa from Portugal's other colonial outposts in Asia and elsewhere, and this continued until the 1950s. In the closing years of the Portuguese empire and Salazar's dictatorship at home, which ended in 1974, Portugal sent political prisoners and African independence leaders to its colonial outpost in Cape Verde (Anderson and Maxwell-Stewart 2013; Coates 2015).

The French transported convicts to its colonies from the mid-sixteenth century until the abolition of transportation in the *Penal Code 1810*. Reintroduced after the abolition of slavery in the French empire in 1848, convicts were sent to the notorious penal colony in French Guyana until 1938. This was also a destination for convicts sent from France's colonies in Africa (Algeria and Senegal) and Indo-China. Throughout the last third of the nineteenth century, New Caledonia in the South Pacific received convicts including political exiles after the 1871 Paris Commune (Anderson and Maxwell-Stewart 2013: 280).

Between the sixteenth and the early twentieth centuries, convicts were transported within the Spanish empire to and amongst its colonies in North and South America, the Caribbean, the South Atlantic, and the Philippines. Convict labour was relied upon both before and after Spanish colonies in South America gained independence in the early nineteenth century. A distinctive feature was the sending of convicts to remote military outposts (presidios), especially in the Southern borderlands of Latin America (Argentina and Chile). There they would serve in the army and/or build and maintain the local military infrastructure. These were regions still substantially under the control of Indigenous peoples. They were also sites of border contestation between the colonising European powers and, later, the newly independent settler states. Convict labour directly served colonising and military ends, subjugating Indigenous peoples and securing national borders (De Vito 2016).

In both tsarist and Soviet eras, Russia relied heavily on internal political exile to Siberia, but additionally it transported about 180 000 convicts to Sakhalin Island in the Pacific between 1850 and 1917 (Anderson and Maxwell-Stewart 2013; Beer 2017; Maxwell-Stewart 2015). The forced labour camps and atrocities of twentieth-century totalitarian dictatorships (Fascist as well as Soviet) are usually seen as so exceptional in scale and brutality as to be aberrant moments in which the ordinary flow of history was interrupted by horrifying regimes led by inhuman monsters. As such, they have come to constitute their own fields of scholarship that others (including criminologists and sociologists of punishment) have left well alone. But there is reason to consider whether insights might be gained from exploring connections with their predecessors in colonial regimes of forced transportation and labour.

Penal transportation was absolutely central to British domestic and colonial penality for three centuries until its complete cessation in the closing years of Britain's empire in India (Anderson 2016; Anderson and Maxwell-Stewart 2013; Arnold 2015). Transportation to Australia is one of the most significant, and well known, of these penal projects but it was far from being the only one (Hughes 1988; Shaw 1966). For two centuries before the American Revolution, Britain transported convicts to its North American and Caribbean colonies (Ekirch 1987). In the modern period, Britain also sent convicts to Bermuda (1824–1863), Gibraltar (1842–1874), the Falklands (1826–1831), and British Guyana in the early nineteenth century. From within Britain's Asian empire, convicts were transported between a wide range of locations, including India, Hong Kong, Ceylon, Burma, and the Straits Settlements (Singapore, Malacca, Penang). Over 80 000 convicts were transported to the Andaman Islands between 1858 and 1939 (Anderson 2016).

The new historical scholarship on convict transportation is not narrowly concerned with transportation as a criminal sentence or form of punishment, but rather seeks to locate it in relation to wider processes of imperial expansion in the modern world and connect it to other forms of forced migration and labour extraction, including slavery and indenture. Questioning the taken-for-granted dichotomy of forced/free in relation to labour and migration that has underpinned the manner in which research on these issues has often been divided up amongst the disciplines, we are urged instead to consider transportation and convict labour in what is posited as a more fluid relationship with other forms of labour control. This also provides a further lens through which we might be led to see convicts as economic and social actors, and convictism (and penal practices more generally) as connected with the changing economic and social structures that marked the advent of modernity.

'Excarcerative' regimes of forced labour in which punishment retains an economic function are shown to be a core element of modern penal policy and practice in many settings and to have survived the advent of a carceral penality centred on the prison, cellular isolation, and bodily discipline. As De Vito (2016: 118) has argued,

> The study of convict labour lies at the crossroads of labour history and the history of punishment. However, in both sub-disciplines convict labour has been traditionally marginalized because of a double teleology: first, the focus on 'free' wage labour has dominated labour (and migration) history, conflating wage labour with capitalism and modernity, and, by contrast, coerced labour with pre-capitalism and pre-modernity; second, in the history of punishment, the quest for the 'birth of the prison' has played a similar role, sketching an alleged shift to the 'modernity' of the penitentiary. The two discourses have also reinforced each other, producing a deterministic narrative of the penitentiary as an instrument for the formation of wage labourers and for factory discipline. Both of these interpretations should be reversed. Building on the evidence presented so far, it is possible to highlight the opportunity offered by the study of convict labour for the study of punishment and labour in the long nineteenth century.

Convict labour fulfilled vital economic and other functions in many Global South colonial settings where prevailing or changing circumstances (be it the abolition of slavery, the hostility of indigenous populations, and/or the paucity of free settlers) ensured no alternative source of labour was available. Adopting a global frame through which to approach penality therefore decentres the penitentiary and carceral discipline as the telos of penal modernisation and points to the multifarious forms, practices, and purposes of penality in the modern world. Convict labour offered a degree of flexibility lacking in other labour regimes and was adaptable to shifting ideas and visions of empire. It could be deployed where needed to serve a variety of needs and functions: building colonial infrastructures; founding entirely new societies (as is arguably the case with transportation to New South Wales and Van Diemen's Land/Tasmania); extending and consolidating colonial power in borderlands (through for example dispossessing indigenous peoples); and redeeming the convicts themselves. Transportation served other purposes in metropolitan and colonial settings from which the convicts were transported. It supplied an effective alternative penalty for serious criminal offenders where the death penalty was falling into disuse and economic cost and prevailing political structures presented major obstacles to domestic penal reform and a penitentiary building programme. This was the case in Britain in the first two thirds of the nineteenth century (Hogg and Brown 2018). Economic, political, and cultural factors also influenced intra-imperial convict transportation, given the frequent reluctance of colonial authorities to 'waste' expenditure on costly infrastructure, like penitentiaries, that was regarded as ill-suited to the 'primitive' mentality of colonial populations, a factor in the transportation of convicts in substantial numbers from India to other penal colonies in British Asia. In both metropolitan and colonial settings, authorities also had recourse to transportation where necessary to suppress political dissent, including in the wake of revolutionary uprisings in nineteenth-century Europe and the 1857 Indian mutiny (Anderson 2016).

The role of convict transportation as an instrument of imperial statecraft also points to important, and arguably under-researched, links between military power (organisation, discipline, and culture) and modern penality. As noted above, convicts were transported to serve in, or otherwise directly support, the military in some settings. More generally, the military were centrally involved in the actual overseas transportation and supervision of convicts and the design, engineering, and management of convict settlements in many places.

This also underlines the fact that it was not just convicts who circulated within imperial networks, but also officials, ideas, plans, blueprints, knowledge, and techniques. And the traffic was multi-directional, between centre and periphery and within the periphery. Speaking of the administration and reform of prisons in England, Edmund Du Cane observed in 1872:

> It is difficult to propose any system now on which some light may not be thrown by our experience in England or in the Colonies. In the history of the latter especially is to be found a great source of knowledge and experience, and so much is our present system the result of, and founded on the transportation system (which ceased entirely only four years ago) that those who wish to acquire a full and connected acquaintance with our views and practice should not fail to study the history and phases of that system.
>
> We have tried, at various times, as portions of our various penal system in the colonies, simple deportation or banishment ;— we have tried assigning convicts to live as servants in families of free people ;—we have tried retaining them under charge of the Government, but hiring out their labour to free people for the benefit of Government ;—we have tried planting them out in bodies in a condition of semi-freedom, to work with pay for Government until employers hired them ;—and we have tried, in England, the exact reverse of this, viz. :—keeping them in isolation for lengthened periods in cells.
>
> (Du Cane 1872: 3–4)

Du Cane wrote directly from experience. As an officer in the Royal Engineers he served for five years in the Swan River penal colony in Western Australia, supervising transported convicts undertaking public works and, at the same time, served as a magistrate in the colony and a visiting magistrate for convict stations. Several years after returning to England he was appointed a director of convict prisons and subsequently oversaw the establishment of a national prison system in the 1870s serving as chair of the National Prison Commission until 1895. He was one of the most (if not the most) influential British prison administrators of the second half of the century.

As Du Cane suggests, the colonies constituted an important laboratory for penal experimentation, many of whose measures influenced administration, policy, and practice in the metropole. In some instances, reform programmes were more readily realised in a practical sense on the *tabula rasa* presented by the colonies than they were in Britain. The idea of the separate system of imprisonment, based on cellular isolation, had been well established for over 50 years before the first prison closely modelled on the penitentiary principle, Pentonville, was built in the early 1840s. The British went on in the later 1840s to build penitentiaries in the remote penal outposts of Norfolk Island and Port Arthur in Van Diemen's Land, before they built further penitentiaries in Britain itself. A juvenile reformatory built on Point Puer at Port Arthur in 1834 predated the construction of any similar institution in England (MacFie and Hargraves 1999). Of more significance, developments in the Australian penal colonies were fundamental in shaping mid-century British penal practice in ways that endured for more than a century and a half thereafter. What became known as the progressive staged system of penal management was a hybrid of the original separate, or penitentiary model, and practices pioneered in the Australian penal colonies. A period of cellular isolation, enforced penitence, and disciplinary labour in Pentonville prison was followed by transportation to Australia where the prisoner would be subject to a forced labour regime or, if of good behaviour, be given a 'ticket of leave' (a form of conditional release) permitting them to work on their own behalf. Later, a further stage—a period of labour in association in a public works prison in England—was interposed between separation in Pentonville and (until its cessation) transportation to the colony. Reforms affecting the release stage—remissions on sentence and conditional early release on licence—were also borrowed from colonial practice in Australia and thereafter became integral elements of British (and Western) penal policy and practice. The measures provided incentives for good behaviour, industriousness, and moral reform, the transition from one stage to the next being subject to positive behavioural and attitudinal change in the prisoner. Alexander Maconochie's marks system, developed by him on Norfolk Island, was also widely adopted as a tool of orderly prison management (see generally on these mid-century British penal developments and their debt to the transportation system, Forsythe 1987: 71–90; on Maconochie and Norfolk Island see Barry 1958; Clay 2001). These measures also served, however uneasily, to reconcile competing visions of prison organisation and penal purpose. Elements of harsh treatment aimed at deterrence and less eligibility combined with reformative elements, isolation, and disciplinary labour with productive labour in association. Early release programmes encouraged individual reform and a more orderly prison environment and, at the same time, reduced the pecuniary burden of the prison system.

With transportation it is important to recognise that the journey itself was an important site of penal innovation, although the pronounced 'terra-centric' bias in conventional North/South discourse (Christopher, Pybus, and Rediker 2007: 1) leads to the neglect of such matters. The tendency to 'privilege large landmasses as uniquely important for human history' (Samson 2011: 244) means oceans appear as no more than 'big empty spaces' on maps (Samson 2011: 249) with the consequence that the significance of journeying in and of itself is generally overlooked. In the context of convict transportation, the sea journey was a site of penal change and reform in relation to forms of spatial organisation, discipline and, in particular, medical supervision that exerted an important and lasting influence on penality. Due to the great risks flowing from epidemics and other diseases at sea, the transports to the Australian penal colonies were from early on accompanied by surgeon-superintendents who were charged with responsibility for discipline as well as the health of convicts and others on board. Medical inspections were also carried out both before embarkation and at disembarkation. The regulation of the health of the convicts, also reflected in attention to diet, sanitation, clothing, hygiene, and habitation, led to steep reductions in mortality both in the passage to the colonies and afterwards. As Maxwell-Stewart observes, 'convict Australia provided the opportunity to impose sanitary and health regimes in a way that was not possible in Britain where *laissez-faire* politics restricted state intervention' (2012: 45; also see Nicholas 1988b). Important components of later penal welfarist regimes (Garland 1985) could, therefore, be said to have originated in certain nineteenth-century convict transportation regimes. It was, of course, dependency on the industry and skills of the convicts, as well as their other economic roles in the fledgling colonies, rather than simply humanitarianism, that motivated attention to their general well-being. In the Australian penal colonies it also necessitated the extension of freedoms and rights denied to felons under British common law (for example, to earn wages and to own, buy and sell property: Kercher 2008).

A reasonable conclusion to draw from this is that the trajectory and many fundamental features of modern British penality, which exerted a powerful influence elsewhere, can only be understood if the imperial context is considered, as this is where many features first appeared. Sometimes they were deliberately adopted as reform measures, but they were often a response to the exigencies of penal management in circumstances where the labour of convicts was critical to colonial economic and social development. Northern penality has a Southern history.

This experience carries other lessons in relation to North Atlantic penological and criminological orthodoxies prevailing at the time. The evidence shows that crime rates fell in the Australian colonies after the cessation of transportation, and rates were certainly much lower than would be expected in convict-descended societies (let alone what had been prophesied by critics of the 'thief colony' and would be suggested by emerging biological theories of crime) (see Braithwaite 2001; Godfrey 2012; Godfrey and Cox 2008; Maxwell-Stewart and Kippen 2015). Other studies have tracked the lives of convicts and shown how so many were enabled to build viable lives away from crime because of the economic and social opportunities afforded them in the unlikely setting of the Australian penal colonies (Female Convicts Research Centre 2012; Frost 2011, 2015; Frost and Hodgson 2013; Frost and Maxwell-Stewart 2001; Kavanagh and Snowden 2015; Smith 2014). Communities settled by a substantially convict population formed into societies that, by the international standards of the time, were law-abiding, egalitarian, and democratic in character. Recognition of the fact at the time might have turned the late nineteenth-century criminological and penal obsession with the biological roots of crime, the habitual criminal, and the problem of recidivism upside down, affording some very different origin stories for a modern criminology.

Penality beyond punishment: coloniality and white men's justice

Recent developments in and around the administration of criminal justice across much of the liberal democratic world have posed afresh the question of how to draw the boundaries around what constitutes punishment so as to ensure respect for the fundamental legal safeguards associated with the power to punish in liberal polities (Zedner 2016). The cardinal liberal precepts are that no individual be subject to the censure and coercion entailed in punishment without having first been proved to be guilty of a crime by an independent tribunal after a fair trial, and such punishment as is imposed should not exceed what is required to reflect the gravity of the crime. Concern has been aroused by the proliferation of coercive measures of various kinds that expand the power of the state in ways that impinge, where they do not outright violate, liberal principles of criminal justice: administrative sanctions, hybrid civil-criminal measures, preventive orders, surveillance systems, and new forms of administrative detention whose purposes have been redefined as non-punitive in order to circumvent the traditional requirements of the criminal process. Some have described this as the emergence of a 'shadow carceral state' (Beckett and Murakawa 2012).

The primary concern in much of this literature is normative: how and where to lay down the boundaries of punishment to ensure respect for liberal, rule of law principles (see, for example, Zedner 2016 and the literature she surveys). Our core concern, on the other hand, is rather with non-normative questions of how we make sense of penal practices historically, politically, and culturally. In particular, we share Garland's (2013: 487–488) emphasis on the importance of apprehending penality in relation to the governmental or public policy contexts in which it operates, the 'problem field' or frames within which it is situated. It is implicit in much of the critical literature on recent penal or quasi-penal developments that offend liberal due process safeguards that these are novel measures, but a Southern perspective and some of the frames it suggests show that illiberal penalities—including measures that are essentially penal in character but justified under some label and purpose other than punishment—have many historical precedents.

One of those frames, as argued at length above, is that of colonial empire. In his study of penality and colonial governance in British India, Brown has stressed that in examining the colonial context, the penal field must be 'broadly defined' (2014: 192) to include a range of military, civil, and administrative powers as well as nominally criminal or penal measures. Repression, including overt and barely restrained violence, was an important component of colonial regimes. The British frequently resorted to open repression against insurrectionary behaviour

by its colonial subjects (see generally Simpson 2001: 59–90) including, to name just a few of the more infamous instances, responses to:
the 1857 Indian 'Mutiny' (after which some mutineers were shot from
canons: Tharoor 2017: 166); the Mau Mau uprising in Kenya (Elkins
2005); and local resistance in 1920s Mesopotamia (today's Iraq) (where
the aerial bombing of villages was conducted as a 'policing' measure or
more accurately, a form of collective punishment: Tanaka 2009).

Massacres of indigenous peoples, often euphemistically labelled
'punitive expeditions', were a frequent occurrence on the Australian
frontier and in the Portuguese and Spanish colonisation of Latin
America. But as Brown (2014) emphasises in his study of colonial
India and Simpson shows for many parts of the British Empire, a
wide variety of coercive measures were relied upon to govern colonial populations. It was, as Brown states, a 'polyvalent enterprise'
(2014: 193), an amalgam of measures adapted to local, and often
changing, conditions and constructions of the problems (and aims)
of colonial rule. Invariably established under colour of law, in most
places measures involved efforts to enlist local assistance, incorporate elements of customary control, and/or exploit tribal, ethnic,
and religious divisions. In any discussion of colonial penality the
exceptional measures adopted until recently in Northern Ireland
should also not be overlooked.

The conditions in colonial settings called forth the need for various
modes of collective control rooted in the fundamental and immutable divide between ruled and rulers, colonial populations and their
colonisers. However, those conditions varied enormously from one
colonial setting to another, dependent on factors such as: the geography and demography of the colony (including the size and distribution
of indigenous populations relative to colonial administrations and
settlers); the character of pre-colonial societies and their hierarchies and
structures of authority; ethnic, tribal, and/or religious divisions in the
existing population; and the nature, pace, and reach of colonisation.

In a country the size of India, for example, and with its vast and
diverse population who were to serve as the principal source of labour
in the colony, a small resident British colonial administration could
never have maintained its rule without the cooperation of local elites
and the participation of others as low-level officials, police officers,

and soldiers. Nonetheless, the repertoire of control measures in India included criminal laws based on the principle of collective punishment. In his study of the genealogy of colonial governmentality in India and its intersections with crime and modes of crime control, Brown examined at length the *Criminal Tribes Act 1871* which criminalised entire communities perceived to be a source of threat to the colonial state. Penal power was directed no longer at the individual, requiring proof of some culpable act, but at whole classes of persons. Numerous tribes were listed as falling under the jurisdiction of the Act (Brown 2014).

Conditions in settler colonies were very different. While the processes of colonisation varied as between different settler countries, and even different regions of the same country, there are definite similarities in the broad pattern (Perry 1996). Taking Australia as our focus here, British colonisation aimed at the more or less complete dispossession of Indigenous peoples. Due to the enormous size and varied physical geography and climatic conditions of the continent and the dispersed character of the Indigenous population, dispossession occurred at a highly uneven pace. Indigenous labour was exploited, and often grossly so, but the foundational assumption of the new society that took shape in the nineteenth century was that Australia was to be 'a white man's country' (Lake and Reynolds 2008), a further expression of the expansion of Britain and its culture, language, laws, and institutions across the globe. That is to say, while Indigenous people were in principle British subjects, the continent was in practice treated as *terra nullius* and land appropriated without regard for prior long-standing Indigenous rights and uses. Resistance to dispossession was violently crushed or treated as criminal. Native police were enlisted in special forces in Eastern Australia to aid in this process. In the early years of colonisation, spanning much of the first half of the nineteenth century and concentrated in the South-East of the continent, imprisonment played little role. Finnane (1997a: 4) notes:

> Imprisonment, after all, is a legalised detention for the trial or punishment of offenders. It operated within the common law assumptions of a jurisdiction over subjects sharing a common heritage. The ambiguous legal position of Aborigines, and the state of guerrilla warfare on the frontiers, meant that the

prisons of the settled parts of Australia were largely filled by the new settlers, not by those who were colonised.

The later colonisation of the West and tropical North of the country, however, was undertaken in 'a different political climate', one in which the imported legal institutions were more firmly established, humanitarian opinion more alert to colonial abuses, and there were higher expectations that 'the formalities of justice' would be observed (Finnane 1997a: 4). In Western Australia, imprisonment was widely used against Aboriginal people, a special prison for Aborigines being built in 1840 on Rottnest Island, just off the coast. By 1905, according to Finnane (1997a: 6), 'Aborigines comprised 32% of the Western Australian prison population, in 1909 more than 42%'. However, their imprisonment rapidly declined after the first decade of the twentieth century, almost certainly because the new regime of administrative segregation under 'protection' legislation (the *Native Welfare Act*) became the preferred means of social control (Finnane 1997b: 38). The imprisonment of Aboriginal people underwent a rapid rise again in Western Australia in the 1970s, after the repeal of the *Native Welfare Act* (Broadhurst 1987: 154). In North Queensland, another island prison for Aborigines was established in 1918 on Palm Island, officially designated a 'penitentiary for troublesome cases' (quoted in Watson 2010: 18). It was a penal settlement but also an institution within the network of Queensland government reserves and missions upon which Indigenous people were forcibly segregated under state 'protection' laws. All the mainland states instituted such regimes from the late nineteenth century, a quasi-penal apparatus of racial control geographically isolated from cities and towns in which virtually every aspect of Indigenous life was subject to supervision by administrators, dubbed 'protectors', positions frequently occupied by local police. First and foremost, the purpose was segregation, a form of racial hygiene aimed at the invisibilisation of Indigenous people. Although the goals and means were frequently in tension, this invisibilisation might also be achieved through assimilation, where this involved efforts to erase Indigenousness and its means of transmission, breaking up families by removing light-skinned children, regulating the right to marry, and suppression of language and culture (Hogg 2001). As what might be regarded as a mode of penal welfarism, the 'protection' regimes inverted the penal welfarist logic described in conventional accounts of penal modernism in the Global North (Garland 1985). Far from thickening social institutions of governance in ways that afforded buffers against carceral interventions and their exclusionary impacts, Indigenous people were brought under very direct forms of administrative control devoid even of judicial oversight. From actual killing fields, which endured in some parts of Northern Australia until the early 1930s, to the segregationist regimes of the twentieth century, the pattern of treatment of Indigenous people in Australia conformed not to venerated liberal principles of British justice, but to the eliminationist logic Wolfe (2006) has identified as laying at the core of settler colonialism.

It is also to be noted that, contrary to the familiar historiography of Western punishment in which corporal punishments gave way to a system of carceral penality in the nineteenth century, bodily punishments and restraints (flogging, use of neck chains, and tying or chaining to trees) remained a crucial instrument of power and control within the local colonial settler order in remote Northern Australia until well into the twentieth century (Hogg 2001: 358–361), as they did in other British colonies (for example, India: Brown 2014: 166–169). Such practices reflected, incorporated, and sustained wider cultural assumptions underpinning the colonial order, centred on what Brown refers to as the 'discourse of insensitivity or debasement' (Brown 2014: 194). Corporal punishments imagined and constructed a particular legal subject, one who was devoid of the capacity for feeling and reason and for whom physical subjection and the sensation of bodily pain, summarily administered, was regarded as the only effective means of control and persuasion. Or as a justice of the Northern Territory Supreme Court put it in 1938, 'The proper punishment for cases of this sort [minor offences], and the only punishment aboriginals appreciate, is a flogging. This has been suggested as the proper punishment for aboriginals by many people who know them' (quoted in Markus 1990: 119). The judge's reference to 'people who know them' was intended as a rebuke to the humanitarian concerns of some missionaries and other outsiders and to contemporary shifts in government policy towards 'welfare' and 'assimilation'. The discourse of debasement was no less an unstated premise of other, ostensibly less harsh, 'protection' policies: systematic and permanent removal of children from their families and communities, for example, necessarily rested on the assumption that Indigenous people were not culturally predisposed to really suffer, or suffer for long, in the face of what for whites would constitute the most grievous loss.

Racialised 'protection' and 'welfare' regimes functioned autonomously of state criminal justice systems, thus limiting contact with the ordinary criminal law until they were dismantled in the 1960s. Thereafter, Indigenous communities were exposed to the full brunt of criminal justice in settings that typically remained deeply hostile to Indigeneity viewing them as a social and hygienic threat to white communities. The very presence of Indigenous people in or on the fringes of townships and urban communities was treated as transgressive of white social norms and public order laws that were assiduously enforced by police. In addition, dispossession and cultural decimation along with exclusion or extreme marginalisation with respect to employment and housing markets, schooling and other services produced entrenched poverty, a widespread sense of despair, severe alcoholism, and heightened conflict and violence in many communities (see Chapter 2).

One of the catastrophic social consequences of this malign history is the massive and ever-increasing scale upon which Indigenous people are imprisoned today. Barely three per cent of the Australian population (Australian Bureau of Statistics (ABS) 2016), Indigenous people account for 27 per cent of the adult prison population and 51 per cent of the juvenile detention population (Pricewaterhouse Coopers 2017). Adults are incarcerated at the national rate of over 2000 prisoners per 100 000 population compared to 154 per 100 000 for the non-Indigenous Australian population (ABS 2016). Comprehensive data on the imprisonment rates of indigenous peoples across the world is not available, but there is good reason to believe that it is generally the case that Indigenous peoples are massively over-represented in the prison populations of other colonial settler societies (including Canada, New Zealand, the US) (United Nations Department of Economic and Social Affairs 2009), as are African-Americans in the US. Yet Indigenous Australians appear to be the most incarcerated people in the world (Anthony 2017). In those parts of Australia—the North and the West—where the history of contact is more recent and where the Indigenous population constitutes a larger share of the whole, these rates are significantly higher again, over 2500 per 100 000 population in the Northern Territory and well over 3000 per 100 000 population in Western Australia (Australian Law Reform Commission 2017: 95).

Garland (2001: 1) has defined mass imprisonment as 'a rate of imprisonment that is markedly above the historical and comparative norm for societies of this type' and that 'ceases to be the incarceration of individual offenders and becomes the systematic imprisonment of whole groups of the population'. The focus has tended to be on the US as 'exceptional' in this regard, but Indigenous incarceration rates in Australia and elsewhere surely qualify as selective mass incarceration and instances of 'penal exceptionalism'. And it should be remembered that incarceration rates afford only a tip-of-the-iceberg glimpse of the degree to which particular groups are entangled with the criminal justice system, given that the reach over time of various forms of correctional supervision is a multiplier of point-in-time prison numbers with deeply destructive collateral effects on families and communities. So, in relation to the indigenous context (in Australia and elsewhere), a Southern perspective seeks to underline, and explicate, the extent to which the criminal justice system is a normalised presence in, and impacts, the lives of entire communities affecting their demographics, social fabric, family structure, inter-generational relationships, political economy, and fosters self-perpetuating spirals of criminalisation. This constitutes a very distinctive penality whose historical roots lie in the 'settler revolution' and the establishment of 'white men's societies' in the Global South (as well as the North).

Patterns of expropriation, exploitation, and segregation have left enduring imprints on all colonial settler societies, whether they are rich or poor by the standards of their Gross Domestic Product (GDP). In the US, slavery, convict leasing, Jim Crow segregation laws, and the mass incarceration of African Americans (Alexander 2010) are all evidence of the South within the North (Currie 2018). In other colonial settler states extreme poverty, serious levels of violence and massively disproportionate incarceration rates are common amongst indigenous populations (United Nations Department of Economic and Social Affairs 2009). Australia sits year in year out near the top of the UN Human Development Index (HDI), causing many to see it more accurately, and notwithstanding its geographical location, as part of the rich Global North. But this masks a deeper reality. Australia is really split between two nations. There is the rich 'neo-Europe' that constitutes the white settler state, but alongside it there are its Indigenous peoples whose HDI sits with that of Cape Verde and El Salvador, about 103rd in the world (United Nations Department of Economic and Social Affairs 2009: 23). Looking at the conditions in which many Aboriginal people live in remote communities some have suggested they approximate a 'failed state' (Dillon and Westbury 2007: 45–47).

Viewed through the historical lens of Southern experience, it becomes apparent that the reconfiguring of the borders of penality to incorporate a repertoire of illiberal measures is no recent development, but one deeply ingrained in and by colonial history. The claims of presentism, that the era of colonialism is long past, that nowadays these societies have moved on, that the old racist laws have been abrogated and principles of non-discrimination and equality in liberty prevail, is mocked by contemporary levels of indigenous incarceration and criminalisation, particularly when we are compelled to view them, as we must, as inescapably linked to past illiberal policy and practice and, thus, perpetuating it in new forms.

There are other respects in which settler colonialism in the Global South offers insights into contemporary problems and issues in the punishment and society literature. There is currently a growing body of important work concerned with 'border penalities' and 'crimmigration' regimes (Aas 2014; Aas and Bosworth 2013; Barker 2017; Fernández Bessa and Brandariz Garcia 2018; Hoang 2018; Stumpf 2006; Weber 2013). These regimes extend state power through new forms of policing, surveillance, and detention which meld elements of criminal justice with state immigration and border controls in the management of particular 'suspect' groups of immigrants and asylum seekers. Prisons increasingly house large numbers of immigrant offenders but are also used as immigration detention centres for 'illegal' immigrants who have committed no crime but are without a valid visa. The latter group are also kept in separate detention facilities that resemble prisons. Non-citizen offenders are increasingly deported as an additional punishment to that imposed by the criminal law, often resulting in long term residents with close family and other ties being removed to a country of birth with which they have few or no connections. In Australia, persons who cannot be deported, because they are stateless or would face persecution in their country of citizenship, may be kept in indeterminate detention.

As described in Chapter 1, the settler revolution, the discovery of 'whiteness' and the project of making 'white men's countries' was an outgrowth of nineteenth century-empire, in particular the British empire's ambition to implant white British populations and institutions in those temperate zones of the world hospitable to the expansion and cultivation of white civilisation (Belich 2011). Lake and Reynolds in *Drawing the Global Colour Line* (2008) provide the most detailed and incisive account of this process. The essential point about 'white men's countries'—which in the Anglo world included Australia, New Zealand, Canada, South Africa, and the US—was that they had to be carved from multi-racial empires. These were empires throughout which slaves, convicts, and indentured labourers had been forcibly circulated to serve the needs of colonisation. Others of diverse origins freely migrated in search of opportunities in these 'new' worlds but, of course, these were not in any way 'new' to the very culturally different native populations who had exercised dominion over them for millennia. Confronted with the fact of such cultural diversity, a racialised article of faith lay at the heart of white nation building, which was further legitimised in the emerging human and social sciences (including medicine, eugenics, and criminology). The capacity for self-government (at both the individual and collective level) was the unique gift of European peoples, more particularly the Anglo-Saxon and Teutonic peoples of Northern Europe, and the free and democratic development of society depended on racial homogeneity. Non-white peoples, by virtue of biology or culture, it was assumed lacked the capacity for self-government and their presence in white society threatened efforts at nation building.

This meant that multi-racial settler states had to be subject to an active programme of 'whitening', a form of what would later in the twentieth century be called 'ethnic cleansing'. This required that the non-white peoples of empire be denied the right of free migration to work and settle in other colonies that whites took for granted. Non-white peoples should be the first to receive passports, not to facilitate their movement but to restrict it. A two-fold strategy was adopted in the aspiring white dominions of empire: on the one hand, the removal, exclusion, or segregation of non-white groups and/or the imposition of restrictions on them (for example, relating to ownership of land, the right to vote, entry to certain occupations, inter-marriage with whites, and so on); on the other, introduction of programmes that encouraged and supported the mass inward migration of white settlers. Lake and Reynolds (2008) demonstrate in detail how these projects in white nation building were inspired and practically shaped by trans-national forms of racial identification and policy exchange. Ideas, methods, and legislative strategies—relating to the outright expulsion of some groups, to immigration restriction, passport controls, and so on—widely circulated backwards and forwards from California, Australia, Natal, Canada, New Zealand, and other settler states. In particular, the technique of the literacy test, pioneered in the American South to disenfranchise black people after Reconstruction, was widely adopted to cloak, however thinly, the racial basis for excluding non-white immigrants in settler states (see Lake 2005). Character tests and health requirements also served as means to exclude certain (non-white groups) as 'undesirable' immigrants. A lexicon incorporating highly flexible criteria of undesirability was elaborated, which remains all-too-familiar today. The nation had to be safeguarded against groups who were prone to moral vice, criminality, and unsanitary habits, who were idle and likely to become a burden on the state, or alternatively would steal jobs and undercut pay and conditions. As Lake and Reynolds (2008: 5) summarise the effect of these efforts, 'in drawing the global colour line, immigration restriction became a version of racial segregation on an international scale'. Lending even greater urgency to these projects at the time were eugenic anxieties aroused by the belief that the non-white peoples of the world were growing in number, power, and assertiveness while white fertility rates were in steep decline.

The military defeat inflicted by Japan on Russia in 1905, the first occasion on which a 'backward' Eastern power had vanquished a European imperial state in the modern age, caused widespread alarm in the West just as it inspired and energised non-white peoples across the world (cf Mishra 2013).

Racially discriminatory immigration laws were repealed in settler states in the same era that saw the dismantling of their segregation regimes aimed at the exclusion of indigenous populations, or in the US at African-Americans. This is a reminder of how closely entwined were the aims, values, and histories of both. As Charles Rowley described it in the Australian context,

> the values that enabled successive generations to accept the degradation of the Aboriginal remnants came to be formulated in the White Australia Policy—a nice indication that the Aboriginal reserves had by the time of our Commonwealth Constitution come to be regarded as 'another country'.
>
> (Rowley 1986: 1)

And like those other feared and despised immigrants, Aboriginal people had to carry passports—or 'dog tags' as they dubbed them— when moving from the reserves into 'white' society (Goodall 1996: 193–226).

Convicts, slaves, natives, immigrants—all groups whose fates on the colonial periphery were often intertwined and around whom distinctive penal and policing strategies and measures were formed in the making of the modern world. The boundaries between them were not always clearly defined. Prior to the late eighteenth century, convicts sent to the plantation colonies in the Caribbean and America were often swept up in the same migration flows with indentured servants, various categories of undesirable (like vagrants, rebels, and orphaned and destitute children) and African slaves. No clear line separated voluntary from involuntary labour, criminal from non-criminal, or white from black (Anderson and Maxwell-Stewart 2013: 271–272; Suranyi 2015). Anderson and Maxwell-Stewart (2013: 272, 284) make the point that from the late eighteenth century, the mingling of convicts with other forms of labour in migration flows gave way to a very different pattern in which convicts were more likely to be sent to designated penal settlements isolated from non-convict populations and 'flows were characterised by complex racial stratifications'. The 'bifurcation of transportation flows on the basis of colour' (Maxwell-Stewart 2015: 175) points to the growing salience of race. Labour regimes based on racial subjection were, of course, pervasive throughout the colonial empires. This may have obviated the need for European convict labour in many of the colonies, but there was also the fear that introducing European convicts would destabilise racially-based labour regimes (Maxwell-Stewart 2015: 175). Race was thus 'a key consideration' (Anderson and Maxwell-Stewart 2013: 283) in the founding of the penal colony in Australia. Maxwell-Stewart suggests that 'One might even go as far as to say that Australia was colonised by convict labour *because* the vast majority of those felons were white' (2015: 175–176, emphasis added). Reflecting this pattern, Europeans convicted in Indian courts were sent to Australia rather than to the convict settlements sprinkled throughout Britain's Asian empire to which Asian convicts were sent (Anderson 2012: 56–92). In the end, no more than a few hundred black convicts were sent to Australia from various parts of the British Empire (Harman 2012; Pybus 2006).

The Australian convict experience demonstrated that convicted felons could transcend their criminal pasts and be restored as full citizens if afforded opportunities to do so, a repudiation of the theories of the day proclaiming the biological roots of crime. But this also critically depended on the fact that the convicts were white. There was a 'convict stain' but it did not extinguish their status as white which ultimately took precedence over their status as felons. The cessation of transportation to Australia closed off the possibility that it would become a caste-based polity and economy and, rather quickly, provided the foundation for democratic self-government in a way that could never have happened if the convicts were not white. This was also possible because of the 'extreme minority status' of the Indigenous population, facilitating the task of rendering them all but invisible in a country being progressively 'whitened' by its new apparatus of immigration controls.

It would be wrong to assume that this dispensation is now of no more than historical interest, that white identities 'constituted in relations of racial domination' (Lake and Reynolds 2008: 110), which underpinned the creation of 'white men's countries', underwent a metamorphosis as the post-colonial, multi-cultural era dawned. In assessing the extent and impact of such transitions it is necessary to consider not only changes in the formal laws and official policies of a particular country, but also the continuing force exerted by modes of informal belonging and exclusion (Hage 1998) that surface in structures of language and affect and in enforcement priorities and practices. Indeed, we appear to have entered a new age of white fear where demands for recognition and substantive equality and genuine acceptance of diversity that threaten white prerogatives are experienced as existential threats to white identity itself. Catch-cries of white victimhood—of white genocide even—appear as the core of a new race politics. Donald Trump's border wall and his throwaway insult that too many immigrants to America come from 'shit-hole countries', together with Brexit and the growing popularity of far right, anti-immigrant parties in Europe all reflect a political phenomenon sweeping across large parts of the rich world demanding ever tougher measures to exclude certain groups, defined by race, ethnicity, and religion. Although certainly novel in some of its aspects, it has disinterred many of the phantasms, ideas, and practices of the past, of earlier regimes of border control, and the anxieties aroused by the movement and mixing of different races and cultures in nineteenth-century conditions of empire. The felt need today to, at least, pay lip service to colour-blindness (a need, it has to be said, that appears to be felt less and less in many places) has seen crime become a crucial proxy for the expression and political manipulation of racial antipathies and penality become yoked ever more tightly to the task of racialised social control through 'crimmigration' regimes, new border penalities, and the extraordinary scale of indigenous incarceration in settler societies.

Comparative penology beyond global neo-liberalism

Simon and Sparks in their introduction to the *The Sage Handbook of Punishment and Society* (2013b) underline the growing interest in the study of punishment and penal developments in the Global South and the East. Relatedly, there is an expanding body of scholarship on comparative penology and the impact of 'globalisation' on punishment (Cavadino and Dignan 2006; Lacey 2008). Regarding the question of globalisation we stress the need to guard against a tendency in some ways the opposite of the one criticised in the first section of this chapter. While our point there was that far too little attention has been accorded the ways in which penality in both North and South was historically shaped by the global context—namely, empire and penal policy as a component of imperial statecraft—there is a risk that national borders and differences will be entirely dispensed with in scholarship that accords a seamlessness to contemporary globalisation and its effects. The most significant and influential expression of this, advanced in the work of Loic Wacquant (see, for example, Wacquant 2009; 2014), depicts penal change (and rising punitiveness) across large parts of the world as a function of the global hegemony of neo-liberalism as a transnational political project related to changes in the relation between the state and the economic, social, and penal fields. The argument, in essence, is that the US model comprising free market economic policies, small government, and punitive management of poverty—sometimes referred to as the 'Washington consensus'—has by way of global US dominance and the policies and initiatives of international institutions like the International Monetary Fund and the World Bank been diffused throughout much of the world. This, it is said, explains the exploding imprisonment rates, harsh criminal justice measures and punitive welfare policies to be found in so many countries. Wacquant's version of the 'neo-liberal penality thesis', for all that it offers fresh and valuable insights on contemporary penal developments around the world, is something of a paradigmatic example of Northern theorising in the contemporary punishment and society literature (for interesting critiques of Wacquant, see Lacey 2013; O'Malley 2015).

By way of contrast, a Southern perspective encourages the development of a comparative penology that seeks to elucidate national and local differences, rejecting a framework in which prisons and penality in the South are analysed as the (imperfect) realisation of penal models and developments based on the Northern experience (see, for example, the collection edited by Dikötter and Brown (2007) on prisons in Africa, Asia, and Latin America, and the Global Prisons Research Network: https://sites.google.com/site/gprnnetwork/home). Latin

America has been a specific focus of Wacquant's research and a testing ground for his neo-liberal penality thesis, which he regards as being confirmed in steeply increasing imprisonment rates throughout most of the continent over the last quarter of a century (Wacquant 2003, 2008; see also Iturralde 2010, 2012). With some exceptions, the same general upward trend in imprisonment rates is a feature of other countries in the Global South. However, much greater attention needs to be given to the specificities of penal policy and practice in particular regions and nations. If we are to grasp how deep or background causes are translated into actual penal effects, it is necessary to have a thicker account of the empirical processes involved in particular contexts that constitute the 'transmission belt' (Garland 2013: 482–483; O'Malley 2015: 15; Sozzo 2018a: 674–676). The recent literature on comparative penology—mostly focused on contexts in the Global North—has variously highlighted different elements, including: constitutional structures; the distribution of decision-making powers; the degree of independence or otherwise of law-making and adjudicative institutions, both from other branches of government and from outside political pressures; bureaucratic structures; electoral systems; party political traditions and processes of social mobilisation and struggle; and media structures and practices (Cavadino and Dignan 2006, 2011; Hamilton 2014; Lacey 2008; Nelken 2010, 2011; Sozzo 2018a; Tonry 2007). While it has been difficult in this chapter to provide these thorough accounts, given the necessary level of generality at which our arguments have had to be pitched, in this section we draw on research on penal developments and trends in Latin America to demonstrate the importance of avoiding analyses of penal change based on North/South diffusion models of explanation.

It is important to recognise that, notwithstanding, the considerable influence of neo-liberalism on Latin American governments since the 1970s in many countries—Argentina (Sozzo 2017a, 2017b, 2018a), Brazil (de Azevedo and Cifali 2017), Venezuela (Grajales and Hernández 2017), Ecuador (Paladines 2017)—left and centre-left governments and governmental alliances consciously forged a 'post neo-liberal' politics around the turn of the century (Sozzo 2017a, 2017b, 2018a). In varying degrees, they pursued agendas to redistribute wealth, re-nationalise some industries and public services, reduce poverty and inequality, build infrastructure, invest in education, and enlarge opportunities for the poorest sections of their societies. In tackling crime and security problems the rhetoric of these governmental alliances emphasised initially preventive strategies and measures, and moderation and reform in the penal realm. But the translation into practice and effects was highly variable and in the best cases was only temporary and partial. For example, in Venezuela, during the governments of Chavez, between 1999 and 2008 there was a very low imprisonment rate, between 69 and 87 inmates per 100 000 inhabitants. But this changed radically after 2008, rising to 172 per 100 000 in 2014 (Grajales and Hernández 2017). This was related to changes in the political rhetoric and orientation of this governmental coalition, in turn related to internal struggles between different groups and the struggles with the political opposition around themes of crime and violence, and to changes in the level of public investment in police forces and the massive adoption of traditional strategies of police saturation in poor urban areas (Grajales and Hernández 2017; Sozzo 2018a: 669–674). Something similar can be observed in the case of Ecuador. During the first government of Correa there was a steep decline in the incarceration rate, from 130 inmates per 100 000 inhabitants in 2007 to 73 inmates per 100 000 inhabitants in 2009 (Paladines 2017). This was the result of a series of policy and legal initiatives oriented towards penal moderation and reflecting the initial rhetoric of the key governmental actors of *Alianza Pais* (the ruling left-wing political alliance) on the themes of crime and punishment. But this suddenly changed in 2010 after an attempted coup d'etat by the National Police, and in the context of struggles with the political opposition on crime and punishment issues and their potential electoral impact. President Correa reversed his rhetoric and strategy and launched several initiatives directed at increasing punitiveness—including a referendum in 2011 that aimed to garner popular support for get tough crime measures and the enactment of a new *Criminal Code* in 2014. In 2014 the incarceration rate had risen to 162 inmates per 100 000 inhabitants—more than double the level of five years before (Paladines 2017). It is very difficult to link these abrupt punitive shifts in Venezuela and Ecuador to the adoption of neo-liberal social and economic policies by these governments in recent years.

These are instances that could be labelled as 'post-neo-liberal punitive turns'. In any case, they present clear obstacles to the thesis that the diffusion of neo-liberalism as a uniform political project across time and space is the deep or background cause of increasing punitiveness in the penal field everywhere.

It is also necessary to reflect that most countries in Latin America suffered under military dictatorships and other forms of authoritarian rule during the twentieth century. Some, notably Columbia, Peru, and Guatemala, remain deeply scarred and divided by decades-long civil wars or insurgencies; and Columbia, Mexico, and El Salvador by the more recent war on drugs. The peacetime paradigm upon which Northern criminology is erected, with its assumptions concerning the normality of the liberal state and liberal penality, is singularly inapt to account for the penal and political trajectories of countries that have spent long periods in the grip of authoritarianism and war, or its after-effects. Analysis that stresses the current impact of neo-liberalism on penality, therefore, needs also to consider its interplay with the effects of recent experiences of dictatorship and state terror and what are often otherwise deeply authoritarian political traditions and profound levels of inequality traceable to the legacies of the colonial past (Sozzo 2016; Ariza and Iturralde 2018). These forces play out very differently in different national settings. For example, the experience of dictator-ship in Argentina and its legacy of fragile state legitimacy, especially where the military and police were concerned, led social democratic governments immediately after the end of the dictatorship in 1983 to establish a truth commission to support the transition to democracy and investigate the crimes of the dictatorship with a view to prosecut-ing and punishing them. Curtailed by the same government later in the 1980s, the initiative was revived after 2003, leading to hundreds of successful high-level prosecutions, making Argentina 'a global leader in human rights prosecutions' and a pioneer in demonstrating the role that transitional justice mechanisms can play in consolidating the path to democracy (Zysman Quirós 2018: 992; see also Sozzo 2013, 2016).

Zysman Quirós makes the critical point, necessarily overlooked in peace-time criminologies, that considering the punishment of state crimes *together* with the punishment of common crimes could yield valuable insights for the sociology of punishment. In Argentina, if not in many other post-dictatorship settings, the abuses of the military and police (and widespread public exposure of those abuses due to the truth commission) appears to have engendered a more parsimonious attitude towards the punishment of common crimes, perhaps because the latter were not perceived to be so serious when juxtaposed to state abuses or because citizens more readily identified with ordinary offenders as being, like themselves, potential victims of state terror and excess. At the same time, and doubtless for the same reasons, a harsh line was maintained and supported against the perpetrators of state crimes (Zysman Quirós 2018: 996). It could be argued, although more research is required, that the efforts to restore the legitimacy of the police also influenced the adoption of innovative policies that aimed to make the state more responsive to the victims of ordinary crime, like women only police stations discussed in Chapter 2. This may also be instructive for other colonial settler states. Although such states may not have experienced dictatorship, they do have a long and dark history of institutionalised human rights abuses against their indigenous populations that have shaped contemporary patterns of indigenous offending, their experiences as victims of crime, and their attitudes to criminal justice institutions. Recognising that the past is never just past, but always impinges on the present, and considering these experiences together, rather than as disconnected in time and space, may afford a better understanding of the contemporary dynamics of penality as well as informing more just and effective policy responses.

Comparative penology, including the above analysis, relies upon imprisonment rates as the most important (if still imperfect) measure of the punitiveness of different societies. The prison is the dominant (if not the sole) frame through which penality in different societies is compared. But if a more in-depth comparative understanding of penality is to be achieved, it is necessary to look beyond the prison (Sozzo 2018b: 49–50). There is also a tendency to focus disproportionate attention on those countries with high rates of imprisonment, the US being the classic case. This may be another instance of the bias that says large is more important and interesting, whether we are referring to land mass or prison populations. Just as 'cities with little crime' (Clinard 1978) and what we can learn from them were often neglected in past criminological scholarship, so prison systems with few prisoners continue to be. More attention needs to be given to seeking out the new and different penal stories that smaller nations in the Global South may have to tell, bearing in mind that they are generally poor as well as small and particularly lacking in academic resources, factors that bear no relationship to the value of their stories.

In Chapter 3 we referred to the neglected subject of island justice, illustrating the point by reference to the Pacific island nation of Tuvalu, one of numerous small island nations in the Pacific. Tuvalu has 'one of the smallest prison populations in the world' (Pratt and Melei 2018: 729). Like many other Pacific nations, it remained a colony (in this case of Britain) until the 1970s. Other Pacific island groups remain today colonies or self-governing territories of the US or France. The Pacific island experience illustrates the variability in the character and effects of colonisation. According to Pratt and Melei (2018), British colonial rule in Tuvalu had a 'protective' effect against other potentially disruptive outside influences, doubtless due to its extreme physical isolation and the fact that it was subject to colonial rule, but not white British settlement. The prison population has been kept small by dispute resolution practices that are a hybrid of traditional customs and authority structures with limited Western Christian and British legal influences. As in so many such nations and communities that have remained relatively isolated from Western influences, social solidarity is maintained with limited reliance on rights-based institutions, positive law, and formal criminal justice structures. As the anthropologist Stanley Diamond (1981: 257) argued some years ago, we have to be wary of law cannibalising custom to the huge detriment of the social solidarity of traditional communities.

The same point was made in Chapter 3 about the Australian Indigenous communities who inhabit the Torres Strait Islands off the Northern coast of Queensland. By virtue of their relative isolation, the Torres Strait Islanders have been able to maintain, to a far greater extent than their Indigenous counterparts on the mainland, a connection with country and their command of vital cultural and material resources when confronting and adapting to the more limited incursions of white society. In consequence, they are more socially cohesive and much less entangled with the penal system than mainland

Indigenous communities (see Scott and Moreton 2018). This is not to romanticise or deny the very real problems island nations and communities face. The major one, and one that threatens their very existence, is climate change—a salutary reminder that these oceans which appear on so many maps and in the Northern imaginary as simply 'big empty spaces', are home to many peoples and are 'connector, facilitator and challenger' (Samson 2011: 249) for those living on, with, and around them. Climate change also underlines the profound planetary reality, of inescapable importance to both North and South, that 'all living things are dependent on Pacific weather systems' (Samson 2011: 249)—an issue taken up in the following chapter.

Conclusion

In this chapter we have identified some of the ways in which contemporary punishment and society scholarship might be 'Southernised' and what that might contribute to our understanding of past and present penal developments across the globe. Our emphasis has been on historical, theoretical, and empirical issues. First, we underlined the historical role of penality as a dimension of imperial statecraft and its impact in shaping many aspects of modern penal development in both North and South, issues that have recently been taken up by historians, but neglected in punishment and society scholarship. Secondly, we examined some of the other ways in which it could be said that contemporary Northern penality has a Southern history, hinging in particular on historical precedents in the racialisation of control practices inside and outside the criminal justice systems of settler societies. Finally, we considered how North to South diffusion models of explanation—in particular the 'neo-liberal penality thesis'—overlooks the specificities of penality and penal developments in Global South countries.

We conclude by simply underlining that the periphery, be it the global periphery or the often overlooked rural or remote periphery of particular societies, can often be the origin of important penal change (whether negative or positive) and innovative ideas and practices. As Donnermeyer (2018) points out of rural peripheries across the globe, while by definition they contain smaller populations and overall account for a shrinking proportion of the global population, there are many more of them from which place-based change is or might be driven. In the nineteenth century, Maconochie's marks system had its origins in Norfolk Island, an eight by five kilometre island speck in the Pacific Ocean. There are more than 20 island nations or self-governing states encompassing thousands of island communities scattered across the vast expanse of the Pacific, often sharing some cultural characteristics, but also with many differences. Some of them have the smallest populations in the world. The tendency in social science to privilege large land masses—graphically reflected and reinforced in cartographic biases that underpin standard representations of the globe in world maps and serve to naturalise a particular (Northern) view of what places are important—means these countries are almost entirely overlooked. Equally the habit of viewing penality through the dominant prism of the prison may cause us to overlook what is most distinctive and often instructive about the penal experience of particular countries. A recent exception, that perhaps proves the rule, are the ideas and practices around restorative justice, many of whose antecedents are in indigenous justice practices. On a different scale, although not unrelated culturally and politically, transitional justice strategies in South Africa, Latin America, and elsewhere in the Global South have provided an example to the world of ways of addressing atrocities and other gross human rights abuses of the past in the process of making the transition to more just, inclusive democratic polities.

Note

1 See the major research project, The Carceral Archipelago: Transnational Circulations in Global Perspective, 1415–1960. Led by Professor Claire Anderson, the project is examining convict transportation in the Caribbean, West Africa, Gibraltar, Russia, Portugal, Latin America, Japan, Australia, and the Indian Ocean, and aims 'to explore penal colonies as engines of global change, to connect convict transportation to enslavement, indenture and other forms of coerced labour and migration, and to define the long-term impacts of penal colonies on economy, society and identity' (University of Leicester nd). https://www2.le.ac.uk/departments/history/research/grants/CArchipelago.

References

Aas KF (2014) Bordered penality: Precarious membership and abnormal justice. *Punishment and Society* 16(5): 520–541. DOI: 10.1177/1462474514548807.

Aas KF and Bosworth M (eds) (2013) *Borders of Punishment: Citizenship, Crime Control, and Social Exclusion*. Oxford: Oxford University Press.

Alexander M (2010) *The New Jim Crow: Mass Incarceration in the Age of Colorblindness*. New York: The New Press.

Anderson C (2009) Convicts and coolies: Rethinking indentured labour in the nineteenth century. *Slavery & Abolition: A Journal of Slave and Post-Slave Studies* 30(1): 93–109. DOI: 10.1080/01440390802673856.

Anderson C (2012) *Subaltern Lives: Biographies of Colonialism in the Indian Ocean World, 1790–1920*. Cambridge: Cambridge University Press.

Anderson C (2016) Transnational histories of penal transportation: Punishment, labour and governance in the British imperial world, 1788–1939. *Australian Historical Studies* 47(3): 381–397. DOI: 10.1080/1031461X.2016.1203962.

Anderson C, Crockett M, De Vito C, Miyamoto T, Moss K, Roscoe K, and Sakata M (2015) Locating penal transportation: Punishment, space, and place c. 1750 to 1900. In Morin KM and Moran D (eds) *Historical Geographies of Prisons: Unlocking the Usable Carceral Past*: 147–167. Oxford: Routledge.

Anderson C and Maxwell-Stewart HJ (2013) *Convict Labour and the Western Empires, 1415–1954*. Oxford: Routledge.

Anthony T (2017) Factcheck Q&A: Are Indigenous Australians the most incarcerated people on Earth? *The Conversation*, 6 June. Available at https://theconversation.com/factcheck-qanda-are-indigenous-australians-the-most-incarcerated-people-on-earth-78528.

Ariza L and Iturralde M (2018) Transformations of the crime control field in Columbia. In Carrington K, Hogg R, Scott J, and Sozzo M (eds) (2018) *The Palgrave Handbook of Criminology and the Global South*: 687–708. Switzerland: Palgrave Macmillan.

Arnold D (2015) Labouring for the Raj: Convict Work Regimes in Colonial India, 1836–1939. In De Vito C and Lichtenstein A (eds) *Global Convict Labour*: 199–221. Leiden: Brill.

Australian Bureau of Statistics (ABS) (2016) Imprisonment rates. *4517.0 - Prisoners in Australia*, 2016, 8 December. Available at http://www.abs.gov.au/ausstats/abs@.nsf/Lookup/by%20Subject/4517.0~2016~Main%20Features~Imprisonment%20rates~12.

Australian Bureau of Statistics (ABS) (2017) Census: Aboriginal and Torres Strait Islander population. *Media Release*, 27 June. Available at http://www.abs.gov.au/ausstats/abs@.nsf/MediaRealesesByCatalogue/02D50FAA9987D6B7CA25814800087E03?OpenDocument.

Australian Law Reform Commission (2017) *Pathways to Justice – An Inquiry into the Incarceration Rate of Aboriginal and Torres Strait Islander Peoples.* Sydney.

Barker V (2017) Penal power at the border: Realigning state and nation. *Theoretical Criminology* 21(4): 441–457.

Barry J (1958) *Alexander Maconochie of Norfolk Island.* Melbourne: Oxford University Press.

Beckett K and Murakawa N (2012) Mapping the shadow carceral state: Toward an institutionally capacious approach to punishment. *Theoretical Criminology* 16(2): 221–244. DOI: 10.1177/1362480612442113.

Beer D (2017) *The House of the Dead: Siberian Exile under the Tsars.* UK: Penguin Books.

Belich J (2011) *Replenishing the Earth: The Settler Revolution and the Rise of the Anglo-World, 1783–1939.* Oxford: Oxford University Press.

Braithwaite J (2001) Crime in a convict republic. *Modern Law Review* 64(1): 11–50. DOI: 10.1111/1468-2230.00307.

Broadhurst R (1987) Imprisonment of the Aborigine in Western Australia, 1957–85. In Hazlehurst K (ed.) *Ivory Scales: Black Australians and the Law:* 153–189. Kensington: University of NSW Press.

Brown M (2014) *Penal Power and Colonial Rule.* Abingdon: Routledge.

Cavadino M and Dignan J (2006) *Penal Systems: A Comparative Approach.* London: Sage.

Cavadino M and Dignan J (2011) Penal comparison: Puzzling relations. In Crawford A (ed.) *International and Comparative Criminal Justice and Urban Governance*: 193–213. Cambridge: Cambridge University Press.

Christopher E, Pybus C, and Rediker M (2007) Introduction. In Christopher E, Pybus C, and Rediker M (eds) *Many Middle Passages: Forced Migration and the Making of the Modern World*: 1–19. Berkeley: University of California Press.

Clay J (2001) *Maconochie's Experiment.* London: John Murray.

Clinard M (1978) *Cities with Little Crime – The Case of Switzerland.* Cambridge: Cambridge University Press.

Coates T (2015) The long view of convict labour in the Portuguese empire, 1415–1932. In De Vito C and Lichtenstein A (eds) *Global Convict Labour:* 144–167. Leiden: Brill.

Currie E (2018) Confronting the North's South: On race and violence in the United States. In Carrington K, Hogg R, Scott J, and Sozzo M (eds) *Palgrave Handbook of Criminology and the Global South*: 43–60. Switzerland: Palgrave Macmillan.

Curthoys A and Lake M (2005) Introduction. In Curthoys A and Lake M (eds) *Connected Worlds: History in Transnational Perspective*: 5–20. Canberra: Australian National University Press.

de Azevedo R and Cifali A (2017) Public security, criminal policy and sentencing in Brazil during the Lula and Dilma Governments, 2003–2014:

Changes and continuities. *International Journal for Crime, Justice and Social Democracy* 6(1): 148–165. DOI: 10.5204/ijcjsd.v6i1.392.

De Vito C (2016) Convict labor in the Southern borderlands of Latin America (ca. 1750s–1910s): Comparative perspectives. In van der Linden M and Garcia MR (eds) *On Coerced Labor: Work and Compulsion after Chattel Slavery*: 98–126. Leiden: Brill.

De Vito C and Lichtenstein A (2013) Writing a global history of convict labour. *International Institute of Social History* 58(2): 285–325. DOI: 10.1017/S0020859012000818.

De Vito C and Lichtenstein A (eds) (2015) *Global Convict Labour*. Leiden: Brill.

Diamond S (1981) *In Search of the Primitive: A Critique of Civilization*. New Brunswick: Transaction Books.

Dikötter F and Brown I (eds) (2007) *Cultures of Confinement: A History of the Prison in Africa, Asia and Latin America*. New York: Cornell University Press.

Dillon M and Westbury N (2007) *Beyond Humbug: Transforming Government Engagement with Indigenous Australia*. West Lakes: Seaview Press.

Donnermeyer J (2018) The rural dimensions of a Southern criminology: Selected topics and general processes. In Carrington K, Hogg R, Scott J, and Sozzo M (eds) *The Palgrave Handbook of Criminology and the Global South*: 105–120. Switzerland: Palgrave Macmillan.

Du Cane E (1872) *An Account of the Manner in which Sentences of Penal Servitude Are Carried Out in England*. London.

Ekirch A (1987) *Bound for America: The Transportation of British Convicts to the Colonies, 1718–1775*. Oxford: Clarendon Press.

Elkins C (2005) *Britain's Gulag: The Brutal End of Empire in Kenya*. London: Pimlico.

Female Convicts Research Centre (2012) *Convict Lives: Women at Cascades Female Factory*, 2nd edn. Hobart: Convict Women's Press.

Fernández Bessa C and Brandariz Garcia J A (2018) 'Profiles' of deportability: Analyzing Spanish migration control policies from a neo-colonial perspective. In Carrington K, Hogg R, Scott J, and Sozzo M (eds) *The Palgrave Handbook of Criminology and the Global South*: 775–796. Switzerland: Palgrave Macmillan.

Finnane M (1997a) Colonisation and incarceration: The criminal justice system and Aboriginal Australians. *Trevor Reese Memorial Lecture*, 11 February. London: Sir Robert Menzies Centre for Australian Studies, Institute of Commonwealth Studies, University of London.

Finnane M (1997b) *Punishment in Australian Society*. Melbourne: Oxford University Press.

Forsythe W (1987) *The Reform of Prisoners 1830–1900*. London: Croom Helm.

Frost L (ed.) (2011) *Convict Lives at the Ross Female Factory*. Hobart: Convict Women's Press.

Frost L (2015) *Abandoned Women: Scottish Convicts Exiled Beyond the Seas*. Sydney: Allen and Unwin.

Frost L and Hodgson AM (2013) *Convict Lives at the Launceston Female Factory*. Hobart: Convict Women's Press.

Frost L and Maxwell-Stewart HJ (eds) (2001) *Chain Letters: Narrating Convict Lives*. Melbourne: Melbourne University Press.

Garland D (1985) *Punishment and Welfare*. Aldershot: Gower.

Garland D (2001) *Mass Imprisonment: Its Social Causes and Consequences*. London: Sage.

Garland D (2013) Penality and the penal state: The 2012 Sutherland Address. *Criminology* 51(3): 475–517. DOI: 10.1111/1745-9125.12015.

Godfrey B (2012) The 'convict stain': Desistance in the penal colony. In Rowbotham J, Muravyeva M, and Nash D (eds) *Shame, Blame and Culpability: Crime and Violence in the Modern State*: 96–108. London: Routledge.

Godfrey B and Cox DJ (2008) The 'Last Fleet': Crime, reformation and punishment in Western Australia after 1868. *Australian and New Zealand Journal of Criminology* 41(2): 236–258. DOI: 10.1375/acri.41.2.236.

Goodall H (1996) *Invasion to Embassy: Land in Aboriginal Politics in New South Wales, 1770–1972*. Sydney: Allen and Unwin.

Gottschalk M (2013) The carceral state and the politics of punishment. In Simon J and Spark R (eds) *The Sage Handbook of Punishment and Society*: 205–240. London: Sage.

Grajales M and Hernández M (2017) Chavism and criminal policy in Venezuela, 1999–2014. *International Journal for Crime, Justice and Social Democracy* 6(1): 166–187. DOI: 10.5204/ijcjsd.v6i1.393.

Hage G (1998) *White Nation: Fantasies of White Supremacy in a Multicultural Society*. Annandale: Pluto Press.

Hamilton C (2014) *Reconceptualising Penality: A Comparative Perspective on Punitiveness in Ireland, Scotland and New Zealand*. Farnham: Ashgate.

Harman K (2012) *Aboriginal Convicts: Australian, Khoisan and Maori Exiles*. Sydney: University of New South Wales Press.

Hoang K (2018) The rise of crimmigration in Australia: Importing laws and exporting lives. In Carrington K, Hogg R, Scott J, and Sozzo M (eds) *The Palgrave Handbook of Criminology and the Global South*: 797–817. Switzerland: Palgrave Macmillan.

Hogg R (2001) Penality and modes of regulating Indigenous peoples in Australia. *Punishment and Society* 3(3): 355–379. DOI: 10.1177/1462474501003003002.

Hogg R and Brown D (2018) Rethinking penal modernism from the Global South: The case of convict transportation to Australia. In Carrington K,

Hogg R, Scott J, and Sozzo M (eds) *The Palgrave Handbook of Criminology and the Global South*: 751–774. Switzerland: Palgrave Macmillan.

Hughes R (1988) *The Fatal Shore: A History of the Transportation of Convicts to Australia 1787–1868*. London: Pan Books.

Iturralde M (2010) Democracies without citizenship: Crime and punishment in Latin America. *New Criminal Law Review* 13(2): 309–322. DOI: 10.1525/nclr.2010.13.2.309.

Iturralde M (2012) O governo neoliberal da inseguranca social na America Latina; semelhanzas e diferencias con o Norte global. In Malaguti V (ed.) *Loic Wacquant e a questao penal no capitalism neo-liberal*: 167–175. Rio de Janeiro: Revam.

Kavanagh J and Snowden D (2015) *Van Diemen's Women: A History of Transportation to Tasmania*. Dublin: The History Press Ireland.

Kercher B (2008) Perish or prosper: The law and convict transportation in the British empire, 1700–1850. *Law and History Review* 21(3): 527–584. DOI: 10.2307/3595119.

Lacey N (2008) *The Prisoners' Dilemma: Political Economy and Punishment in Contemporary Democracies*. Cambridge: Cambridge University Press.

Lacey N (2013) Punishment, (neo)|liberalism and social democracy. In Simon J and Sparks R (eds) *The Sage Handbook of Punishment and Society*: 260–280. London: Sage.

Lake M (2005) From Mississippi to Melbourne via Natal: The invention of the literacy test as a technology of racial exclusion. In Curthoys A and Lake M (eds) *Connected Worlds: History in Transnational Perspective*: 209–230. Canberra: Australian National University Press.

Lake M and Reynolds H (2008) *Drawing the Global Colour Line: White Men's Countries and the Question of Racial Equality*. Carlton: Melbourne University Press.

MacFie P and Hargraves N (1999) The empire's first stolen generation: The first intake at Point Puer 1834–39. *Tasmanian Historical Studies* 6(2): 129–154.

Markus A (1990) *Governing Savages*. Sydney: Allen and Unwin.

Maxwell-Stewart H (2012) Convicts, slaves and prison inmates: The voyage to Australia in comparative perspective. In Fullagar K (ed.) *The Atlantic World in the Antipodes: Effects and Transformations since the Eighteenth Century*: 33–51. Newcastle upon Tyne: Cambridge Scholars Publishing.

Maxwell-Stewart H (2015) Convict labour extraction and transportation from Britain and Ireland, 1615–1870. In De Vito C and Lichtenstein A (2015) *Global Convict Labour*: 168–196. Leiden: Brill.

Maxwell-Stewart H and Kippen R (2015) 'What is a man that is a bolter to do? I would steal the Governor's axe rather than starve': Old lags and recidivism in the Tasmanian penal colony. In Miller V and Campbell J (eds) *Transnational Penal Cultures: New Perspectives on Discipline, Punishment and Desistance*: 165–183. London: Routledge.

Mishra P (2013) *From the Ruins of Empire: The Revolt against the West and the Remaking of Asia*. London: Penguin Books.

Nelken D (2010) Denouncing the penal state. *Criminology and Criminal Justice* 10(4): 329–338. DOI: 10.1177/1748895810382382.

Nelken D (2011) Theorising the embeddedness of punishment. In Melossi D, Sozzo M, and Sparks R (eds) *Travels of the Criminal Question*: 65–94. Oxford: Hart.

Newburn T (2010) Diffusion, differentiation and resistance in comparative penality. *Criminology and Criminal Justice* 10(4): 341–352.

Newburn T and Sparks R (eds) (2004) *Criminal Justice and Political Cultures: National and International Dimensions of Crime Control*. Devon: Willan.

Nicholas S (ed.) (1988a) *Convict Workers: Reinterpreting Australia's Past*. Melbourne: Cambridge University Press.

Nicholas S (1988b) The care and feeding of convicts. In Nicholas S (ed.) *Convict Workers: Reinterpreting Australia's Past*: 180–198. Melbourne: Cambridge University Press.

O'Malley P (2015) Repensando la penalidad neoliberal. In *Delito y Sociedad* 40: 11–30.

Paladines J (2017) The 'Iron Fist' of the Citizens' Revolution: The punitive turn of Ecuadorian left-wing politics. *International Journal for Crime, Justice and Social Democracy* 6(1): 186–204. DOI: 10.5204/ijcjsd.v6i1.394.

Perry R (1996) *From Time Immemorial: Indigenous Peoples and State Systems*. Austin: University of Texas Press.

Pratt J and Melei T (2018) One of the smallest prison population in the world under threat: The case of Tuvalu. In Carrington K, Hogg R, Scott J, and Sozzo M (eds) *The Palgrave Handbook of Criminology and the Global South*: 729–750. Switzerland: Palgrave Macmillan.

Pricewaterhouse Coopers (2017) Closing the gap on Indigenous incarceration could save almost \$19bn in 2040. *Press Room*, 25 May. Available at https://www.pwc.com.au/press-room/2017/indigenous-incarceration.html.

Pybus C (2006) *Black Founders: The Unknown Story of Australia's First Black Settlers*. Sydney: University of New South Wales Press.

Rowley C (1986) *Recovery: The Politics of Aboriginal Reform*. Ringwood: Penguin Books.

Rusche G and Kirchheimer O (2003 [1939]) *Punishment and Social Structure*. New Brunswick: Transaction Publishers.

Samson J (2011) Pacific history in context. *Journal of Pacific History* 46(2): 244–250. DOI: 10.1080/00223344.2011.607273.

Scott J and Moreton J (2018) Understanding crime and justice in Torres Strait Islander communities. In Carrington K, Hogg R, Scott J, and Sozzo M (eds) *The Palgrave Handbook of Criminology and the Global South*: 587–610. Switzerland: Palgrave Macmillan.

Shaw AGL (1966) *Convicts and the Colonies: A Study of Penal Transportation from Great Britain and Ireland to Australia and Other Parts of the British Empire*. London: Faber and Faber.

Simon J and Sparks R (eds) (2013a) *The Sage Handbook of Punishment and Society*. London: Sage.

Simon J and Spark R (2013b) Introduction: Punishment and society: The emergence of an academic field. In Simon J and Spark R (eds) *The Sage Handbook of Punishment and Society*: 1–23. London: Sage.

Simpson AWB (2001) *Human Rights and the End of Empire*. Oxford: Oxford University Press.

Smith B (2014) *The Luck of the Irish: How a Shipload of Convicts Survived the Wreck of the Hive to Make a New Life in Australia*. Sydney: Allen and Unwin.

Sozzo M (2013) Transicion a la democracia y politica penal en Argentina. In Amaral B (ed.) *Justicia criminal y democracia*: 195–238. Madrid: Marcial Pons.

Sozzo M (2016) Democratization, politics and punishment in Argentina. *Punishment and Society* 18(3): 301–324. DOI: 10.1177/1462474516645689.

Sozzo M (2017a) Postneoliberalism and penality in South America: By way of introduction. *International Journal for Crime, Justice and Social Democracy* 6(1): 135–147. DOI: 10.5204/ijcjsd.v6i1.391.

Sozzo M (2017b) A postneoliberal turn? Variants of the recent penal policy in Argentina. *International Journal for Crime, Justice and Social Democracy* 6(1): 207–225. DOI: 10.5204/ijcjsd.v6i1.390.

Sozzo M (2018a) Beyond the 'neo-liberal penality thesis'? Punitive turn and political change in South America. In Carrington K, Hogg R, Scott J, and Sozzo M (eds) *The Palgrave Handbook of Criminology and the Global South*: 659–686. Switzerland: Palgrave Macmillan.

Sozzo M (2018b) The renaissance of the political economy of punishment from a comparative perspective. In Brandariz JA, Melossi D, and Sozzo M (eds) *The Political Economy of Punishment. Visons, Debates and Challenges*: 37–64. Routledge: London.

Stumpf J (2006) The crimmigration crisis: Immigrants, crime, and sovereign power. *American University Law Review* 56: 367–419.

Suranyi A (2015) Indenture, transportation, and spiriting: Seventeenth century English penal policy and 'superfluous' populations. In Jennings E and Donoghue J (eds) *Building the Atlantic Empires: Unfree Labor and Imperial*

States in the Political Economy of Capitalism, ca. 1500–1914: 132–159. London: Brill.

Tanaka Y (2009) British 'humane bombing' in Iraq during the interwar era. In Tanaka Y and Young M (eds) *Bombing Civilians: A Twentieth Century History*: 8–29. New York: The New Press.

Tharoor S (2017) *Inglorious Empire: What the British Did to India*. Brunswick: Scribe.

Tonry M (2007) Determinants of penal policy. In Tonry M (ed.) *Crime, Punishment and Politics in Comparative Perspective*: 1–48. Chicago: Chicago University Press.

United Nations Department of Economic and Social Affairs (2009) *State of the World's Indigenous Peoples*. New York: United Nations.

University of Leicester (nd) *The Carceral Archipelago: Transnational Circulations in Global Perspective, 1415–1960*. Available at http://www2.le.ac.uk/depart ments/history/research/grants/CArchipelago (accessed 25 May 2017).

Wacquant L (2003) Towards a dictatorship over the poor? Notes on the penalization of poverty in Brazil. *Punishment and Society* 5(2): 197–205. DOI: 10.1177/146247450352004.

Wacquant L (2008) The militarization of urban marginality: Lessons from the Brazilian metropolis. *International Political Sociology* 1(2): 56–74. DOI: 10.1111/j.1749-5687.2008.00037.x.

Wacquant L (2009) *Punishing the Poor: The Neoliberal Government of Social Insecurity*. Durham: Duke University Press.

Wacquant L (2014) The global firestorm of law and order: On punishment and neo-liberalism. *Thesis Eleven* 122(1): 72–88. DOI: 10.1177/0725513614536136.

Watson J (2010) *Palm Island: Through a Long Lens*. Canberra: Aboriginal Studies Press.

Weber L (2013) *Policing Non-Citizens*. Abingdon: Routledge.

Wolfe P (2006) Settler colonialism and the elimination of the native. *Journal of Genocide Research* 8(4): 387–409. DOI: 10.1080/14623520601056240.

Zedner L (2016) Penal subversions: When is a punishment not punishment, who decides and on what grounds? *Theoretical Criminology* 20(1): 3–20. DOI: 10.1177/1362480615598830.

Zysman Quirós (2018) Building social democracy through transitional justice: Lessons from Argentina 1983–2015. In Carrington K, Hogg R, Scott J, and Sozzo M (eds) *The Palgrave Handbook of Criminology and the Global South*: 991–1010. Switzerland: Palgrave Macmillan.

Legislation cited

Comprehensive Organic Criminal Code 2014 (Ecuador).
Criminal Tribes Act 1871 (India).
Native Welfare Act 1963 (WA).
Penal Code 1810 (France).

5

ENVIRONMENTAL INJUSTICE AND THE GLOBAL SOUTH

Introduction

This book has discussed thus far the way in which criminological knowledges are partially, inequitably, and ineffectually created and dispersed within dominant Northern hegemonic discourses of power, prestige, and control. As we have noted, our intention is to reconceptualise and emancipate the North/South relationship and move beyond the depiction of the South as a fixed and static intellectual geographical region. Our project is to begin to envisage and explore the dynamic, historical, and asymmetrical relations between North and South and the global processes that have always connected them in various ways. Issues relating to climate change and the environment provide insights into the disadvantages and detriments of the South perpetuated by global divides and knowledge hegemonies.

The Intergovernmental Panel on Climate Change's (IPCC) most recent report categorically identifies the realities of human-induced global warming and climate change (IPCC 2013a). This unequivocal position has been further independently endorsed by the world's leading climate scientists who conclude that human activity is directly responsible for rapidly declining human health, biodiversity loss, and rising global levels of air pollution (Watts et al. 2017). The intersection between climate change and criminology has only recently been forged within innovative discourses in green criminology. Indeed for some, the emerging connections between green criminology and science 'are precisely where green criminology has eclipsed orthodox criminology' (Lynch and Stretesky 2010, 2014: 80). Moreover, Goyes, and South (2017a: 167) argue that 'a green criminology did not just appear' but was influenced by a series of events, movements, and discourses beyond the Anglophone and the Global North to capture the lived experiences of peoples in the Global South disproportionately affected by climate change and environmental despoliation. The fusing of discourses in both green and Southern criminology provides a new and dynamic intellectual excursion for examining and redressing environmental injustices on a global scale. Or, as Brisman, South, and Walters (2018: 25) argue, 'Southern criminology and green criminology are both powerful reactions against the status quo in criminology and provide standpoints from which to reconsider the contemporary causes and distribution of various forms of inequality, exploitation and harm.'

This chapter explores the hegemonic political and corporate power of Northern elites and the ways in which such governing principles substantially and unjustly contribute to environmental degradation and destruction in the Global South. It also examines the pervasiveness of climate denial in certain Northern corridors of power and how such rationales victimise and deprive peoples of the Global South of their fundamental human rights. The intention here is, therefore, to identify how Northern environmental governance is pervasive and influential in the corridors of global power. It also seeks to explore the embeddedness of denial and misinformation within 'Platonic' analyses of power and ignorance. It argues that Northern political dismissiveness of climate change and its associated deleterious environmental impacts is not only a recipe or agenda for those in positions of power to exploit for profitable economic and political pursuits, but more importantly, is culturally imbued within contemporary notions of truth and knowledge. That is, those in positions of Northern power and entitlement, not only further their political and capital aspirations through the perseverance of a political platform that enriches their ideological and profitable existence but one that self-identifies them as agents of self-preservation entitlement and enhancement. Finally, the chapter examines the inequitable distribution of the impacts of climate change (Mendelsohn, Dinar, and Williams 2006), with poorer nations, notably in the Global South, experiencing the disproportionate amount of 'natural disasters', forced migration, and scarcity of essential natural resources.

Climate politics and Northern power

The United Nations (UN) Secretary General, António Guterres, recently referred to climate change as 'the most systemic threat to humankind' and called on world leaders to lower their countries' greenhouse gas emissions (Sengupta 2018). This view is grounded in mounting scientific evidence that identifies the perils facing humans from global warming and climate change (Wildlife Conservation 2018). For example, the World Economic Forum's twelfth annual *Global Risks Report* (2017) places climate change as the most pressing and significant problem facing humanity's ongoing safety and security. The threats posed by nuclear weapons, military and rogue dictatorships, and political corruption are deemed less dramatic than the perils presented by global warming and its impacts on humans and non-human species alike (World Economic Forum 2017). Such predictions have been endorsed and alluded to by the global scientific community. The Intergovernmental Panel on Climate Change, established in 1988 by the World Meteorological Organization, comprises thousands of scientists across 120 countries. Acting on a voluntary basis and providing assessments of government climate policy and the threats and impacts of climate change (IPCC 2013a), this organisation continues to highlight the impending perils of climate change. Recent research from an elite group of scientists attached to the IPCC have reported that the two degrees Celsius target established by the *Paris Agreement* will be exceeded by 2050 taking the planet into 'game over' territory before the turn of the next century (Friedrich et al. 2016). Moreover, the UN Secretary-General, mentioned above, has further publicly described the world's response to climate change as being 'a mess' (Grimm 2017). This pronouncement is alarming given that 200 countries agreed to the terms of the *Paris Agreement* (Uwiringiyimana 2016), with 148 nations having now ratified it, pledging their allegiance to reduce greenhouse gas emissions (UN Framework Convention of Climate Change 2017).

It is now emerging that the targets of the *Paris Agreement* did not go far enough to arrest the imminent and undeniable dangers presented by global warming and climate change (Mengel et al. 2018).

However, some powerful leaders are neither heeding the words of the UN Secretary-General nor the overwhelming scientific evidence of reputable scholars. Consider, United States (US) President Donald Trump's position on climate change: 'It's called weather, it changes and you have storms and you have rain and you have beautiful days' (Donald Trump, then presidential candidate and now 65th President of the United States, cited in Vincent 2015).

The nationalistic and US-centric values of Trump typified by the comment above, and his disregard for the impacts of climate change, were no better exemplified than by his withdrawal from the landmark *Paris Agreement*. In doing so, he stated it

> is simply the latest example of Washington entering into an agreement that disadvantages the United States to the exclusive benefit of other countries, leaving American workers—who I love—and taxpayers to absorb the cost in terms of lost jobs, lower wages, shuttered factories, and vastly diminished economic production.
>
> (The White House 2017)

Indeed, it should be noted that Trump's withdrawal from the *Paris Agreement* occurred in the very week that scientists reported that global greenhouse gas emissions, notably in the Global South, including carbon dioxide, methane, and nitrogen oxide were at their highest levels in 800,000 years (Meinhausen 2017; Slattery 2017; World Meteorological Organization 2017). Moreover, Trump's decision coincided with 5000 square kilometres of the Larsen C ice shelf in the South Pole being perilously close to detaching (Amos 2017); and that new evidence pointed to rapid species extinction from climate change (Pacifici et al. 2017). President Trump's position was in stark contrast to his predecessor who had referred to the *Paris Agreement* as 'the best chance we have to save the one planet we have' (BBC 2015) and the UN Secretary-General has since called on the 'world to remain united in the face of climate' (Grimm 2017). The US withdrawal from a pact involving 197 countries now leaves it with Syria and Nicaragua as the only two nations not to submit and agree to the *Paris Agreement* (Zatat 2017). The outpouring of dismay at President Trump's decision has been widespread with calls for his impeachment as well as those suggesting he is a 'climate criminal' (Cohn 2017; Poyla 2017). This presidential leadership premised on climate denial has cascaded throughout the US administration with the Environmental Protection Agency's head systematically dismantling environmental regulations and funding; and an Energy Secretary challenging reputable climate science (DiChristopher 2017; Savage 2017).

It is not our intention here to traverse the global armada of responses to Trump's decisions, and that of his administration (for further discussion on this topic see, Friedman et al. 2017). The purpose here is to apply Trump's politics of ignorance to a Northern governing rationality that dangerously impacts the natural environments in the Global South. In doing so, we wish to highlight the words of economic Nobel Laureate's Paul Krugman's recent article and the objection to his President's decision to withdraw from the *Paris Agreement*, namely his *New York Times* piece entitled, 'Making ignorance great again' (Krugman 2017). In his view, political leadership in the US, indeed republicanism, 'doesn't do substance, it doesn't assemble evidence, or do analysis to formulate or even justify its policy position. Facts and hard thinking aren't wanted, and anyone who tries to bring such things into the discussion is the enemy' (2017: 1). Indeed, Trump's dramatic cuts to university and scientific funding demonstrate his administration's disdain for knowledge and intellectual expertise (Mervis 2017).

Northern hegemony and Platonic ignorance

It is important to note that not only are the politics and knowledges of the Global North powerful in discourse, debate, and decisions about climate change and environmental preservation, but even 'ignorance' is equally effective in capturing and colonising centre stage to the detriment of the Global South. Amidst the international condemnation, embarrassment, anger, and disbelief of President Trump's climate change denial, Professor Klugman's succinct critique, mentioned above, struck us as a poignant observation of the grave decision-making of powerful Northern political and corporate elites who deny climate change. The future of our planet teeters on the precipice of environmental destruction and concomitant species extinction and our hopes, dreams, and values are encapsulated and placed in the palms of a doctrine of 'ignorance'; one that does not represent the majority world, but favours a dominant Northern minority who hold the integrity of nature hostage for their unfounded, unwanted and demarcated values.

As Latour has persuasively argued in his 'Europe as refuge' (2017: 80):

> If there is no planet, no earth, no soil, no territory to house the Globe of globalization to which all countries claimed to be heading, what should we do? Either we deny the existence of the problem, or else we seek to come down to earth. For each of us, the question now becomes: 'Are you going to keep nursing dreams of escape, or are you going to search for a land in which you and your children might live?' This is what now divides people, much more than knowing whether you are politically on the right or the left. The United States had two solutions. By finally realizing the extent of the change in circumstances, and the hugeness of their responsibility, they could finally become realistic, leading the free world out of the abyss; or they could sink into denial. Trump seems to have decided to leave America to dream on for a few more years, delaying the possibility of coming down to earth and dragging other countries down into the abyss.

The classical Greek philosopher Plato and founder of the Academy in Athens debated extensively about the relationship between knowledge, belief, wisdom, and ignorance (see *Republic, Parmenidas and Theaetetus*). In Plato's *Apology* he analyses Socrates's claim to 'knowing nothing' and the pervasiveness of ignorance (Matthews 2003: 6). In Socrates's dialogue of 'what is knowledge?' Plato summarises and identifies three types of knowledge: 'knowledge as perception', 'knowledge as true belief', and 'knowledge as true belief or judgement with an account' (Bostock 1988). For Plato, an absence of knowledge is ignorance, akin to hunger and thirst or the 'emptying of the bodily condition'. Ignorance is the 'emptying of the condition of the soul', and like thirst and hunger can only be rectified by 'filling' or 'intellectual nourishment' (Harte 2013: 21). However, with Trump and other climate deniers discussed shortly, there is no attempt to 'fill the void'. The lack of content or evidence is used as a form of power as one 'believes' and 'trusts' in their own opinion and that of fellow deniers. Indeed, the filling of the void comes from others with whom the void is combatable. As such, knowledge becomes ignorance, as those with power seek the voices and views of those who sustain their position. This is often referred to as the 'supply chain trust' where creator and dispenser and recipient share benefits from the knowledge imparted (Lambert and Cooper 2000).

Plato challenges us to question the dominant knowledges in society and why certain opinions prevail above others to create the status quo. An important dimension to Platonic knowledge is its reliability and one's willingness to 'trust' in the veracity of the wisdom imparted. Moreover, knowledge must have two key dimensions for the author: a belief that what is said is true, and an ability to justify or substantiate the belief (Pigliucci 2012). The legitimation of knowledge, therefore, is bound not only in its justifiable factual truth, but in its acceptance. The ability to distort facts and provide counter narratives become powerful tools in the hands of those who can shape the contours of truth. President Trump is a master at this, he dismisses facts and scientific evidence as 'fake news' and in its place his Twitter account becomes the font of knowledge—the words from the horse's mouth, undistorted by a 'corrupt' and self-serving media. If you demonise the scientific expert, as Trump routinely does with his 'war on science' (The Editorial Board 2017), you legitimate 'the other'. In the case of Trump and climate denial, it is the 'experience' and 'opinion' of 'the other' or those that provide his inner circle, who become the informed and authoritative 'other'. Such individuals and their partisan accounts are elevated to the status of the 'scientific citizen' (Braham 2016; Ritchie et al. 2016). In times when legitimate scientific debate has been polarised and stymied by an equilibrium of evidence, governments have turned to the experiences, views, and logic of the public to cast the die in what is otherwise an undecided, contested, and uncertain debate (Walters 2011). The voice of 'opinion' becomes a powerful tool, notably when it is controlled and cajoled by those in positions of political power. Here, we see that ignorance is capable of asserting different kinds of power

(Smith 2012). This is especially the case when the 'ignorant are ignorant of their ignorance' (see Code 2004).

The sociology of knowledge is a well-established field and scholars have long debated the relationship between knowledge, politics, and power (Foucault 1981). Critiques of 'expert knowledge' abound in the sociology of knowledge literature and have contributed to understandings of the importance of 'local/contextual/tacit' knowledge (Bourdieu 1991). These critiques at both policy and local contexts support a democratisation of knowledge, but rarely attempt to interrogate links between knowledge ownership and production, how certain knowledge gains 'authority', and the power effects of particular knowledge appropriation and insertion into influential discourses. There is a sense that the critiques of scientific knowledge and the focus on its limitations has displaced a concern for the materialist aspects of (scientific) knowledge—the way this knowledge production is increasingly privatised, controlled, and selectively deployed by corporate and state interests, and how this is transformed into economic and political power. The Trump administration and its dissemination of ignorance as a self-styled truth seeks to colonise and dominate alternative narratives about issues such as global warming and climate change. It is here that ignorance is at its most powerful: when the influence and charisma of those in political authority assert their positions with a personally stylised rhetoric, substantiated or justified only by favourable and sympathetic voices within a powerful inner circle. It is a kind of distorted Weberian soft power, where political authority and charisma through legally and democratically recognised avenues combine to legitimate and create 'truth' that is not only adopted, but followed and imbued within cultural mores (Nye 2004; Zafiroski 2007). So not only is criminological knowledge distorted by the global organisation of social science which privileges the wealthy countries of the Global North, but so is political discourse. Hence the importance of Trump's denialism in setting the tone for political discourse elsewhere in the world.

Climate change denial and Northern lobbying

As mentioned, irrespective of mounting scientific evidence that global warming is occurring and that humans are responsible for climate change and its devastating impacts including, for example, the sinking of low lying Pacific nations (Union of Concerned Scientists 2018; Young 2017), the deniers of this scientific fact comprise a powerful Northern lobby (Frumhoff and Oreskes 2015). Indeed, the link between climate change denial in the Global North and politically conservative think tanks has been well established, where non-peer reviewed books and articles are disseminated as powerful 'science' in a persuasive attempt to control, censure, and neutralise the overwhelming caucus of reputable empiricism which identifies the undeniable existence of global warming and its devastating effects (Dunlap and Jacques 2013).

The global climate change deniers are at their largest and most powerful in the United States. Indeed, the culture of climate denial in the Global South—in Asia, Africa, Latin America, and Australasia—is comparatively very small (Xifra 2016). Moreover, it is conservative white males that disproportionately represent the greatest number of climate change deniers in the US (McCright and Dunlap 2011). Indeed, in the small pockets of climate denial that exists in social democratic and political progressive nations, it is also conservative white males that uphold and perpetuate positions of denial to further the status quo of trade and fiscal hegemony and prosperity (Jylhä et al. 2016). For instance, in Australia the climate deniers in politics are among the white men of the National and Liberal political party coalition.

The climate denial movement in the United States is an organised and institutionalised facet of contemporary social life (Oreskes and Conway 2012). A number of influential 'think tanks' including the Cato Institute, American Enterprise Institute and the Heartland Foundation openly attack climate change research as the 'climatism cartel' accusing pro climate change advocates of skewing government priorities and funding left academic research with anti-Republican outcomes (Bohr 2016). Moreover, research into climate change is currently systematically halted and dismantled by the US administration (McKie 2017) and vast budget cuts have been made to clean and renewable energy initiatives (Greshko, Parek, and Howard 2018). It has been widely reported that President Trump selected Scott Pruitt, a well-known climate denier, to head the Environmental Protection Agency (Pooley 2017). Trump has also disbanded a federal advisory committee on climate change (Rosten 2018; Tollefson 2017) and has installed severe tariffs on solar panels which will have devastating employment and growth impacts on the renewable energy sector (Eckhouse, Natter, and Martin 2018). The US President is supported in the Senate by senior Republican figures, such as Jim Inhofe who chairs the Environment and Public Works Committee. He has notoriously thrown snowballs in the Senate during unseasonable cold spring to mock the science of global warming and has declared that climate change 'is the greatest hoax ever perpetuated against the American people' (Kluger 2015). Indeed, Trump continues to appoint climate sceptics to senior government positions, which has many commentators concluding that climate change deniers are 'running the administration' (Holden 2018).

This is at odds with 70 per cent of the US public who believe that human-induced climate change is happening and 75 per cent support laws to reduce carbon emissions (Marlon et al. 2016; Popovich, Schwartz, and Schlossberg 2017). However, with Trump's withdrawal from the *Paris Agreement*, and his ongoing support for fossil fuels, it is unlikely that the US public will see their nation's second highest greenhouse gas emitter status reduced during this presidential term (We-Haas 2017). That said, the ability of the US public to investigate and potentially further their resolve on issues of climate change is undermined by an administration that suppresses access to information. Indeed, the ability to distil and synthesise climate change evidence in the US has recently proven very difficult for the public. President Trump has ordered thousands of pages of climate change-affirming research be deleted from the webpages of the US Environmental Protection Agency (Griffin 2017). The reliable access and free flow of official government decision-making and its supporting evidence is a hallmark of a progressive democratic society (Chang 2002); however, such access in the US is continually curtailed by powerful deniers—ignorance has become the pervasive discourse. A recent study of social media in the US identifies that 'fake news' or misinformation is far more popular and believable than the truth (Meyer 2018). This will be good news for those who perpetuate ignorance and deny access to alternative narratives.

Furthermore, multibillion dollar Northern energy corporations have actively sponsored the voices of opposition to global warming and, as such, have been described as the 'heart and soul of climate denial' in the US (Goldenberg and Bengtsson 2016). The powerful and affluent corporate deniers in the US have also attempted to polarise society and actively obstruct policies that seek to protect the environment (Farrell 2016). It is clear that the funding of climate change denial in the US is big business and often originates from untraceable sources. According to one study between 2003 and 2010, more than 140 'foundations' transferred $US558 million into climate denying organisations. The author of this comprehensive study concluded that, 'the climate change countermovement has had a real political and ecological impact on the failure of the world to act on global warming' (Bruille quoted in Fischer 2013: 8). This distortion and denunciation of justifiable scientific evidence for economic gains proves immensely powerful when supported and perpetuated by the influential political corridors of the Global North.

Furthermore, in recent years we have witnessed emerging discourses in knowledge politics (Grundmann and Stehr 2003). The German cultural studies expert Nico Stehr has written extensively on the ways that science and technology have coalesced around market forces to dominate the agendas of politics and innovation (Stehr 2005). In this hierarchy of knowledge, it is science and notably its market branding in 'innovation' that triumph and assert a dominant position in political priorities. For many commentators this science-driven era of knowledge politics is viewed as the 'scientification of public policy' (Frickel 2013: 23) where the values and needs of people are secondary to the aspirations and discoveries of science. Indeed, technological innovation is becoming embedded in social life in the ways that individuals perceive and interact with their worlds. As Bourdieu's work on hexis has argued, individual mannerisms and choices to resolving perceived problems or creating opportunities are almost instinctively found in modern technologies (Bourdieu 1991). This is more evident than ever with mobile phones and their applications, high-speed wireless communications, as well as satellite tracking, computer implants, and emerging initiatives with drones, artificial intelligence, driverless cars, and 3D printing (World Economic Forum 2017). To be lacking technological instinctiveness in contemporary society—to use Bourdieu, is to be a digital dinosaur, to be out-of-date; all things modern, progressive, forward-looking and problem solving often have a technological edge in world. The late Harvard Professor of Business, Juma Calestous, recognised as one of the most influential Africans of all time, argues that 600 years of history reveals that people 'resist new technologies when they substitute for, rather than augment, our humanity . . . but we eagerly embrace them when they support our desire for inclusion, purpose, challenge, meaning and alignment with nature' (Calestous 2016). It is here that the climate deniers, primarily from the Global North, have captured debate on global warming. They have systemically eroded the democratisation of knowledge and in its place is emerging a knowledge politics (grown out of ignorance, self-interest, and the desire to maintain power and profit) that emphasises specific scientific developments that the public may embrace, yet serve to enhance economic innovation at the expense of social innovation. Therefore, we observe massive increases in funding in the US for scientific and technology innovation to enhance the military apparatus, to explore space, and to strengthen domestic security. In times when threats of terrorism are heightened, and when the Doomsday Clock has been set at two minutes to midnight (Bulletin of Atomic Scientists 2018), the climate change deniers supplant new hope in the minds of the public in military strength and space exploration. All this occurs with a political handover to private industry which is deemed to have the expertise and know-how to manage and deliver on projects that will enhance and secure humanity (Cloud 2018; Wall 2018). Climate change continues to be a presented as a hoax and has even been removed by Trump as a threat to the United States (Lieven 2018). At the same time, we are not witnessing the implementation of universal healthcare, or increases in social services, but the exact opposite, with huge cuts to welfare and human service (Wilts 2018). Of course, the corporate tentacles of climate denial are embedded in the fossil fuel industry (Union of Concerned Scientists 2015) and in those technological innovations all receiving presidential support through tax cuts and Pentagon appointments (Mazzoni 2017).

Global warming and Southern dislocation

It is not only the climate denying ideologies of the powerful Global North that have shaped political discourse, negatively impacted on renewables and furthered the planet destructive technologies powered by fossil fuels. It is also the environmentally unjust practices of the powerful North that continue to marginalise, contaminate, and dislocate the Global South. The three economic powerhouses in Europe and North America, namely the United States, Russia, and Germany are also in the top five carbon dioxide emitting nations (Smith 2017). Whilst many commentators rightly point to China and India as part of the top five polluting nations, they are also among the most polluted countries and they are also, unlike their Northern polluting partners, rapidly transitioning away from fossil fuels to a range of renewable technologies.

Of course, such critical views of China, in particular, overlook that developing countries of the Global South are playing economic and industrial catch up and have to date made very little contribution to the accumulated stock of greenhouse gas emissions when compared to Northern countries. This biased appraisal of 'current' emissions fails to acknowledge the historical contexts of global pollution and thus represents a further example of the static, divided, and unevenly balanced North/South relations. Indeed, according to the recent United Nations Climate Change report, it is China and India who 'lead' the world in energy transition in green and clean alternatives (United Nations Climate Change 2017: 1) and who continue to receive the praise and adulation of global environmental groups (Shackleman 2017). It is not surprising that the top ten most polluted countries in the world are all in the Global South where air quality is compromised, water contaminated, and food security threatened (Smith 2017). Moreover, the capitalist excesses of the Global North are inextricably linked to the marginalisation and forced migration of millions of people more commonly referred to as 'climate refugees' (Barnes and Dove 2015) or 'environmental refugees' (Seelye 2001). According to the United Nations Refugee Agency, more than 21 million people are forcibly displaced each year as a result of human-induced global warming and its impacts on food and freshwater (UN High Commission for Refugees 2017); almost 90 per cent are from the Global South (Brisman

2015; Guha-Sapir and Hoyois 2015). It has been widely reported that low-lying South Pacific nations are threatened by rising sea levels. Islands, such as the Maldives, Tuvalu, Palau, and Kiribati, with little or no carbon footprint are victims of the perilous impacts of free trade ideologies and excessive greenhouse gas emissions that have underpinned powerful nations of the Global North. As the Ambassador of Tuvalu to the United Nations alarmingly stated more than a decade ago as his nation continues to be engulfed by the surrounding seas, 'The world has moved from a global threat once called the Cold War, to what now should be considered the Warming War. Our conflict is not with guns and missiles but with weapons from everyday lives—chimney stacks and exhaust pipes' (His Excellency, Afelee Pita, Ambassador of Tuvalu to the United Nations, 17 April 2007 cited in Walters 2012: 89). Such warnings have become realised as threats posed by global warming engulf the 1000 low lying South Pacific islands. As such, Pacific Island leaders remain united and outspoken on the polluting trade-centric ideologies of the G7, however, their appeals continue to fall on global deaf ears (Pearl 2017). In response to rising sea levels, some nations have begun 'purchasing' land from other countries in order to resettle entire populations. This is occurring in relation to Kiribati, where 24 square kilometres of land have been purchased from the Fijian Government to undertake entire 'wholesale population resettlement' for Kiribati peoples. This process presents a host of legal and social dilemmas for the nation of Fiji, which itself already suffers from rising sea levels and the threat of population displacement (Bilimoria, unpublished). Climate change refugees are also being relocated to some of the most unstable and violent countries in the Pacific, such as Bougainville, adding to the catastrophic effects of their relocation, as discussed in Chapter 2.

Whilst the nations of the Global South experience disproportionate human dislocation (see Gross 2017), we are also witnessing the emergence of 'privatised green enclaves'. The 'Eko Atlantic' in Nigeria, for example, is a proposed vision for the future—an ultra-elite and privileged metropolis for the super-rich, protected by private security from the impoverished, who dwell beyond the guarded walls. This has been described by some as the new emerging 'climate apartheid'—'a world in which the rich and powerful exploit the global ecological crisis to widen and entrench extreme inequalities and seal themselves off from its impacts' (Lukacs in Brisman, South, and Walters 2018: 302). Nigeria's Eko Atlantic is a ten square kilometre multi-billion dollar development along the Lagos shoreline, funded by transnational corporations and banks that seek to establish a self-governing enclosed metropolis of unprecedented living splendour on land rescued from the rising seas. Indeed, the project is premised on a capitalist response to 'arresting the ocean's encroachment.' The developers describe the project as:

> an entire new coastal city being built on Victoria Island adjacent to Lagos, Nigeria, to solve the chronic shortage of real estate in the world's fastest-growing megacity. It is a focal point for investors capitalising on rich development growth based on massive demand—and a gateway to emerging markets of the continent.
>
> (Eko Atlantic 2017: 1)

It is estimated that this mega ecofriendly city that has been advertised to match the magnificence of Paris' Champs-Elysees and New York's Fifth Avenue, will house 250 000 of Africa's wealthiest people in a location where two-thirds of the population live in poverty (Winsor 2015). It is important to note that Eko Atlantic was originally conceived in 2003 as a retaining wall to prevent shoreline erosion caused by climate change and rising seas.

> What was, therefore, designed to be an architectural feature to save coastal Nigeria *for everyone* has evolved into 'the African Dubai'—a walled sanctuary of grandeur where the country's richest one per cent have their futures secured, whilst the impoverished locals are evicted from their surrounding homes to make way for the world's most expensive development.
>
> (Brisman et al. 2018: 345)

Northern monopolies and Southern exploitation

The Institute of Environmental Science and Technology at the Universitat Autonoma de Barcelona coordinates the Environmental Justice Atlas, the world's largest database that identifies and catalogues social conflicts emerging from environmental injustice (Environmental Justice Atlas 2018). It is a comprehensive overview of existing legal and social struggles depicting government and corporate exploitation of environmental resources including water, soil, and food. It is compiled by advocates, lawyers, and victims and seeks to both expose government and corporate exploitation for the trauma, deprivation, and injustice caused by, for example, land grabs, logging, toxic dumping, and mining. At present there are 2427 'live cases' involving litigation and social protest over widespread environmental destruction—90 per cent of cases are in the Global South (Environmental Justice Atlas 2018).

It is perhaps unsurprising, given their biodiversity richness, that the countries of the Global South are the targets of illegal corporate plunder of their flora, fauna, and natural resources. Goyes, Mol, Brisman, and South (2017) provide a unique and innovative edited collection, entitled *Environmental Crime in Latin America*, that examines the exploitative practices of commerce, the plunder and ruination of lands by mining extraction, the mono aqua and agricultural practices that destroy bio-diversity, the dispossession of Indigenous peoples' land and way of life, and the theft of wildlife in Latin America. The editors of this compendium have undertaken to correct the blind spots of Northern criminology and contribute to the huge ongoing project of de-colonising the theoretical toolbox of social science to render visible that which Eurocentric thought silenced for centuries. Furthermore, as peoples of the Global South continue to protest and stand up against corporate power and defend their bio sovereignty, they are increasingly the victims of death and injury. Indeed, four environmental activists/ defenders are killed weekly with the top five most dangerous places for people protecting their natural resources against corporations and corrupt governments, all coming from the Global South (McCarthy 2018). The exploitation of the Global South, driven by Northern ideologies of free-trade, can be examined in more detail by looking at two examples, namely food and water. As discussed in Chapter 1, the establishment of colonial empire shaped power relations between the North and South with a lasting economic and geopolitical legacy. Similarly, there exist environmental legacies of injustice that are continually fuelled and compounded US global supremacy, the dominance of economic institutions, such as the International Monetary

Fund and World Bank, as well as the monopolies and exploitations facilitated by Northern corporate power.

It is widely reported that the peoples of the Global South experience a disproportionate amount of food and water insecurity (Brisman, South, and Walters 2018; UN Department of Economic and Social Affairs 2017). If we first examine food security or food justice (Alkon and Agyeman 2011) we observe that the vast networks or food 'superhighways' have become normalised within contemporary developed societal discourses of human consumption. Transnational free-market flows and economic expansionism continue to advantage affluent nations. Foods from near and far fill the supermarket trolleys and stack the pantries of the 'global kitchens' of the developed world often within a non-critical and hedonistic vacuum. The globalisation of food has changed the way people eat, shop, and live. A visit to any supermarket across Europe or North America in mid-winter may result in the purchase of: Shamouti oranges from Israel; savoy cabbage from France; Angeleno plums from Australia; alpine nectarines from South Africa; aromatic ginger from Brazil; asparagus tips from Peru; freshly picked blueberries from Poland; onions from Argentina, bananas from Cameroon; organic beans from Zambia; and so on. Such purchases have become routine daily consumer practice in a market that demands endlessly and immediately available fresh global produce, and at discount and competitive prices. For the developing, highly indebted, and majority world of the Global South, the tale of readily accessible and cheap food, available in diverse abundance, is a distant and unimaginable dream—a mere fable. With one billion people suffering from hunger or food insecurity, the global industry of food for the majority world results in vast amounts of edible produce discarded, all in the name of 'consumer choice' and 'freshness'.

It is anticipated that the human population will increase to 9.7 billion by 2050 (UN Department of Economic and Social Affairs 2015), and current food production arguably needs to double, making food security one of the greatest global challenges (Breene 2016). The challenges of long-term 'equitable' global food access and security are further compounded by resource scarcity, environmental degradation, biodiversity loss, and climate change. These issues are arguably caused and aggravated by the spread of corporatised and monopolised food systems in the Global North. For some, humanitarian crises associated with food shortages and injustices are emerging 'global security threats' with unimaginable human suffering; for others, it is fiscal opportunity, a flourishing market with unprecedented profits for savvy global corporate food monopolies (Shepherd 2011; Siegenbeek van Heukelom 2011). The term 'food security' has been in use for at least 40 years, first emerging at the World Food Congress in 1974 (Carolan 2013). Earlier uses of food security referred to availability and access of food, as well as its sustainability, nutritional value, and sustainable livelihoods for food producers. More recently, it has been argued that the term food security needs to be 'reclaimed' due the term being hijacked (Carolan 2013) or captured (Carney 2011) by corporate actors advocating privatised and market-driven solutions to the global food supply.

The United Nations Food and Agriculture Organisation (2017: 2) has argued for some time that global food security is not a production issue but an ideological problem stating that 'there is more than enough food produced in the world to feed everyone, yet 815 million go hungry'. This global inequity in food distribution is exacerbated by G7 countries, the World Trade Organization and food governance policies, tariffs, and trade agreements that privilege and prioritise Northern markets and consumers (Sommerville, Essex, and Le Billon 2014). As the UN Educational, Scientific and Cultural Organisation (2010: 1) has persuasively argued:

> The terms of international trade favour the North. The rich world keeps the South wedded to commodity production by putting up tariff barriers to manufactured goods. Barriers and clothing alone cost poor countries $53 billion a year in lost trade—this equals the total of all Western aid to the South. Ironically, marinating poverty in the South means poor countries can buy less of the manufactured goods the rich are so eager to supply.

It is perhaps, therefore, unsurprising that the economically powerful countries of the Global North should experience food excess whilst the people of the Global South starve. It has been argued that the United States wastes up to 50 per cent of its overall food supply (Gunders 2012). According to the UN's Food and Agriculture Organization, European countries discard 100 million tonnes of food waste each year (Hepker 2014). The United Kingdom (UK) is the most food wasteful country in Europe, discarding almost 90 million tonnes of food (Sedghi 2015). While some of this wastage is related to health and safety regulations and household excess, it is also about corporate profit and the marketing of freshness and consumer choice. We live in a world of both opulent food abundance and desperate life-threatening food shortage. In response to this, there have been recent moves to global land acquisition by financial investors that have been couched in arguments of food security, yet at both local and national levels, loss of access to productive land has brought about greater food insecurity, particularly for small-scale farmers and others dependent on land and forest resources in developing nations (Borras and Franco 2010; Borras et al. 2011; Lyons, Richards, and Westoby 2014). This is also evident in the stated aim of

> the New Alliance on Food Security and Nutrition, a partnership between the powerful G8 countries, and corporations, to mobilize domestic and foreign private investments in African agriculture, bring agricultural innovations to scale, and reduce the risk borne by vulnerable economies and communities.
>
> (Yara International 2015 in Brisman et al. 2018)

This public/private neo-liberal policy purports to relieve 50 million people from hunger by expanding industrialised agriculture in the African continent and thereby increasing production. However, the 'Alliance' has been subject to intense criticism for relieving rural Africans of their land and livelihoods, and thus exacerbating poverty and food insecurity (McKeon 2014; Monbiot 2013). The main challenges remain: addressing food security through social, economic, and distributive justice (Carolan 2013; Patel 2007).

Similarly, the monopolisation of global freshwater supplies by Northern corporations has witnessed devastating scarcity and social conflict in the Global South (Brisman et al. 2018; Goyes et al. 2017). For example, in 2015, more than 280 million people across 24 countries had their water supplied by one of the world's top 50 private contractors (Bluefield Research 2015). Since 1990, the rate of public-private partnerships for water provision and sanitation in developing countries has steadily increased. The freshwater industry is estimated to be worth $US1 trillion a year. The world's top five earning water companies—all based in the US, UK, and France—report global annual revenue exceeding $US84 billion (Brisman et al. 2018). What is now becoming a common story is that large water monopolies are returning huge profits to shareholders, whilst increasing prices to consumers and paying little or no tax (Wright 2016). The contested legal arrangements that seek to uphold equitable distribution and sustainability also permit the control and exploitation of sovereign water resources for commercial purposes. The Dublin Principles paved the way for the rise of corporate water monopolies to protect and represent sovereign nations' best interests. Within this burgeoning industry are new corporate conglomerates such as Aquaduct Alliance (owned by Goldman Sachs, General Electric, Coco Cola, Dow Chemicals, United Technologies, Talisman Energy, and Bloomberg), now emerging as dominant global water entrepreneurs. These large transnational corporations, some with dubious and reprehensible records of water abuse and contamination, are now creating databases that chart water supplies and identify risks and opportunities for business. The profits for transnational water monopolies are immense. For investment advisors and hedge fund managers, the global freshwater scarcity is providing 'serious profit opportunities for those in the know. . . The Aqueduct Alliance database/ maps will show where those opportunities are located. . . If you play it right. . . the results of this impending water crisis can be very good' (Nelson 2012: 1).

Southernising green criminology

The United Nations' Intergovernmental Panel on Climate Change has referred to global warming as human-induced climate change as a 'weapon of mass destruction'; indiscriminatingly annihilating entire species including the potential extinction of the human race (Mohammed 2014). The need to protect the natural environmental and curtail its destruction and exploitation has been reflected in a growing amount of international debates that seek to reduce human-induced environmental impacts. Criminology is part of this global challenge, specifically green criminology that has blossomed into a range of critical perspectives examining environmental concerns within notions of power, harm, and justice (Walters, Westerhuis, and Wyatt 2013). Green criminology continues to evolve as a dynamic knowledge of resistance and innovation, one that challenges mainstream crime discourses, and critically examines the policies and practices of contemporary governments and corporations. It is a collection of new and thought-provoking voices within the criminological lexicon, and its engagement with diverse narratives seeks to identify, theorise, and respond to environmental issues of both global and local concern. The expansion of green criminological perspectives serves to harness and mobilise academic, activist, and governmental interests to preserve, protect, and develop environmental issues. In 2013, South and Brisman compiled the first *International Handbook of Green Criminology*, and in their introduction they describe green criminology as a 'capacious and evolving perspective' where 'diversity is one of its great strengths' (Brisman and South 2013: 4). An important component of this intellectual enterprise is its 'horizon-scanning'—to look to the future and predict the issues and actions of global collective concern (White and Heckenberg 2014). As such, green criminology continues to engage with issues of climate change and species decline (Lynch, Long, and Stretesky 2015). Southern criminology and green criminology complement each other in various ways, not only in terms of their central concerns regarding that which has been overlooked but also with respect to how their history is illuminated by the idea of a 'project of retrieval' (see Goyes and South 2017a), noted above. Both Southern criminology and green criminology have recognised and emphasised the problems of bias, inequalities and injustice woven into the global flows of knowledge, wealth, and resources.

The Southernising of the green criminological agenda opens new trajectories by critiquing the impact of Northern environmental knowledges on the peoples of the South. For example, Goyes, Mol, Brisman, and South (2017) have recently published an edited collection of essays on environmental harm in Latin America. They argue that a truly transnational green criminology needs to 'ensure that the environmental crimes and harms affecting the lands of the peoples of the Global South are bought to the forefront' (Goyes et al. 2017: 2). The idea behind this compendium of essays came from the editors' realisation that green criminology had largely overlooked the Global South. The first theme considers how hierarchies of knowledge have historically overlooked the environmental plunder of the Global South. Specifically, the chapter by Rojas-Páez illustrates well how the Eurocentric understandings of law, crime and justice have historically misrepresented the peoples of the Global South as barbarians—uncivil—less than human (Rojas-Páez 2017: 62). He argues that this hierarchy of knowledge has persisted from colonial to post-colonial eras to justify imperial projects of 'genocides, slavery and environmental degradation' (2017: 63). This chapter draws on De Sousa Santos's theory of border epistemologies to explain how the dominant epistemology excluded knowledge about the historical experience of the colonised. Indigenous knowledges practices, for example, were systematically subjugated by ruling colonial and post-colonial powers. The historical injuries of the colonial period are relevant to understanding the continuation of harms in post-colonial worlds of the Global South (Rojas-Páez 2017: 70), also a key idea in our project.

Consequently, a second theme taken up in this compendium is about the centrality of colonial and post-colonial power relation to understanding the dynamics of ecological plunder in Latin America. Mondaca's chapter situates the growth of the salmon industry, mining and mono agricultural and aqua cultural activities within the historical context of the colonialisation of the Archipelago of Chiloé, a group of 40 or so islands that remained loyal to its Spanish colonisers during Chile's War of Independence (1810–1818) (Mondaca 2017). Historically treated as inferior, strange, and remote he argues the legacy of colonialism racialised relations between the people of the Archipelago and those of mainland Chile (2017: 32–37). The group of islands was neglected for 150 years, until a 'new extractivism' emerged under Pinochet's dictatorship. The Archipelago then became an internal territory whose abundance of natural resources (mainly copper, salmon, and Eucalypt plantations) were plundered, through what Mondaca describes as a violent process of neo-liberalism 'that has caused the inhabitants of Chiloé to lose (their territory and their identity)' (2017: 50).

The volume's third theme is the violence of colonialism, a theme often overlooked in the field of criminology as explained in the introduction to this book, but not in *Environmental Crime in Latin America*. Many of the chapters provide vivid details of how the commodification of nature (land, sea, water, air and, non-human life) and exploitation of subaltern peoples from the Global South were violently dispossessed, and turned into slaves as part of the modern 'civilising' processes undertaken by European colonial powers. Two places where this occurred in the 1800s in the colonial period were the Congo and the Amazon jungles. In both places slaves were subject to horrific punishments if they failed to deliver their quota of rubber (Rojas-Páez 2017: 58). Private militia who meted out violent punishments went hand in hand with slavery. Today, private security, armed forces, and militia continue to be used to police contested commercial activities (especially mining) in Columbia, Peru, Honduras, Brazil, and Argentina. Goyes and South liken the activities of transnational commercial enterprises in Latin America to the East India company, 'employing new —yet familiar—methods to plunder, seize land and gain power over natural products' (Goyes and South 2017: 189).

Not surprisingly, another theme throughout *Environmental Crime in Latin America* is the dispossession and in some cases genocide of subaltern groups of indigenous peoples, Afro-descendants of slavery, and campesino communities of Latin America, by the capricious activities of palm oil extraction, mining, dam construction, and aqua and agricultural development, to name but a few. In Columbia alone the Permanent Peoples Tribunal, an international body based on the *Universal Declaration of the Rights of Peoples*, found that the existence of 28 Indigenous communities was in jeopardy due to neo-liberal modes of development and commercialisation (Rojas-Páez 2017: 76). The final section of the volume contains three chapters on illegal wildlife trafficking—mainly due to demand for exotic reptiles, birds, and pets from the jungles of the Amazon (Nassaro 2017: 45). Wildlife trafficking involves the abduction and death of millions of animals on an annual basis (Sollund 2017: 215). The central problem is that traffickers enjoy a sense of impunity because wildlife trafficking is not a priority of border control, surveillance, or policing in Latin American countries. The failure to prioritise policing or preventing the abuse of animals is part of another hierarchy—one that elevates human life over non-human life. In this hierarchy of value the killing of animals—what Beirne terms 'theriocide' (2014: 49)—is not considered a crime. Until there is species justice for non-humans that recognises theriocide, too little will be done to prevent wildlife trafficking.

In a similar vein, the highly acclaimed and internationally renowned environmental lawyer, Polly Higgins, has developed the term 'ecocide' (Higgins 2010; Higgins, Short, and South 2012: 4) to place deliberate and reckless acts of mass environmental destruction within the criminal domain. As such 'ecocide' is 'the extensive damage, destruction to or loss of ecosystems of a given territory, whether by human agency of by other causes, to such an extent that peaceful enjoyment by the inhabitants of that territory has been severely diminished' (Higgins 2010: 3). If humans are responsible for this ecological loss, then Higgins argues that ecocide should be included in the *Statute of Rome* where perpetrators of mass environmental destruction can be convicted in similar ways to offenders processed for crimes against humanity (Higgins 2015).

Criminalising ecocide

The language of ecocide as a legal term is premised on notions of a human right to a clean and safe environment, and the need to protect and conserve biodiversity. The threats and impending perils posed by climate change deniers and global warming have recently witnessed the invoking of human rights for pending litigation. For example, there are legal proceedings being brought against political leaders in an attempt to hold them responsible for climate change. The Trump Administration withdrawal from the *Paris Agreement* has seen 21 children and young adults continue to pursue their case against the US Government using the 'doctrine of public trust' argument. In essence, the position draws on the US Constitution as well as international principles of intergenerational equity (Weiss 2008) and argues that governments must do whatever they can to hold the planet's future environmental integrity intact for the enjoyment of the next generation. Failure to do so is a breach of international responsibilities. President Trump has attempted to throw out the young person's case in the Federal Ninth circuit Court by filing a writ of mandamus, stating that an order should 'end this clearly improper attempt to have the judiciary decide important questions of energy and environmental policy to the exclusion of elected branches of government' (Walters 2018: 82). The Trump administration attempt to strike out the litigation was denied by Judge Aiken (Geiling 2018). In February 2018, environmental activists in the UK won their third case in the High Court against the British Government for 'unlawful' levels of air pollution in a case that marked the responsibilities of governments to protect citizens from green gas emissions and provide a safe and clean environment (Leary 2018). There are also emerging cases where governments are suing fossil fuels companies for climate change. The New York City Government has stated that it plans to sue the top five fossil fuels companies in the US for $5 billion for 'their contribution to climate change' (Lauder 2018).

The emerging legal pushback against the corporate and politically powerful actions of climate change denial form part of a broader discourse in 'green justice' (see Kibert 2001). As a concept, 'green justice' has been used by activists and left scholars to examine environmental injustice, namely, the plight of the poor and powerless at the hands of affluent, industrial economies (Alier 2000). Others have used the phrase to discuss environmental law and policy and the use of court processes (Hoban and Brooks 1996; Walters and Westerhuis 2013). Therefore, the usage of the term 'green justice' resonates not only in discourses of protest, resistance, and anti-capitalism, but also within legal debates about the role of law. This position recognises that the vast majority of greenhouse gas emissions are caused by fossil fuel combustion, deforestation, and the industrial activities of the world's most economically wealthy and powerful nations. This activity continues to have devastating consequences for the world's lowest producing emission countries.

International justice and transnational legal processes are emerging through protocols and inter-state agreements that seek to regulate and prevent illicit corporate activity within the complex webs of global markets (Likosky 2002). With increasing concerns about climate change and its impacts on air, food, and water security, it is imperative that a legally constituted and representative system of justice evolve. The recognition of anthropocentric environmental damage and the need for ecological sustainability has ensured that discourses of risks, rights, harm, responsibility, and liability have become part of Southern green criminology (Brisman, South, and Walters 2018). Moreover, the involvement of citizens in environmental activism that continues to emerge in the Global South has been pivotal to the progression and development of environmental policies and regulation. Environmental movements are becoming central in the identification, detection, and prevention of environmental crime. Their resources, technologies, databases, and personnel are increasingly utilised by law enforcement agencies to police, regulate, and prosecute both organised and localised environmental crime. Here, environmental activism, through technology and networks of action, local alliances, as well as appeals to citizens and officials, elevate the social movement to a reliable and reputable status which is inculcated into government and regulatory structures. Environmental activism becomes not mere representative democracy but participatory democracy with both a visible presence and impact. As such, with public and political integration it becomes a new and important form of environmental governance. Networks of green activists have become important in environmental law enforcement and are increasingly drawn upon by official agencies for intelligence. As such, the plight of those seeking to protect and preserve the environment through vocal and direct public action has been both risky and dangerous. It is estimated that environmental activists or 'defenders' are dying at the rate of four per week globally, often murdered by individuals representing corporate interests exploiting the land for economic growth (Global Witness 2017). In these instances, environmental activists are perceived as a threat to the corporations and states that seek to deny climate change and seek profit through the exploitation of natural resources.

Quo Vadis

This chapter concludes that Northern economics, governance, and decision-making within contexts of climate change are politically and commercially powerful. It is not a mere agenda that determines a willingness to see the planet spiral into imminent and impending peril, it is a politics of being that undermines the democratisation of knowledge, the expression of free speech, and the realisation of inalienable rights. The danger of climate denial and embedded agnosia from Northern powerful elites discussed in this chapter cannot be overemphasised because global publics are unwittingly conditioned to comply and conform to governing authorities through historical, institutional, and cultural notions of 'trust'. Such trust is too often centred on the powers of the Global North that have historically, and controversially, provided the intellectual, imperial and colonial leadership of all things 'progressive' and 'democratic'.

Yet, we have witnessed resistance and dissent and it forms an essential part of political accountability and global justice. There is mounting intellectual and social pushback against climate change deniers through discourse, litigation, and direct action. Much of this action is coming from the Global South where the impact of global change is disproportionately felt for reasons already described. Such action is increasingly dangerous in a world governed by demagogues and corporate moguls who seek power and control through the exploitation of the environment and its natural resources. However, it is through mobilised resistance that embraces the voices, knowledges, and experiences of the Global South that the divisive and environmentally destructive policies and actions of the economically and politically backed climate change deniers will be consigned to the historical trash cans of the future. Or as the world's leading human geographer and former panellist of the IPCC, Professor Hulme, has recently noted

> we can't solve climate change with numbers . . . We can actually only deal with climate change through the human imagination . . . Science will not be able to adjudicate on what we should or should not do . . . We have invented another human tradition—we call it politics—to resolve those sorts of challenges.
>
> (cited in Sellah 2018: 1)

References

Alier JM (2000) Retrospective environmentalism and environmental justice movements today. *Capitalism, Nature, Socialism* 11(4): 45–50. DOI: 10.1080/10455750009358939.

Alkon A and Agyeman J (2011) *Cultivating Food Justice: Race, Class and Sustainability*. Cambridge: MIT Press.

Amos J (2017) Antarctic ice crack takes major turn. *BCC News*, 31 May. Available at http://www.bbc.com/news/science-environment-40113393.

Barnes J and Dove MR (2015) Introduction. In Barnes J and Dove MR (eds) *Climate Cultures: Anthropological Perspectives on Climate Change*: 1–21. New Haven and London: Yale University Press.

BBC (2015) COP21: Paris climate deal: best chance to save planet. *BBC News*, 13 December. Available at http://www.bbc.com/news/science-environment-35086346.

Beirne P (2014) Theriocide: Naming animal killing. *International Journal for Crime, Justice and Social Democracy* 3(2): 49–66. DOI: 10.5204/ijcjsd.v3i2.174.

Bilimoria N (unpublished) Mapping policies and legal approaches in Fiji for climate-induced cross-border migration by Pacific Islanders. PhD Thesis. Brisbane, Australian: Queensland University of Technology.

Bluefield Research (2015) *Provide Water Utilities: Global Rankings and Company Strategies*. Boston: Bluefield Research.

Bohr J (2016) The climatism cartel: Why climate deniers oppose market-based mitigation policy. *Environmental Politics* 25(5): 812–830. DOI: 10.1080/09644016.2016.1156106.

Borras SM and Franco J (2010) Towards a broader view of the politics of global land grab: Rethinking land issues reframing resistance. *ICAS Working Paper Series* 1(May).

Borras SM, Hall R, Scoones I, White B, and Wolford W (2011) Towards a better understanding of global land grabbing: An editorial introduction. *The Journal of Peasant Studies* 38(2) 209–216. DOI: 10.1080/03066150.2011.559005.

Bostock D (1988) *Plato's Theaetetus*. Oxford: Oxford University Press.

Bourdieu P (1991) *Language and Symbolic Power*. Cambridge: Harvard University Press.

Braham E (2016) The rise and rise of citizen science. *Positive News*, 14 December. Available at https://www.positive.news/2016/science/24628/rise-rise-citizen-science/.

Breene K (2016) Food security and why it matters. *World Economic Forum*, 18 January. https://www.weforum.org/agenda/2016/01/food-security-and-why-it-matters/.

Brisman A (2015) 'Multicolored' green criminology and climate changes achromatopsia. *Contemporary Justice Review* 18(2): 178–196. DOI: 10.1080/10282580.2015.1025629.

Brisman A and South N (2013) Introduction. In South N and Brisman A (eds) *Routledge International Handbook of Green Criminology*: 1–24. London Routledge.

Brisman A, McClannhan B, South N, and Walters R (2018) *Water, Crime and Security in the Twenty-First Century: Too Dirty, Too Little, Too Much*. London: Palgrave.

Brisman A, South N, and Walters R (2018) Southernizing green criminology: Human dislocation environmental injustice and climate apartheid. *Power Justice and Resistance* 4(1): 21–39.

Bulletin of Atomic Scientists (2018) Timeline: It is 2 minutes to midnight. *Doomsday Clock*. Available at https://thebulletin.org/clock/2018 (accessed 9 May 2018).

Calestous J (2016) *Innovations and Its Enemies: Why People Resist New Technologies*. Oxford: Oxford University Press.

Carney M (2011) The food sovereignty prize: Implications for discourse and practice. *Food and Food Ways* 19(3): 169–180. DOI: 10.1080/07409710.2011.599767.

Carolan M (2013) *Reclaiming Food Security*. London: Routledge.

Chang N (2002) *Silencing Political Dissent: How Post-September 11 Anti-Terrorism Measures Threaten Our Civil Liberties*. New York: Seven Stories Press.

Cloud D (2018) Trump proposes huge increase in military spending. *Los Angeles Times*, 12 February. Available at http://www.latimes.com/nation/la-na-trump-defense-20180212-story.html.

Code L (2004) The power of ignorance. *Philosophical Papers* 33(3): 291–308. DOI: 10.1080/05568640409485144.

Cohn M (2017) Trump's climate withdrawal is an impeachable offense. *Truthout*, 6 June. Available at http://www.truth-out.org/news/item/40838-trump-s-climate-withdrawal-is-an-impeachable-offense.

DiChristopher T (2017) Energy Secretary Rick Perry says CO_2 is not the main driver of climate change. *CNBC Energy*, 19 June. Available at https://www.cnbc.com/2017/06/19/energy-sec-rick-perry-says-co2-is-not-the-main-driver-of-climate-change.html.

Dunlap RE and Jacques PJ (2013) Climate change denial books and conservative think tanks: Exploring the connection. *The American Behavioral Scientist* 57(6): 699–733. DOI: 10.1177/0002764213477096.

Eckhouse B, Natter E, and Martin C (2018) President trump slaps tariffs on solar panels in major blow to renewable energy. *Time*, 22 January. Available at http://time.com/5113472/donald-trump-solar-panel-tariff.

Eko Atlantic (2017) About us. Available at http://www.ekoatlantic.com/about-us/ (accessed 26 April 2018).

Environmental Justice Atlas (2018) About us. Available at https://ejatlas.org/about (accessed 2 May 2018).

Farrell J (2016) Corporate funding and ideological polarization about climate change. *Proceedings of the National Academy of Sciences of the United States of America PNAS* 113(1): 92–97.

Fischer D (2013) 'Dark money' funds climate change denial effort. *Scientific American*, 23 December. Available at https://www.scientificamerican.com/article/dark-money-funds-climate-change-denial-effort/.

Foucault M (1981) *The History of Sexuality*, Vol 1. Harmondsworth: Penguin.

Frickel S (2013) Knowledge politics. *Mobilizing Ideas*, 1 April. Available at https://mobilizingideas.wordpress.com/2013/04/01/knowledge-politics/.

Friedrich T, Timmerman A, Tigchelaar M, Timm O, and Ganapolski A (2016) Nonlinear climate sensitivity and its implications for future greenhouse warming. *Science Advances* 2(11). DOI: 10.1126/sciadv.1501923.

Frumhoff P and Oreskes O (2015) Fossil fuel firms are still are still bankrolling climate denial lobby groups. *The Guardian*, 25 March. Available at https://www.theguardian.com/environment/2015/mar/25/fossil-fuel-firms-are-still-bankrolling-climate-denial-lobby-groups.

Geiling N (2018) Federal court denies Trump's last-ditch attempt to derail the youth climate lawsuit. *Think Progress*, 7 March. Available at https://thinkprogress.org/federal-court-denies-trump-writ-mandamus-climate-lawsuit-4c489af5dad2/.

Global Witness (2017) The Defenders tracker, *The Guardian*, 13 July. Available at https://www.theguardian.com/environment/ng-interactive/2017/jul/13/the-defenders-tracker.

Goldenberg S and Bengtsson H (2016) Biggest US coal company funded dozens of groups questioning climate change. *The Guardian*, 13 June. Available at https://www.theguardian.com/environment/2016/jun/13/peabody-energy-coal-mining-climate-change-denial-funding.

Goyes D and South N (2017a) Green criminology before 'green criminology': Amnesia and absences. *Critical Criminology* 25(2): 165–181. DOI: 10.1007/s10612-017-9357-8.

Goyes D and South N (2017b) The injustices of policing, law and multinational monopolization in the privatization of natural diversity: Cases from Colombia and Latin America. In Goyes D, Mol H, Brisman A, and South N (eds) *Environmental Crime in Latin America: The Theft of Nature and the Poisoning of the Land*: 187–212. London: Palgrave.

Goyes D, Mol H, Brisman A, and South N (eds) (2017) *Environmental Crime in Latin America: The Theft of Nature and the Poisoning of the Land*. London: Palgrave.

Greshko M, Parek L, and Howard B (2018) A running list of how Trump is changing the environment. *National Geographic*, 24 April. Available at https://news.nationalgeographic.com/2017/03/how-trump-is-changing-science-environment/.

Griffin A (2017) Donald Trump orders Environmental Protection Agency to delete all climate change information from its website. *The Independent*, 25 January. Available at http://www.independent.co.uk/

life-style/gadgets-and-tech/news/donald-trump-environmental-protection-agency-website-climate-change-global-warming-a7544621.html.

Grimm N (2017) UN Secretary-General calls on the world to remain united in the face of climate change. *ABC News*, 31 May. Available at http://www.abc.net.au/news/2017-05-31/un-calls-on-world-to-remain-united-in-face-of-climate-change/8576642.

Gross M (2017) Refugee displacement at seven-decade high. *Giz Press*, 25 June. Available at http://gizpress.com/2017/06/25/united-nations-refugee-displacement-at-seven-decade-high.html (no longer active).

Grundmann R and Stehr N (2003) Social control and knowledge in democratic societies. *Science and Public Policy* 30(3): 183–188. DOI: /10.3152/147154303781780524.

Guha-Sapir D and Hoyois P (2015) *Estimating Populations Affected by Disasters: Review of Methodological Issues and Research Gaps.* Brussels: Centre for Research on the Epidemiology of Disasters. https://sustainabledevelopment.un.org/content/documents/7774UN%20Note%20on%20affected%20-%20Final%20version.pdf.

Gunders D (2012) Wasted: How America is losing up to 40 percent of its food from farm to fork to landfill. *NRDC Issue Paper* (August).

Harte V (2013) Plato's politics of ignorance. In Harte V and Lane M (eds) *Politeia in Greek and Roman Philosophy*: 139–154. Cambridge: Cambridge University Press.

Hepker C (2014) Food waste reduction could help feed world's starving. *BBC World Business Report*, 3 July. Available at http://www.bbc.com/news/business-28092034.

Higgins P (2010) *Eradicating Ecocide: Laws and Governance to Prevent the Destruction of Our Planet.* London: Shepheard-Walwyn.

Higgins P (2015) *Eradicating Ecocide: Exposing Corporate and Political Practices Destroying the Planet*, 2nd edn. London: Shepheard-Walwyn.

Higgins P, Short D, and South N (2012) Protecting the planet after Rio – the need for the crime of ecocide. *Criminal Justice Matters* 90(1): 4–6. DOI: 10.1080/09627251.2012.751212.

Hoban T and Brooks R (1996) *Green Justice: The Environment and the Courts*, 2nd edn. Boulder: Westview Press.

Holden E (2018) Climate change skeptics run the Trump administration. *Politco*, 7 March. Available at https://www.politico.com/story/2018/03/07/trump-climate-change-deniers-443533.

Intergovernmental Panel on Climate Change (IPCC) (2013a) Climate change 2013: The physical science basis. *IPCC Assessment Report* 5.

Intergovernmental Panel on Climate Change (IPCC) (2013b) What is the IPCC? *IPCC Factsheet.*

Jylhä K, Cantal C, Akrami N, and Milfont T (2016) Denial of anthropogenic climate change: Social dominance orientation helps explain the conservative male effect in Brazil and Sweden. *Personality and Individual Differences* 98 (August): 184–187. DOI: 10.1016/j.paid.2016.04.020.

Kibert N (2001) Green justice: A holistic approach to environmental injustice. *Journal of Land Use and Environmental Law* 17(1): 169–182.

Kluger J (2015) Senator throws snowball! Climate change disproven. *Time*, 27 February. Available at http://time.com/3725994/inhofe-snowball-climate/.

Krugman P (2017) Making ignorance great again. *New York Times*, 5 June. https://www.nytimes.com/2017/06/05/opinion/trump-gop-paris-climate-accordhtml?mcubz=0&_r=0.

Lambert D and Cooper M (2000) Issues in supply chain management. *Industrial Marketing and Management* 29(1): 65–83. DOI: 10.1016/S0019-8501(99)00113-3.

Latour B (2017) Europe as refuge. In Geaselberger H (ed.) *The Great Regression*: 78–87. Cambridge: Polity.

Lauder J (2018) New York City sues fossil fuel giants over climate change. *Triple J Hack*, 11 January. Available at http://www.abc.net.au/triplej/programs/hack/nyc-climate-change-lawsuit/9321138.

Leary K (2018) Activists are suing governments over the state of the environment – and winning. *Futurism*, 28 February. Available at https://futurism.com/environmental-activists-are-suing-governments-over-climate-change-and-winning/.

Lieven A (2018) The only force that beat climate change is the US army. *Foreign Policy*, 9 January. Available at http://foreignpolicy.com/2018/01/09/the-only-force-that-can-beat-climate-change-is-the-u-s-army/.

Likosky M (ed.) (2002) *Transnational Legal Processes: Globalisation and Power Disparities*. London: Butterworths.

Lynch M and Stretesky P (2010) Global warming global crime: A green criminological perspective. In White R (ed.) *Global Environmental Harm: Criminological Perspectives*: 62–84. Devon: Willan.

Lynch M and Stretesky P (2014) *Exploring Green Criminology: Toward a Green Criminological Approach*. Surrey: Ashgate.

Lynch M, Long M, and Stretesky P (2015) Anthropogenic development drives species to be endangered: Capitalism and the decline of species. In Sollund R (ed.) *Green Harms and Crimes: Critical Criminology in a Changing World*: 117–146. London: Palgrave Macmillan.

Lyons K, Richards C, and Westoby P (2014) *Carbon Violence: The Real Cost of Carbon Markets. The Impacts of Green Resources and Plantation Forestry in Uganda*. California: The Oakland Institute.

Marlon J, Howe P, Mildenberger M, and Leiserwitz A (2016) Yale climate opinion maps – US 2016. *Yale Program on Climate Change Communication*.

Available at http://climatecommunication.yale.edu/visualizations-data/ycom-us-2016/?est=happening&type=value&geo=county (accessed 31 April 2018).

Matthews G (2003) Socratic ignorance. *Philosophic Exchange* 33(1): 776–789.

Mazzoni M (2017) Top 10 climate deniers in Trump administration. *Eco Watch*, 20 December. Available at https://www.ecowatch.com/climate-deniers-in-trump-administration-2518894384.html.

McCarthy J (2018) These are the five deadliest countries for environmental activists. *Global Citizen*, 14 July. Available at https://www.globalcitizen.org/en/content/5-deadliest-countries-for-environmental-activists/.

McCright A and Dunlap R (2011) Cool dudes: The denial of climate change among conservative white males in the United States. *Global Environmental Change* 21(4): 1163–1172. DOI: 10.1016/j.gloenvcha.2011.06.003.

McKeon N (2014) New alliance for food security and nutrition: A corporate coup? *The Transnational Institute Agrarian Justice Programme: Policy Paper* (May).

McKie R (2017) Republicans accused of obstructing satellite research on climate change. *The Guardian*, 5 November. Available at https://www.theguardian.com/science/2017/nov/05/donald-trump-accused-blocking-satellite-climate-change-research.

Meinhausen M (2017) Greenhouse gas factsheets. *Australian-German Climate and Energy College*. Available at http://climate-energy-college.org/ghg-factsheets (accessed 31 May 2017).

Mendelsohn R, Dinar A, and Williams L (2006) The distributional impact of climate change on rich and poor countries. *Environment and Development Economics* 11(2): 159–178. DOI: 10.1017/S1355770X05002755.

Mengel M, Nauels A, Rogeli J, and Schleussner CF (2018) Committed sea-level rise under the Paris Agreement and the legacy of delayed mitigation action. *Nature Communications* 9(601): advance access. https://www.nature.com/articles/s41467-018-02985-8.

Mervis J (2017) Research is an afterthought in first Trump budget. *Science*, 20 March. http://www.sciencemag.org/news/2017/03/research-after-thought-first-trump-budget.

Meyer R (2018) The grim conclusions of the largest-ever study of Fake News: Falsehoods almost always beat out the truth on Twitter penetrating further faster and deeper into the social network than accurate information. *The Atlantic*, 8 March. Available at https://www.theatlantic.com/technology/archive/2018/03/largest-study-ever-fake-news-mit-twitter/555104/.

Mohammed A (2014) Kerry calls climate change weapon of mass destruction. *Scientific American*. https://www.scientificamerican.com/article/kerry-calls-climate-change-weapon-of-mass-destruction1/.

Monbiot G (2013) Africa let us help – just like in 1884. *The Guardian*, 11 June. http://www.theguardian.com/commentisfree/2013/jun/10/african-hunger-help-g8-grab.

Mondaca E (2017) The Archipelago of Chiloé and the uncertain contours of its future: Coloniality, new extractivism and political-social re-vindication of existence. In Goyes D, Mol H, Brisman A, and South N (eds) *Environmental Crime in Latin America: The Theft of Nature and the Poisoning of the Land*: 31–55. London: Palgrave.

Nassaro MRF (2017) Wildlife trafficking in the state of São Paulo, Brazil. In Goyes D, Mol H, Brisman A, and South N (eds) *Environmental Crime in Latin America: The Theft of Nature and the Poisoning of the Land*: 245–260. London: Palgrave.

Nelson J (2012) Who's profiting from the water crisis? *New Internationalist*, 1 May. https://newint.org/features/2012/05/01/water-crisis-profit-opportunity/.

Nye J (2004) *Soft Power: The Means to Success in World Politics*. London: Hartlett.

Oreskes N and Conway E (2012) *Merchants of Doubt: How a Handful of Scientists Obscured the Truth from Tobacco Smoke to Global Warming*. London: Bloomsbury.

Pacifici M, Visconti P, Butchart S, Watson J, Cassola F, and Rondinini C (2017) Species traits influenced their response to recent climate change. *Nature Climate Change* 7: 205–208. DOI: 10.1038/nclimate3223.

Patel R (2007) *Stuffed and Starved: Markets Power and the Hidden Battle for the World Food System*. Melbourne: Black Inc.

Pearl H (2017) Pacific Island leaders express dismay at US leaving Paris climate accord. *SBS News*, 2 June. Available at https://www.sbs.com.au/news/pacific-island-leaders-express-dismay-at-us-leaving-paris-climate-accord.

Pigliucci M (2012) *Answers for Aristotle How Science and Philosophy Can Lead Us to a More Meaningful Life*. New York: Basic Books.

Pooley E (2017) Donald Trump's EPA pick imperils science – and Earth. *Time*, 19 January. Available at http://time.com/4635162/scott-pruitt-science-denial/.

Popovich N, Schwartz J, and Schlossberg T (2017) How Americans think about climate change, in six maps. *New York Times*, 21 March. Available at https://www.nytimes.com/interactive/2017/03/21/climate/how-americans-think-about-climate-change-in-six-maps.html.

Poyla G (2017) Climate criminal Trump contributes 20% of Worlds annual carbon debt increase. *Counter Current*, 1 June. Available at http://www.countercurrents.org/2017/06/01/climate-criminal-trump-america-contributes-20-of-worlds-annual-carbon-debt-increase/.

Ritchie E, Davis J, Martin J, and Maclagen S (2016) National Science Week: The rise of citizen science is great news for our native wildlife. *ABC News: Science*, 17 August. Available at http://www.abc.net.au/news/science/2016-08-17/how-citizen-science-can-help-australias-native-wildlife/7753712.

Rojas-Páez G (2017) Understanding environmental harm and justice claims in the global south: Crimes of the powerful and peoples' resistance. In Goyes D, Mol H, Brisman A, and South N (eds) *Environmental Crime in Latin America: The Theft of Nature and the Poisoning of the Land*: 57–83. London: Palgrave.

Rosten E (2018) Climate scientists exiled by Donald Trump to reconvene at Columbia University and continue research. *Independent*, 5 January. Available at http://www.independent.co.uk/environment/donald-trump-climate-change-scientists-columbia-university-earth-institute-research-environment-a8143696.html.

Savage C (2017) E.P.A threatens to stop funding Justice Dept. environmental work. *The New York Times*, 27 September. Available at https://www.nytimes.com/2017/09/27/us/politics/scott-pruitt-epa-justice-department-funding.html.

Sedghi A (2015) UK tops chart of EU food waste. *The Guardian*, 23 May. Available at https://www.theguardian.com/world/2015/may/22/uk-tops-chart-of-eu-food-waste.

Seelye K (2001) Global warming may bring new variety of class action. *The New York Times*, 6 September.

Sellah A (2018) Science can't solve climate change – better politics can, former IPCC scientist say. *ABC News: Science*, 2 May. Available at http://www.abc.net.au/news/science/2018-05-02/why-science-cant-solve-climate-change/9711364.

Sengupta S (2018) Biggest threat to humanity? Climate change, U.N. Chief Says. *The New York Times*, 29 March. Available at https://www.nytimes.com/2018/03/29/climate/united-nations-climate-change.html.

Shackleman J (2017) How China and environmentalists became unlikely bedfellows. *Bloomberg*, 6 November. Available at https://www.bloomberg.com/news/articles/2017-11-06/how-china-drew-respect-from-greens-while-boosting-its-pollution.

Shepherd B (2011) Food security should be about feeding the hungry, not making a profit. *The Conversation*, 20 September. Available at https://theconversation.com/food-security-should-be-about-feeding-the-hungry-not-making-a-profit-3309.

Siegenbeek van Heukelom T (2011) A human approach to food security: Land grabs in the limelight. *Journal of Human Security* 7(1): 6–20. DOI: 10.3316/JHS0701006.

Slattery C (2017) Greenhouse gases higher than any time in 800,000 years 'shows definite human effect'. *ABC News*, 1 June. Available at http://www.abc.net.au/news/2017-06-01/greenhouse-gases-database-shows-co2-ch4-n2o-rising-relentlessly/8578918.

Smith N (2012) Plato on the power of ignorance. In Kamtekar R (ed.) *Virtue and Happiness: Essays in Honour of Julia Annas*: 51–73. Oxford: Oxford University Press.

Smith O (2017) Mapped: The world's most polluted countries. *The Telegraph*, 2 January. Available at https://www.telegraph.co.uk/travel/maps-and-graphics/most-polluted-countries/.

Sollund R (2017) The use and abuse of animals in wildlife trafficking in Colombia: Practices and injustice. In Goyes D, Mol H, Brisman A, and South N (eds) *Environmental Crime in Latin America: The Theft of Nature and the Poisoning of the Land*: 215–243. London: Palgrave.

Sommerville M, Essex J, and Le Billon P (2014) The global food crises and the geopolitics of food security. *Geopolitics* 19(2): 239–265. DOI: 10.1080/14650045.2013.811641.

Stehr N (2005) *Knowledge Politics: Governing the Consequences of Science and Technology*. Abingdon: Routledge.

The Editorial Board (2017) President Trump's war on science. *New York Times*, 9 September. Available at https://www.nytimes.com/2017/09/09/opinion/sunday/trump-epa-pruitt-science.html.

The White House (2017) Statement by President Trump on the Climate Paris Accord. *The White House Office of the Press Secretary*, 1 June. https://www.whitehouse.gov/the-press-office/2017/06/01/statement-president-trump-paris-climate-accord.

Tollefson J (2017) US Government disbands climate science advisory committee. *Nature*, 20 August. Available at https://www.nature.com/news/us-government-disbands-climate-science-advisory-committee-122484.

Union of Concerned Scientists (2015) Documenting the fossil fuel industry's climate deception. *Got Science*, July. Available at https://www.ucsusa.org/publications/got-science/2015/got-science-july-2015.

Union of Concerned Scientists (2018) *Scientists Agree: Global Warming is Happening and Humans are the Primary Cause*. Available at https://www.ucsusa.org/global-warming/science-and-impacts/science/scientists-agree-global-warming-happening-humans-primary-cause (accessed 24 April 2018).

United Nations (UN) Climate Change (2017) China and India lead global renewable energy transition. *Report*, 21 April. Available at https://unfccc.int/news/china-and-india-lead-global-renewable-energy-transition.

United Nations (UN) Department of Economic and Social Affairs (2015) World population projected to reach 9.7 billion by 2015. *News*, 29 July. Available at http://www.un.org/en/development/desa/news/population/2015-report.html.

United Nations (UN) Department of Economic and Social Affairs (2017) Water and food security. *International Decade for Action 'Water for Life' 2005–2015*. Available at http://www.un.org/waterforlifedecade/food_security.shtml (accessed 24 April 2018).

United Nations (UN) Educational, Scientific and Cultural Organisation (2010) *FAO Strategies for Improving Food Security*. Available at http://www.unesco.org/education/tlsf/mods/theme_c/popups/mod14t04s01.html (accessed 24 April 2018).

United Nations (UN) Food and Agriculture Organization (2017) *How Close Are We to Zero Hunger: The State of Food Security in the World*. Available at http://www.fao.org/state-of-food-security-nutrition/en/ (accessed 28 April 2018).

United Nations (UN) Framework Convention of Climate Change (2017) *The Paris Agreement*. Available at https://unfccc.int/process/the-paris-agreement/what-is-the-paris-agreement (accessed 24 April 2018).

United Nations (UN) High Commissioner for Refugees (2017) Frequently asked questions on climate change and disaster displacement: Displacement linked to climate change is not a future hypothetical – it's a current reality. *News*, 6 November. Available at http://www.unhcr.org/en-au/news/latest/2016/11/581f52dc4/frequently-asked-questions-climate-change-disaster-displacement.html.

Uwiringiyimana C (2016) Nearly 200 nations agree binding deal to cut greenhouse gas emissions. *Reuters*, 16 October. Available at http://www.reuters.com/article/us-un-climatechange-deal-idUSKBN12F02T.

Vincent M (2015) Climate change: Trump says 'it's called weather', Obama says it 'will define this century'. *ABC News*, 25 November. Available at http://www.abc.net.au/news/2015-11-23/climate-change-clashes-in-us-politics/6961546.

Wall M (2018) Trump's 2019 NASA budget request puts moon ahead of the space station. *Space.Com*, 21 February. Available at https://www.space.com/39671-trump-nasa-budget-2019-funds-moon-over-iss.html.

Walters R (2011) *Eco Crime and Genetically Modified Food*. London: Routledge.

Walters R (2012) Air crimes and atmospheric justice. In South N and Brisman A (eds) *Routledge International Handbook of Green Criminology*: 134–149. Oxford: Routledge.

Walters R (2018) Climate change denial: Making ignorance great again. In Barton A and Howard T (eds) *Ignorance, Power and Harm: Agnotology and the Criminological Imagination*: 79–100. London: Palgrave.

Walters R and Westerhuis D (2013) Green crime and the role of environmental courts. *Crime, Law and Social Change* 59(3): 279–290. DOI: 10.1007/s10611-013-9415-4.

Walters R, Westerhuis D, and Wyatt T (eds) (2013) *Emerging Issues in Green Criminology: Exploring Power Justice and Harm.* London: Palgrave.

Watts N, Amann M, Ayeb-Karlsson S, Belesova K, Bouley T, Boykoff M, Byass P, Cai W, Campbell-Lendrum D, Chambers J, Cox P, Daly M, Dasandi N, Davies M, Depledge M, Depoux A, Dominguez-Sales P, Drummond P, Ekins P, Flahault A, Frumkin H, Georgeson L, Ghanei M, Grace D, Graham H, Grojsman R, Haines A, Hamilton A, Hamilton I, Hartinger S, Johnson A, Kelman I, Keisewetter G, Kniveton D, Liang L, Lott M, Lowe R, Mace G, Sewe M, Maslin M, Mikhaylov S, Milner J, Latifi A, Moradi-Lakeh M, Morrissey K, Murray K, Neville T, Oreszczyn T, Owfi F, Pencheon D, Pye S, Rabbaniha D, Robinson E, Rocklov J, Schutte S, Shumake-Guillemt J, Steinbach R, Tabatabei M, Wheeler N, Wilinson P, Gong P, Montgomery H and Costello A (2017) The Lancet countdown on health and climate change: From 25 years of inaction to a global transformation of public health. *The Lancet* 391(10120): 581–630. DOI: 10.1016/S0140-6736(17)32464-9.

We-Haas M (2017) How America stacks up when it comes to green-house gas emissions. *The Smithsonian*, 2 June. Available at https://www.smithsonianmag.com/smart-news/how-America-stacks-up-greenhouse-gas-emissions-180963560/.

Weiss E (2008) Climate change, intergenerational equity, and international law. *Vermont Journal of Environmental Law* 9: 615–627.

White R and Heckenberg D (2014) *Green Criminology: An Introduction to the Study of Environmental Harm.* London: Routledge.

Wildlife Conservation (2018) *Global Warming: The Next Threat to Humanity.* Available at http://mirpurifoundation.org/programs/wildlife-conservation/global-warming-the-next-threat-to-humanity/ (accessed 24 April 2018).

Wilts A (2018) Donald Trump's budget proposal cuts social welfare and massively increases federal deficit. *The Independent*, 12 February. Available at http://www.independent.co.uk/news/world/americas/us-politics/trump-budget-plan-deficit-increase-cut-social-welfare-border-wall-infrastructure-a8207216.html.

Winsor M (2015) Nigeria's new city: Eko Atlantic construction in Lagos fuels criticism and praise. *IBTimes*, 11 August. Available at http://www.ibtimes.com/nigerias-new-city-eko-atlantic-construction-lagos-fuels-criticism-praise-2048964.

World Economic Forum (2017) *The Global Risks Report 2017.* Geneva, Switzerland.

World Meteorological Organization (2017) Greenhouse gas concentrations surge to new record. *Press Releases*, 30 October. Available at https://public.wmo.int/en/media/press-release/greenhouse-gas-concentrations-surge-new-record.

Wright O (2016) Private companies earn billions via rip-off charges. *The Independent*, 13 January. Available at http://www.independent.co.uk/home-news/private-water-companies-earn-billions-via-rip-off-charges.

Xifra J (2016) Climate change deniers and advocacy: A situational theory of publics approach. *American Behavioral Scientist* 60(3): 276–287. DOI: 10.1177/0002764215613403.

Young M (2017) Pacific Island nations urge world leaders to act as islands expected to sink. *News.com.au*, 25 November. Available at http:/www.news.com.au/technology/environment/pacific-island-nations-urge-world-leaders-to-act-as-islands-expected-to-sink/news-story/9416ac17 26d1f8d02a1ae435924e364f.

Zafiroski M (2007) *The Protestant Work Ethic and the Spirit of Authoritarianism Puritanism and Democracy and the Free Civil Society*. New York: Springer.

Zatat N (2017) Paris Agreement: Donald Trump will be joining Nicaragua and Syria as non-members of climate change accords. *Independent*, 2 June 2017. Available at http://www.independent.co.uk/news/world/americas/us-politics/paris-agreement-donald-trump-nicaragua-syria-climate-change-accords-not-members-global-warming-a7768441.html.

Human rights instruments

Paris Agreement (2016) Treaties-XXVII.7.d, opened for signature 16 February 2016, entered into force 4 November 2016.

Rome Statute of the International Criminal Court [*Statute of Rome*] (1998) 2187 UNTS 90, opened for signature 17 July 1998, entered into force 1 July 2001.

Universal Declaration of the Rights of Peoples (2001) UNPO General Assembly, entered into force 17 February 2001.

6

SOUTHERNISING CRIMINOLOGY

A journey

In 2016, when three of the present authors published an article entitled 'Southern Criminology' in the *British Journal of Criminology*, we were surprised at the immediate and widespread interest it generated. There has been much debate, including some fierce critique, at Asian, American, Australian, British, and European conferences. We are grateful for the vast amount of feedback, largely supportive, from colleagues offering a diversity of theoretical, empirical, and multidisciplinary suggestions. Indeed, the purpose of all good academic debate is to engage peers in constructive dialogue to generate new and exciting ideas. Of course, no worthwhile intellectual exchange is without its protagonists, and in these early days of this exchange we value the critical and insightful input of Max Travers and his questioning of whether a Southern criminology is even possible (Travers 2017). Moreover, Cunneen's scepticism on whether Southern criminology can deliver on the democratisation of knowledge if it does not adopt an 'indigenous lens', is serious food for thought (Cunneen 2018). Our response is that both authors miss a major point about Southern criminology. The first, is that it's not a new narrative or criminological brand, as Moosavi (2018) points out, but rather a way of harnessing and expanding the experiences, biographies, and knowledges of the Global South, that are often unheard, for the purpose of advancing human rights and global justice. Second, it is an open-ended project that is inclusive of multiple subaltern voices including indigenous voices, and that seeks to address the historical violence of colonisation and the coloniality of gender. Nevertheless, that the *general* idea appeared to resonate suggested that we were not alone in our intellectual journey towards injecting innovative theoretical and empirical knowledge into the field of criminology from the Global South. One of the more positive effects to date has been the rapid development of new, and strengthening of existing, East/South, South/South, and South/North relationships and collaborations.

Asia provides some lessons regarding the challenges facing those seeking a more globally-oriented criminology from the Global South. As Liu (2009) has noted, the term 'American criminology' has a global currency, to the extent that we can place it with names, traditions, institutions, journals, and associations. Indeed, criminology has become institutionalised in the United States to an extent not comparable anywhere else in the world, despite many other countries in the Global North having introduced criminology as a distinct discipline for undergraduate and post-graduate study during the latter part of the twentieth century. Liu observes that the 'international community' of criminologists mostly comprises scholars from the Global North and mostly involves a (English-speaking) dialogue across the North Atlantic. In 1999, only 16 in 1000 presentations at the premier North American (and world) criminology meeting were about Asia, the majority of these being on China. In a quantitative analysis of criminology publications focusing on Asia, Belknap (2016) found the country most frequently represented in English in Northern journals was Japan, followed by China and India. This noted, the first English language criminology publication on an East Asian nation only appeared in 1970. Further, growth in criminological publishing has been largely restricted to Japan and a small group of newly industrialised East Asian nations, such as China, Singapore, Taiwan, and South Korea, and while the quantity of papers with a focus on Asia has increased in recent years, the interest in Asia has remained mostly comparative and most researchers remain affiliated with the institutions of the Global North.

Where theory has been appropriated, it has often been highly selective. For example, Hirschi's social bonding control theory has been used frequently in Chinese research because of a perceived consistency with Chinese cultural values (Belknap 2016; Lee and Laidler 2013). Similarly, social disorganisation theory has also been widely taken up, presumably because it is well-suited to a society where social inequalities, of the kind best interpreted through a critical lens, are officially non-existent.

The Northern dominance of global criminology is attested to in the translation of Northern research for adoption in courses elsewhere in the world. Further, many of the world's most successful scholars in the Global South were trained in Northern traditions and schools. It is somewhat ironic that the texts which travel North–South contain so little or no information specific to the countries where they are adopted. For example, in one of the best-selling British criminology texts, not only was India absent from its index, but Iran, Iraq, and Italy were included in the 'I' section. This is truly beguiling, given that the three former nations are non-English speaking, are not Commonwealth nations, and do not share historical links to the extent Britain and India do. In Australia, while local texts written by local scholars are often adopted in criminology programs, most of the examples cited are derived from the Global North.

Despite these difficulties, there has been criminological expansion in countries such as China. Examples of this growth include national organisations such as the Chinese Society of Criminology and the Chinese Juvenile Delinquency Research Association. The Chinese criminologist Jianhong Liu has been a great advocate for 'Asian criminology'; in 2006, he co-founded the *Asian Journal of Criminology* and, shortly thereafter, he became the first President of the Asian Criminology Society. The *Asian Journal of Criminology* is experiencing considerable success for such a young journal (now ranked a Q1), likewise in 2017 the *International Journal of Crime, Justice and Social Democracy* sky-rocketed into the international rankings as Australia's top law and criminology journal as a Q2. Such elevations, within a ranking system dominated by Northern indexes, reveal the rising value and contributions of Southern voices across a range of social sciences.

From the earliest musings of the Southern criminology project links were quickly forged with the Asian Criminological Society.

In mid-2017, the Asian Society of Criminology and the Crime and Justice Research Centre (CJRC) at Queensland University of Technology (QUT) co-hosted a conference in Cairns, Northern Australia entitled *Crime and Justice in Asia and the Global South*, attended by scholars from over 27 countries from Africa, Latin America, the Caribbean, the Pacific, Asia, Europe, North America, and Australasia. In November 2018, the now-called Crime, Justice and Social Democracy Research Centre will further this democratisation of knowledge by co-hosting an international congress on Southern perspectives in law, crime, and justice at the Universidad Nacional de Litoral, Santa Fe, Argentina. Again, this is an innovative and trailblazing event.

In our experience, there are so many criminological lessons to be learned from South America, yet such voices are stifled by Northern hegemonic power and tradition; as well as the reluctance of so many in the English-speaking world to traverse language barriers and actively access and engage with the knowledges and cultures of others. That said, it is important to note that Southern criminology is not just a 'Southern' thing, and that it resonates well beyond any geographical divide. The large numbers of Northern scholars whose interest, engagement, and support have been catalysed by the concept of Southern criminology is testament to the appeal of an intellectual project that seeks inclusivity, diversity, and innovation. The Southernising project steers a tricky path along what the Bengali social scientist Chakrabarty (2007) calls conceptual pragmatism. This is a pragmatism that accepts knowledge is so embedded with metropolitan thought it is not possible to completely disentangle it. But it is possible to pluralise, democratise, and de-centre knowledge production by injecting it with theory and innovation from non-Anglophone cultures. Liu's body of work is an example.

Liu (2017) has recently begun to develop what he has referred to as an 'Asian paradigm' in criminology which emphasises the importance of collectivism, conflict avoidance, notions of shame, and holistic thinking. He observes that a central objective of Asian justice is to restore harmony to groups, such as the family or community. He has also noted a more significant place exists for informal or customary law in China. Belknap (2016) has provided an extensive outline of recent Asian contributions to criminological theory and practice, in a range of areas including intimate partner violence, green criminology, and policing.

Nevertheless, on a broader level, criminology in the Global South is fractured by language barriers, diversity in legal systems and crime control practices, and resource limitations (Liu 2009). English language dominance (Faraldo-Cabana 2018) has, for example, ensured that Latin America has been marginalised from international criminological debates notwithstanding its long criminological tradition (del Olmo 1999) and substantial output of social research on crime and criminal justice. Global South criminology is also limited by local political and cultural attitudes towards crime and deviance, which often fail to acknowledge criminology as a legitimate scholarly enterprise, placing it instead at the periphery of the social sciences or seeing it as a technical enterprise (Lee and Laidler 2013). Lee and Laidler (2013) observed that there were only five criminology departments in Asia as of 2013. Today, there are even fewer in Latin America and only a handful of undergraduate criminology programs. Moreover, the post-colonial nature of funding, access to data, and research prioritisation has meant that where criminology has achieved some degree of institutionalisation it is mostly in the form of administrative criminology, often linked to aspirations to professionalise criminal justice personnel like police. This was also a prominent feature of the early development of criminology in Australia (Carson and O'Malley 1989; Finnane 2012). And while administrative criminology has shown a capacity to move beyond functional research in Northern contexts, cultural, political, and institutional constraints have hampered this shift in other settings, such as the Asian context (Lee and Laidler 2013). Lack of public funding has also resulted in much research in the Asian setting consisting of short term applied projects conducted by outside agencies, such as consultancy firms or international donors. This often results in research agendas developed externally that are culturally insensitive and/or non-responsive to local needs (Lee and Laidler 2013). These factors have undoubtedly limited the possibility for more theoretical and critical traditions to develop locally in Asia and doubtlessly in other places.

However, it is also important to recognise that if we consider the entire field of social research on crime and justice, and not only the work of those who directly identify as criminologists, we find critical work in abundance in many settings—including Latin America, Australia, and New Zealand. This work features feminist, neo-Marxist, post-structuralist, and left-realist perspectives, to name a few. It is undertaken by sociologists, historians, political scientists, anthropologists, lawyers, and others who apply the tools of their various disciplines, and typically also interdisciplinary insights, to criminological questions. They frequently consort with criminologists at conferences and publish in criminology journals, but they continue to foreground their primary discipline as their principal intellectual identity. This highlights what Garland refers to as 'one of the constitutive dynamics of criminology', 'its incessant raiding of other disciplines for new ideas with which to pursue, renew and enrich the criminological project' (2011: 303–304). In consequence it could be said that criminology is in a perpetual state of identity crisis (Bosworth and Hoyle 2011). But this is to be counted as a major strength and we wholeheartedly agree with Garland's caveat that any trend towards the greater autonomy of criminology from other foundational disciplines and emerging fields of research is something to be firmly resisted. Indeed, from a Southern perspective, we would argue (and hopefully in earlier chapters have practically demonstrated) that the range of disciplines and fields with which criminology might fruitfully engage is broader than perhaps has traditionally been the case in the Global North. John Braithwaite typifies the intellectual ethos described and commended by Garland. Recently, he has played a pioneering role in the development of both Asian criminology and global peace-building criminology, after making major contributions to other fields across his career (Braithwaite 2015, 2018; Braithwaite and Wardak 2013; Wardak and Braithwaite 2013). Unsurprisingly, he recently argued for the importance of making Southern criminology 'less criminological' (Braithwaite 2018: 974), an argument with which we fully concur.

It is clear then that criminology's reach and presence in the Global South has been highly uneven. Where it has secured an institutional foothold, this has frequently been in a form that reflects its dependence on, and deference to, imported concepts, theories, and methods and those core assumptions underpinning the dominant Northern criminological paradigm examined in Chapter 1. Elsewhere a form of criminology that took shape as an auxiliary to the liberal nation state, sharing its definitions and understandings of crime, criminal justice and punishment, may be of limited use. In Chapter 4, we referred to problems with analyses of penal developments in Latin America that take no account of their past histories of dictatorship and authoritarian government. Dixon (2013) has recently referred to the 'aetiological crisis' in post-apartheid South African criminology. And criminology may fail to speak at all to those post-colonial or neo-colonial settings that pertain in many parts of the world in which civil war, recent past histories of violent conflict and/or foreign intervention relegates the idea of a well-resourced, stable nation state to the realm of extreme contingency, if not (in some places) outright fantasy.

In confronting these issues, Southern criminology faces definite risks and major challenges. It also imposes intellectual responsibilities. The chief risks—which caveats in Chapter 1 regarding what Southern criminology *is not* addressed—relate to closure and evangelism (see Carlen 2010). Carlen argues that all good knowledge is critical and that it

> should be: open; constantly recognising, questioning, and if necessary, denying the conditions of its existence; and neither 'trimming' to make them politically correct or 'clubbing'—that is, pulling its punches either to conform with contemporary academic fashions or political prejudices.
>
> (Carlen 2010: 349)

It is essential to safeguard against any verdant field of inquiry turning into a space that must be fortified and defended, its intellectual fruits compared and promoted not simply as different but as succeeding and subsuming others. This is why we underline the importance of holding to that general vision of criminology described by Garland earlier and typified in the work of John Braithwaite. We prefer to conceive of the project as a journey (and the metaphor is carefully chosen) with unknown destinations and involving an open invitation to others. The Southernising of criminology is one step in the journey toward the development of a robust transnational criminology that invents methods and concepts which bridge global divides and enhance the democratisation of knowledge, a journey toward cognitive justice. We are mindful of the intellectual quest to claim new territory and that is not a quest we are on. We do not seek a distinctive identity as a sub-discipline or brand within criminology.

Throughout this book we have discussed the implications of the Southern criminology project in the field of production and circulation of knowledge about crime and crime control. We have shown various ways in which the criminological concepts and arguments constructed in the Global North reflect the problems and contexts around which they were formed and how this feature makes them, in some cases, inadequate to describe and understand problems and contexts of the Global South. In this way, we have advocated the need to generate a theoretical and empirical inventiveness from the Global South capable of carrying out this task and, on different topics, we have exemplified its deployment, establishing other questions (and hopefully providing answers to some) that could enrich the debate in this field.

We have also referred at various times to the question of the transfer of state policies and interventions related to crime control, which are complexly intertwined with the travels of ideas on these issues that occur in the academic field, between the Global North and South. The project of Southernising criminology also aims to make a contribution to this discussion (Cain 2000; Cohen 1982; Ellison and Pino 2012; Jones and Newburn 2006; Karstedt 2001; Melossi, Sozzo, and Sparks 2011; Newburn and Sparks 2004; Sozzo 2011, 2014). Policy transfer between North and South has a long history that is embedded in the dynamics of colonialism and neo-colonialism and more recent shifts in the nature of empire. Peripheral contexts, in this framework, have again typically played a dependent role, seeking to adopt forms of crime control that were moulded in the central contexts as a mechanism oriented towards incorporation into what is defined as 'civilisation' and modernity. Think about the international diffusion of the prison as a penal technique during the nineteenth century and the first half of the twentieth century. Accompanying this diffusion were various attempts to organise prison operation for different purposes—correction, dissuasion, retribution—combining differently education, work, religion, isolation, and surveillance. Institutions were erected that symbolized 'penal modernisation' in places far away from the Northern scenarios in which this form of punishment was born and consolidated through a long process since the sixteenth century. For example, in Latin America this process started with the House of Correction in Rio de Janeiro, whose construction began in 1834 and ended in 1850 (Bretas 1996: 104), and with the Penitentiary of Santiago de Chile that began to be built in 1844 but only functioned fully after 1856 (León 2003: 429). However, these processes of importation have frequently been subjected to dynamics of 'metamorphosis'. Since Southern actors put into operation these Northern originating institutions and practices of crime control in the face of local problems and contexts, they are marked by a series of peculiarities, which leads them to generate modifications and adaptations that give these imported objects unique features (Sozzo 2011: 186–187, 2014: 17–24, 39–50). For example, the chronic lack of resources and the fragility of Latin American states during the nineteenth century meant that the ambitious projects of installing a system of 'modern', 'civilised' prisons promoted by sectors of the elites, frequently resulted in the creation of a handful of institutions that embodied the appeal to emulate the Global North coexisting with a majority of spaces of confinement that articulated high rates of abandonment and violence, what amounted to truly 'punitive swamps' (Caimari 2004: 109–124; see also Aguirre 2009: 216–220).

As we saw in Chapter 4, these processes of importing the 'modern' and the 'civilised' from the North to the South did not imply that European powers in the colonies have not assiduously employed other 'backward' penal techniques (such as genocide of indigenous peoples, the death penalty, other corporal punishments, and various forms of violence not formally defined as penal measures). On the contrary the process of colonisation and settlement in the colonies was a very violent process, as discussed in both Chapters 2 and 4, and this long openly illiberal tradition constituted a dark and forceful legacy in penal dynamics and practices after the processes of independence from the European metropoles. At the same time, as we also discussed in Chapter 4, in this context the specific penal technique of convict transportation was practised over many centuries and in its dynamics functioned to connect Global North and South in the form of the transfer from the European metropoles to the colonies of condemned individuals. Convict transportation constituted an important dimension of colonisation with many different effects both at the imperial centre and in the periphery. In this sense, it is evident that crime control histories in peripheral contexts are much more complex than the simple reproduction of the patterns of historical transformation through processes of importation of what is defined as 'modern' or 'civilised'.

The Southernising of knowledge encourages a detailed exploration of these specificities of crime control in the contexts of the Global South, with regard to both the past and the present. But it is also important to account for the dynamics of policy transfer from the Global North to the Global South anchored in colonial and neo-colonial relations. Transforming these North–South transfers into an object of inquiry by itself also implies thinking of them as processes that often go beyond mere adoption, providing an account of the metamorphoses involved, including complex modes of modification and adaptation to local problems and contexts (see Blaustein 2015). These complexities can only be made visible from thorough explorations of policy transfers (for examples, see Sozzo 2011). At the same time, it involves the careful analysis of the actors that participate in these transfer dynamics and their mutations. Beyond the traditional role of state authorities and officials and academics from the North and South that have a long past, in the present key new agents appear: experts uncoupled from the academic world (advisors, consultants), private companies that are dedicated to selling various types of services linked to security and criminal justice policies, non-governmental, not-for-profit organisations, and supranational organisations (such as various United Nations agencies) (Blaustein 2016; Blaustein, Pino, and Ellison 2018; Wacquant 2009). This pluralisation of actors, and the instant communication of the current technological era, make North-South travels of crime control techniques and practices much more complex than in the past. North-South travels then become a fertile field of studies from the perspective of Southern criminology, focusing on particular state policies and institutions— from community policing to situational crime prevention, from plea bargaining to probation, and beyond. While much has been done in this direction, much remains to be done.

However, the project of Southernising criminology is not only interested in this dimension of North–South transfers. It is vital to reconstruct, both in the past and in the present, the travels in the opposite direction, from the Global South to the North, even though they have been less frequent and powerful. In Chapter 4, we have referred to travels in that direction during the nineteenth century between the British colonies of Oceania and the metropolis, from the 'marks system' to the 'ticket of leave' (see also Hogg and Brown 2018: 756–763). But there are other significant examples, even today, that must be examined. Perhaps, the most prominent case is the global diffusion of 'restorative justice' that incorporates elements originally drawn from peripheral contexts—including ideas and practices of indigenous peoples of Australia, New Zealand, Asia (Latha and Thilagaraj 2013; Liu 2009) and Africa (Tutu 1999: 51–52). In turn, these innovations have been the object of hybridisations in the Global North—but also in different contexts of the Global South (Braithwaite 2017; Braithwaite and Zhang 2017). This process, in which diverse Southern contexts inform the design of state policies and institutions related to crime control for Northern scenarios, provides stories about the conditions of possibility for other paths of future reform and innovation.

If South-North transfers have been frequently neglected, even by those researchers interested in decolonising the production of knowledge in the field of criminology, South-South transfers have been even more so. It is critical to reverse this absence and place this theme at the centre of research agendas. The already mentioned example of the diffusion of 'restorative justice' offers multiple possibilities in this sense. Another relevant field of exploration is the different ways of dealing with atrocities, genocides, and massive human rights violations in different peripheral contexts in recent decades; commonly encompassed under the concept of 'transitional justice', the exchanges and influences between different forms pose important questions (Braithwaite 2018; Zysman Quirós 2018). A further area of interest (discussed in Chapter 2) is the emergence of women's police stations (WPS) in South America since the 1980s. WPS grew as a form of specialised intervention to respond to gender violence and have transferred to various peripheral settings—from South Africa to India, from Kosovo to the Philippines (Hautzinger 2007; Jubb et al. 2011; Macdowell Santos 2005; Perova and Reynolds 2017). The investigation of these South-South journeys is a key source of lessons, both for the theoretical and political reflection of researchers, and for state and non-state agents that work in peripheral contexts, seeking to nurture a kind of equal and open cooperation across borders.

The project of Southernising criminology seeks, therefore, to actively involve itself with the question of the transfer of state institutions and practices related to crime control, both from a theoretical and political point of view. This obviously implies setting aside the colonising lenses of 'benign transfer' (Cohen 1982) and 'occidentalism' (Cain 2000) to pioneer formulations of the problem from a critical standpoint. But this does not necessarily mean adopting a radically inverse perspective, which tends to deny the possibility of any dialogue between the Global North and South on the terrain of crime control institutions and practices. Southernising criminology implies placing the dynamic of North-South travels at the centre of a critical view, addressing them in all their complexity and plurality, highlighting both their perverse outcomes but also their potentialities—how they reproduce dependence, how they frequently modify and adapt, and how these change over time. But it also means paying equal attention to South–North and South–South travels, as processes that break with the global political and cultural hierarchy in the past and in the present, and provide lessons for both the theoretical and political imagination. Much remains to be done.

The primary challenge lies in redefining the geographic and symbolic limits of criminology to create globally connected systems of knowledge. In this sense, Southernising criminology is just a step in the journey toward the development of a trans-national criminology that is inclusive of the experiences and perspectives of a plurality of voices from the Global South.

References

Aguirre C (2009) Carcel y sociedad en America Latina 1800–1940. In Kingman Garces E (ed.) *Historia social urbana. Espacios y flujos*: 209–252. Quito: Flacso.

Belknap J (2016) Asian criminology's expansion and advancement of research and crime control practices. *Asian Criminology* 11(4): 249–264. DOI: 10.1007/s11417-016-9240-7.

Blaustein J (2015) *Speaking Truths to Power: Policy Ethnography and Police Reform in Bosnia and Herzegovina*. Oxford: Oxford University Press.

Blaustein J (2016) Exporting criminological innovation abroad: Discursive representation, 'evidence-based crime prevention' and the post-neoliberal development agenda in Latin America. *Theoretical Criminology* 20(2): 165–184. DOI: 10.1177/1362480615604892.

Blaustein J, Pino N, and Ellison G (2018) Crime and development in the Global South. In Carrington K, Hogg R, Scott J, and Sozzo M (eds) *The Palgrave Handbook of Criminology and the Global South*: 205–221. London: Palgrave.

Bosworth M and Hoyle C (eds) (2011) *What Is Criminology?* Oxford: Oxford University Press.

Braithwaite J (2015) Rethinking criminology through radical diversity in Asian reconciliation. *Asian Journal of Criminology* 10(3): 181–183. DOI: 10.1007/s11417-014-9200-z.

Braithwaite J (2017) Hybrids politics for justice: The Silk Road of restorative justice II. *Restorative Justice. An International Journal* 5(1): 7–28. DOI: 10.1080/20504721.2017.1294795.

Braithwaite J (2018) Criminology, peacebuilding and transitional justice: Lessons from the Global South. In Carrington K, Hogg R, Scott J, and Sozzo M (eds) *The Palgrave Handbook of Criminology and the Global South*: 971–990. London: Palgrave.

Braithwaite J and Wardak A (2013) Crime and war in Afghanistan, Part 1: The Hobbesian solution. *British Journal of Criminology* 53(2): 179–196.

Braithwaite J and Zhang Y (2017) Persia to China: The Silk Road of restorative justice I. *Asian Journal of Criminology* 12(1): 23–38. DOI: 10.1007/s11417-017-9244-y.

Bretas ML (1996) What the eyes can't see: Stories from Rio de Janeiro's prisons. In Salvatore R and Aguirre C (eds) *The Birth of the Penitentiary* in *Latin America: Essays on Criminology, Prison Reform and Social Control 1830–1940*: 101–122. Austin: University of Texas Press.

Caimari L (2004) *Apenas un delincuente. Crimen, castigo y cultura en la Argentina, 1880–1955*. Buenos Aires: Siglo XXI.

Cain M (2000) Orientalism, occidentalism and the sociology of crime. *British Journal of Criminology* 40(2): 239–260. DOI: 10.1093/bjc/40.2.239.

Carlen P (2010) *A Criminological Imagination*. Surrey: Ashgate.

Carrington K, Hogg R, and Sozzo M (2016) Southern Criminology. *British Journal of Criminology* 56(1): 1–20. DOI: 10.1093/bjc/azv083.

Carrington K, Hogg R, Scott J, and Sozzo M (eds) (2018) *The Palgrave Handbook of Criminology and the Global South*. London: Palgrave.

Carson K and O'Malley P (1989) The institutional foundations of contemporary Australian criminology. *Australian and New Zealand Journal of Criminology* 25(3): 333–355. DOI: 10.1177/144078338902500301.

Chakrabarty D (2007) *Provincializing Europe: Post-Colonial Thought and Difference*, 2nd edn. Princeton: Princeton University Press.

Cohen S (1982) Western crime control models in the third world: Benign or malignant? *Research in Law, Deviance and Social Control* 4: 85–119.

Cunneen C (2018) Indigenous challenges for Southern Criminology. In K Carrington, Hogg R, Scott J, and Sozzo M (eds) *The Palgrave Handbook of Criminology and the Global South*: 19–42. London: Palgrave.

del Olmo R (1999) The development of criminology in Latin America. *Social Justice* 26(2): 19–45.

Dixon B (2013) The aetiological crisis in South African criminology. *Australian and New Zealand Journal of Criminology* 46(3): 319–334. DOI: 10.1177/0004865813489697.

Ellison G and Pino N (2012) *Globalization, Police Reform and Development: Doing It Western Style?* Basingstoke: Palgrave.

Faraldo-Cabana P (2018) Research excellence and Anglophone dominance: The case of law, criminology and social science. In Carrington K, Hogg R, Scott J, and Sozzo M (eds) *The Palgrave Handbook of Criminology and the Global South*: 163–182. London: Palgrave.

Finnane M (2012) The origins of criminology in Australia. *Australian and New Zealand Journal of Criminology* 45(2): 157–178. DOI: 10.1177/0004865812443682.

Garland D (2011) Criminology's place in the academic field. In Bosworth M and Hoyle C (eds) (2011) *What Is Criminology?*: 298–317. Oxford: Oxford University Press.

Hautzinger S (2007) *Violence and the City of Women*. Berkeley: University of California Press.

Hogg R and Brown D (2018): Rethinking penal modernism from the Global South: The case of convict transportation to Australia. In Carrington K,

Hogg R, Scott J, and Sozzo M (eds) *The Palgrave Handbook of Criminology and the Global South*: 751–774. London: Palgrave.

Jones T and Newburn T (2006) *Policy Transfer and Criminal Justice.* Buckingham: Open University Press.

Jubb N, Comacho G, D'Angelo A, Hernández K, Macassi I, Meléndez L, Molina Y, Pasinato W, Redrobán V, Rosas C, and Yáñez G (2011) *Women's Police Stations in Latin America: An Entry Point for Stopping Violence and Gaining Access to Justice.* Quito: CEPLAES, IDRC.

Karstedt S (2001) Comparing cultures, comparing crime: Challenges, prospects and problems for a global criminology. *Crime, Law and Social Change* 36(3): 285–308. DOI: 10.1023/A:1012223323445.

Latha S and Thilagaraj R (2013) Restorative justice in India. *Asian Journal of Criminology* 8(4): 309–319. DOI: 10.1007/s11417-013-9164-4.

Lee M and Laidler K (2013) Doing criminology from the periphery: Crime and punishment in Asia. *Theoretical Criminology* 17(2): 141–157. DOI: 10.1177/1362480613476790.

León MA (2003) *Encierro y corrección. La configuración de un sistema de prisiones en Chile (1800–1911).* Santiago: Universidad Central de Chile.

Liu J (2009) Asian Criminology – challenges, opportunities and directions. *Asian Journal of Criminology* 4(1): 1–9. DOI: 10.1007/s11417-009-9066-7.

Liu J (2017) The new Asian paradigm: A relational approach. In Liu J, Travers M, and Chang LYC (eds) *Comparative Criminology in Asia*: 17–32. New York: Springer.

Macdowell Santos C (2005) *Women's Police Station. Gender Violence and Justice in Sao Paulo, Brazil.* Basingstoke: Palgrave.

Melossi D, Sozzo M, and Sparks R (eds) (2011) *The Travels of the Criminal Question: Cultural Embeddedness and Diffusion.* Oxford: Hart.

Moosavi L (2018) Decolonizing criminology: Syed Hussein Alastas on crimes of the powerful. *Critical Criminology* (published online 15 June 2018).

Newburn T and Sparks R (2004) *Criminal Justice and Political Cultures. National and International Dimensions of Crime Control.* Cullompton: Willan Publishing.

Perova E and Reynolds SA (2017) Women's police stations and intimate partner violence: Evidence from Brazil. *Social Science and Medicine* 174: 188–196. DOI: 10.1016/j.socscimed.2016.12.008.

Sozzo M (2011) Cultural travels and crime prevention in Argentina. In Melossi D, Sozzo M, and Sparks R (eds) *Travels of the Criminal Question: Cultural Embeddedness and Diffusion*: 185–215. Oxford: Hart.

Sozzo M (2014) *Viagems culturais e questao criminal.* Rio de Janeiro: Revan.

Travers M (2017) The idea of a Southern Criminology. *International Journal of Comparative and Applied Criminal Justice. Epub ahead of print* 26 October. DOI: 10.1080/01924036.2017.1394337.

Tutu D (1999) *No Future Without Forgiveness*. London: Rider.

Wacquant L (2009) *Punishing the Poor: The Neoliberal Government of Social Insecurity*. Durham: Duke University Press.

Wardak A and Braithwaite J (2013) Crime and war in Afghanistan: Part II: a Jeffersonian alternative? *British Journal of Criminology* 53(2): 197–214. DOI: 10.1093/bjc/azs066.

Zysman Quirós D (2018) Building social democracy through transitional justice. In Carrington K, Hogg R, Scott J, and Sozzo M (eds) *The Palgrave Handbook of Criminology and the Global South*: 991–1010. Basingstoke: Palgrave.

INDEX